KT-475-136

PENGUIN BOOKS

The Venetian Empire

Jan Morris, who is Anglo-Welsh by parentage, divides her time between her library-house in North Wales, her *dacha* in the Black Mountains of South Wales and travel abroad. She has been to Manhattan every year since 1953, makes an annual visit to Venice, and has spent much of her life wandering and writing.

Her books include the *Pax Britannica* trilogy (*Heaven's Command*, *Pax Britannica* and *Farewell the Trumpets*), the autobiographical *Conundrum* and *Pleasures of a Tangled Life*, *Venice*, *Oxford*, *Spain*, *The Matter of Wales*, *Among the Cities*, *Manhattan '45* and *Hong Kong: Epilogue to an Empire*. She has also published six volumes of collected travel essays and edited *The Oxford Book of Oxford*. Her first work of fiction, *Last Letters from Hav* (Viking 1985, Penguin 1986), was shortlisted for the Booker Prize. Many of her books are published by Penguin.

Jan Morris

The
Venetian Empire

A Sea Voyage

Penguin Books

For Suki Provstgård Morys

PENGUIN BOOKS

Published by the Penguin Group
27 Wrights Lane, London W8 5TZ, England
Viking Penguin Inc, 40 West 23rd Street, New York, New York 10010, USA
Penguin Books Australia Ltd, Ringwood, Victoria, Australia
Penguin Books Canada Ltd, 2801 John Street, Markham, Ontario, Canada L3R 1B4
Penguin Books (NZ) Ltd, 182–190 Wairau Road, Auckland 10, New Zealand

Penguin Books Ltd, Registered Offices: Harmondsworth, Middlesex, England

First published in an illustrated edition by Rainbird 1980
Published in Penguin Books 1990
10 9 8 7 6 5 4 3 2 1

Copyright © Jan Morris, 1980
All rights reserved

Made and printed in Great Britain by
Cox and Wyman Ltd, Reading, Berks.
Filmset in Linotron Bembo by
Rowland Phototypesetting Ltd, Bury St Edmunds, Suffolk

Except in the United States of America,
this book is sold subject to the condition
that it shall not, by way of trade or otherwise,
be lent, re-sold, hired out, or otherwise circulated
without the publisher's prior consent in any form of
binding or cover other than that in which it is
published and without a similar condition
including this condition being imposed
on the subsequent purchaser

Contents

The Venetian Empire

→···· Maritime trade routes

| 0 | | 100 | | 200 | | 300 miles |

| 0 | 100 | 200 | 300 | 400 | 500km |

Introduction

FOR SIX CENTURIES the Republic of Venice, set resplendently in its lagoon at the head of the Adriatic Sea, was an imperial power. Like many another medieval city-state, it extended its authority gradually over the countryside round about, and at the height of its success ruled much of north Italy, as far south as Ancona, inland almost to Milan. But in a more properly imperial kind, it acquired too over the years a dominion overseas, a colonial empire in the classic sense – *Stato da Mar* in the Venetian vernacular – and it is this romantic entity, scattered through the world's loveliest seas, that is the subject of my book. It is a traveller's book, geographically arranged, but space and time are jumbled in it, and I have wandered at will from the landscapes and sensations of our own day into events, suggestions and substances of the past.

I call the Venetian Empire an entity, but it often feels more like an abstraction. The Venetians were never without overseas possessions, from the time my story starts at the end of the twelfth century until the fall of the Venetian Republic at the end of the eighteenth century. Rome apart, theirs was the first and the longest-lived of the European overseas empires. Their imperialism, though, was piecemeal and opportunist. They had first become rich by collecting the products of the east, shipping them home to Venice, and dispatching them through Europe: their empire was contrived to protect and develop this activity, and was accordingly pragmatic to a fault. It adapted all too easily to circumstance. The Venetians were exporting no ideology to the world. They were not hoping to found lesser states in their own image. They had no missionary zeal. They were not great builders, like the Romans. They were not fanatics, like the Spaniards.

They were above all money-people – every Venetian, wrote Pope Pius II in the fifteenth century, was a slave to 'the sordid occupations of trade'. If their overseas adventures gave them a sense of patriotic fulfilment too, that is because during their years of national virility the Venetians were intensely proud of their republic and its institutions, and carried their loyalty into everything they did. Pride and profit were inextricably mingled. As the oarsmen of a Venetian galley said, when they found themselves trapped in the Golden Horn during the Turkish capture of Constantinople in 1453, 'where our wares are, there is our house . . . We have decided to die upon this galley, which is our home' – and seizing their swords, they prepared to repel boarders beneath the banner of St Mark, the patron and protector of all things Venetian.

It was an empire of coasts and islands, distributed along the republic's trading routes to the orient. Its entire population was probably never more than 400,000, but it extended in scattered bits and pieces from the Adriatic in the west to Cyprus in the east, and northward far into the Aegean. It was never, so to speak, definitive. It had no moment of completion. It was changing all the time, and its possessions varied enormously in style, size and longevity.

Some were mere isolated fortresses on an alien shore. Some were great centres of transhipment or naval power, where the merchant galleys could find food, water and repairs, and the warships could base their patrols. Some were settlement colonies: Venetian families settled permanently in Crete and Corfu, for instance, and others held Aegean islands as feudal estates. In some places Venice stayed so long that her presence seemed almost geological: in others, hardly had her soldiers stormed the walls than the flag came down again and the galleys vanished into the sea, their punitive duties done. A place like Koroni, in Greece, was Venetian during three separate periods of its history, in the intervals being ruled variously by French knights, Greek emperors and Turkish sultans: and to add to the complexity of it all, so many of the Venetian possessions have changed their names, at one time or another, that I have felt obliged to include a gazetteer at the back of the book, to explain where is where.

The Venetians, nevertheless, did try to make a unity of this ungraspable congeries. Despite appearances, theirs was a severely centralist empire. Everything looked towards Venice, to the Signory at the summit, just as the merchant convoys which were the imperial *raison d'être* were all sailing to and from one grand destination, Venice herself. When the empire was at its most dynamic it was very tightly run. All colonial trade with Venice had to be carried in Venetian ships. All surplus colonial produce had to go to Venice. All Adriatic trade was channelled through the lagoon. Officials sent from Venice governed all the chief colonies, under various titles – governor, rector, bailie, prefect, lieutenant – and the defence of the realm was always in the hands of Venetian noblemen.

Lower in the hierarchy the indigenes were usually allowed some share in government, but the last word came always from Venice, and there was no devolution of real power to the colonies, and no colonial representation at the imperial capital. There is no pretending that it was a very enlightened empire. No improving instinct guided the Venetians, such as tempered the pugnacity of the British empire-builders later, and their standards of government varied from the impersonally efficient to the incorrigibly corrupt. 'If you want the Dalmatians to be loyal,' the theologian Paolo Sarpi advised the Signory in 1615, 'keep them ignorant and hungry . . . As for your Greek subjects, wine and bastinados should be their share.' In many of their possessions they were intensely disliked. Orthodox Greeks, after a few generations of Venetian Catholic rule, frequently welcomed the arrival of the Muslim Turks – who, if they had unappealing weaknesses for mass slaughter, arson and disembowelment, at least did not despise their subjects as bumpkin schismatics.

In other places, though, it is fair to say, the authority of Venice was sentimentally beloved. Great trust was placed in the distant

Signory itself, as against its officials on the spot, and sometimes indeed the subject peoples were more resolute in its defence than the Venetians themselves, when Turks or Genoese, pirates or hostile feudalists disembarked impertinently on its foreshores.

More than most empires, the Venetian was single-minded in its function. It did not in itself make Venice rich – keeping the colonies probably cost more than the revenues they supplied. Strategically, as the centuries passed, it became more of a burden than an asset. It did, it is true, provide jobs and chances for members of the ruling nobility, but it was an empire of small places, and it attracted no mass migration from the mother city.

No, this was specifically a mercantile empire. Beneath the guns of its scattered strongpoints the merchantmen could sail with confidence on their enterprises: and in an age when seamen preferred to spend their nights ashore, the existence of so many Venetian havens meant that a voyage from the lagoon to the east was in effect a series of stages from one Venetian port to the next: Venice – Poreč – Split – Durrës – Corfu – Methoni – Kithira – Crete – Cyprus – Beirut. In the fifteenth century, say, a Venetian ship need put in at no foreign harbour all the way from its owner's quay to the warehouses of the Levant.

Many enemies beset those routes, but one in particular loomed over Venetian prospects almost from the start. The Ottoman Turks first burst into history, from their Anatolian homeland, at the beginning of the twelfth century. Four centuries later they had taken Constantinople, were masters of the Arab world, and had advanced into Europe as far as Vienna. The truest thread of Venetian imperial history is the republic's long defensive action, lasting on and off for three hundred years, against the power of this colossus. Venice was the most exposed and vulnerable of the European Powers in the long contest between Islam and Christianity, and for most of her imperial history she was intermittently at war with the Turks: even before her own expansion had reached its limits, the Signory was losing its first possessions to the Porte.

But at the same time Venice depended upon the Muslim trade. Her relationship with Islam was always ambiguous. Though she took part in more than one Crusade, she hung on to her trading stations in Syria and Egypt: even while she fought the Turks, she maintained her commercial contacts within their territories, and at the height of the antagonism indeed allowed Turkish merchants to establish their own business centre on the Grand Canal in Venice. However appallingly the Turks used her, she was generally swift to appease them. While she represented herself to the west as the lonely champion of Christendom, to Islam she liked to appear as a sort of neutral service industry: when in 1464 some Muslim passengers were seized from a Venetian ship by the militantly Christian Knights of St John, at Rhodes, within a week a Venetian fleet arrived off the island, an ultimatum was delivered, the Knights were overawed, and the infidels were delivered safely to Alexandria with fulsome hopes, we may assume, of continuing future favours.

The Venetian Empire was a parasite upon the body of Islam, but as the centuries passed this became an increasingly uncomfortable status. If the Venetians needed Islam, Islam did not greatly need Venice, and in four fierce wars and innumerable skirmishes the Turks gradually whittled away the republic's eastern possessions. One by one the colonies fell, until at the moment of Venice's own extinction as a state, in 1797, she had nothing much left but the Ionian Islands, off the coast of Greece, and a few footholds on the eastern shore of the Adriatic – properties useless to her anyway by then, except as reminders of the glorious past.

Venice was never *primarily* an imperial power, and her surpassing interest to historians and travellers of all periods has been only indirectly due to empire. As we make our own journey we must remind ourselves now and then of the great things always happening at the imperial capital far away. The city itself gradually reached the apex of its magnificence as the most luxurious place in Europe – La Serenissima, The Most Serene Republic – and the Venetian constitution was refined into the subtle and watchful oligarchy, under its elected Doges, that was the wonder of the nations. The Venetian bureaucracy was developed into a mighty instrument of power and permanence. For a century a vicious war was waged against the most persistent of Venice's European rivals, Genoa, culminating in a dramatic final victory actually within sight of the city. The mainland estate, the *terrafirma*, was created and consolidated, while repeatedly Venice was drawn into the vast dynastic and religious conflicts of the rest of Europe. More than once the republic was formally excommunicated by the Pope for its heretical tendencies. Several times it was decimated by plague. A succession of great artists brought glory to the city: a slow enfeeblement of the national will eventually brought it ignominy.

For like all states, the Venetian Republic waxed and waned. It reached the apogee of its reputation, perhaps, in the fifteenth century, but its decline was protracted. The stalwart character of the people imperceptibly softened. The integrity of the ruling nobles was corroded by greed and self-indulgence. The rise of superpowers, the Ottoman Empire to the east, the Spanish Empire to the west, put Venice, whose population never exceeded 170,000, out of scale in the world: the more progressive skills of northern mariners, Dutch and English, outclassed her on her native element, the sea. New political organisms, new ideas and energies left the republic an anachronism among the nations of Europe: until at last in 1797 Napoleon Bonaparte, declaring, 'I will be an Atilla to the Venetian State', sent his soldiers into the lagoons and put an end to it all, to the glory of progress and the sorrow of romantics everywhere. Wordsworth spoke for them all, in the heyday of Romanticism, when he wrote his sonnet, 'On the Extinction of the Venetian Republic':

> Once did She hold the gorgeous East in fee:
> And was the safeguard of the west: the worth
> Of Venice did not fall below her birth,
> Venice, the eldest Child of Liberty.
> She was a maiden City, bright and free;
> No guile seduced, no force could violate;
> And, when she took unto herself a Mate,
> She must espouse the everlasting Sea.
> And what if she had seen those glories fade,
> Those titles vanish, and that strength decay;
> Yet shall some tribute of regret be paid

When her long life hath reached its final day:
Men are we, and must grieve when even the Shade
Of that which once was great, is passed away.

All this we should keep at the corner of our mind's eye, then, as we sail the sunlit seas, clamber the flowered fortress walls, admire the heroes and deplore the villains of the *Stato da Mar*: and I have included a chronological table too, after the gazetteer, to try and put our voyage into historical perspective. These islands, capes and cities of the sea were distant reflections of a much greater image. It is only proper that we start our journey through them, as we shall end it, in the very eye of the sun, on the brilliant and bustling waterfront before the palace of the Doges.

Pre-Imperial

*Prospects from the Piazzetta – a very
particular city – come of age – a pious
commitment – setting sail*

THE MOST GLITTERING of all the world's belvederes, the most
suggestive of great occasion and lofty circumstance, is surely the
Piazzetta di San Marco, the Little Piazza of St Mark, upon the
waterfront at Venice. Two marble columns stand in it, one
crowned with a peculiar winged lion of St Mark, the city's patron
saint, the other with a figure of St Theodore, his predecessor in
that office, in the company of a crocodile: and if you stand between the two of them, where they used to hang malefactors long
ago, you may feel yourself almost to be part of Venice, so infecti-
ous is the spirit of the place, and so vivid are all its meanings.

Immediately behind you is stacked the ancient fulcrum of the
city: the pinkish mass of the Doge's Palace, the arcane gilded
domes of the Basilica beyond, the towering Campanile with the
angel on its summit and the sightseers thronging its belfry, the
arcaded elegance of the Piazza San Marco, Napoleon's 'finest
drawing-room in Europe', from whose recesses, if the season is
right, the wistful strains of competing café orchestras sigh and
thump above the murmur of the crowd. To the west, beyond the
golden weather-vane of the Customs House (held by a figure of
Fortune and supported on its great sphere by two muscular
Atlases), the Grand Canal sweeps away between an avenue of
palaces towards the Rialto. To the east the Riva degli Schiavoni
disappears humped with bridges and lined with hotels past the
ferry-boats, the tugs and the cruise-liners at their berths towards
the distant green smudge of the Public Gardens.

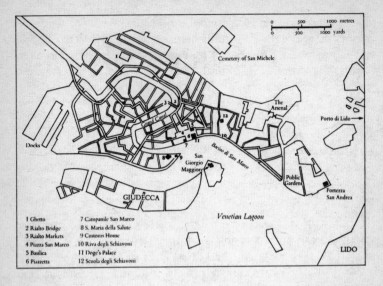

Venice

Immediately in front of you, the ever shining and shifting proscenium of this theatre, lies the Bacino di San Marco, the Basin of St Mark, for a thousand years the grand harbour of Venice. It is dominated from this viewpoint, as by some monumental piece of stage scenery, by the towered island of San Giorgio Maggiore, and it is streaked around the edges with mudbanks when the tide is low, and speckled, as it opens into the wide lagoon, with the hefty wooden tripods that mark the deep-water passages out to sea.

Night and day the ships go by. Sometimes a great freighter passes, hugely out of proportion, its riggings, aerials and radar-scanners gliding away queerly through roofs and chimney-pots towards the docks. Sometimes a cruise ship prances in. Ever and again there come and go the indomitable *vaporetti*, the water-buses of Venice, deep in the water with new arrivals from the railway station and the car parks, and sometimes the yellow-funnelled Chioggia steamer hoots, shudders a little, backs away from her moorings and sets off into the lagoon. The gondolas, if it is the tourist season (for gondolas nowadays tend to be hibernatory craft) progress languidly here and there, a flutter of ribbons from gondoliers' straw hats, a trailing of honeymoon fingers over gunwales. Portentous official launches hasten from office to conference. Speedboats of the rich speed away to the Lido or Harry's Bar. A grey customs launch detaches itself with a bellow from its berth beyond San Giorgio and ominously roars off in pursuit of contraband (or possibly lunch).

It is a restless scene. The ships are never satisfied, the tourists mill and churn. The water itself has no surf or breakers, but often seems to be chopped, in a peculiarly Venetian way, into a million little particles of light-reflecting vapour, rather like ice-fragments, giving the surface of the lagoon a dancing, prismatic quality. The Piazzetta is never static, never silent, and never empty of life: it has been in this condition, night and day, since the early Middle Ages, and every now and then it has been the setting of one of those spectacular displays of pageantry and purpose which have always been essential to the style of Venice.

Captains-General of the Sea, for example, have set off with their squadrons for distant campaigns. Enormous regattas have celebrated holy days or victories. Visiting potentates or holy men have been welcomed. In 1374 Henry III of France sailed in on a ship rowed by 400 Slavs, with an escort of fourteen galleys, a raft upon which glass-blowers created fanciful objects from a furnace shaped like a marine monster, an armada of fantastically decorated floats circling all around, and a welcoming arch designed by Palladio and decorated jointly by Tintoretto and Veronese. In 1961 Queen Elizabeth II of England arrived in her royal yacht, while from the gun-turret of her escorting destroyer a solitary Scottish piper, kilts swirling in the breeze, head held high like cock-o'-the-walk, played a proud if inaudible Highland melody. I myself have seen a dead Pope come in, golden-masked and gilt-coffined on the poop of a ceremonial barge, to a heavy swish of oars and the rhythmic beat of a galley-master's drum.

On 8 November 1202, 'in the octave of the Feast of St Remigius', one such spectacle, never to be forgotten by the Venetians, began the transformation of their city-state into a maritime empire: for on that fine day of a St Martin's summer the

11

octogenarian and purblind Enrico Dandolo, forty-first Doge of Venice, boarded his red-painted galley in the Basin, beneath a canopy of vermilion silk, to trumpet calls, priestly chanting and the cheers of a mighty fleet lying all around, and set in motion the events of the Fourth Crusade – which were presently to make him and all his seventy-nine successors, at least in name, Lords of a Quarter and a Half-Quarter of the Roman Empire.

Venice had been in existence for some five hundred years already. Born out of the fall of Rome, when her first rickety townships were built within the fastness of the lagoon, she had become a client of the Byzantine Empire, which had its headquarters in Constantinople, alias Byzantium, now Istanbul, and was the eastern successor to Rome's glories. Through the first centuries of their history, while much of western Europe endured the Dark Ages of barbaric regression, the Venetians had organized their affairs within the fold of Byzantine power. Sometimes they availed themselves of Byzantine protection, sometimes they acted as mercenaries for Byzantium, and so loyal had they been to the suzerainty that one of the more fulsome of the emperors had called Venice 'Byzantium's favourite daughter'.

In 1202, accordingly, this was in many respects a Byzantine city, though of a very particular kind. The impact it had upon strangers was much the same then as now: the marvellous spectacle of a city built upon mudbanks, its walls rising directly out of the lagoon, was perhaps even more astonishing in those days, when laborious journeys over the wild Alps, or perilous voyages through the Mediterranean, deposited the stranger at last upon this marvellous strand. The earliest townscape picture we have of Venice, a fourteenth-century miniature in the Bodleian Library at Oxford, seems to have been painted in a kind of daze: fantastically coloured domes and turrets crown the scene, suave white swans float around, and a sightseer in the Piazzetta is looking up at the lion on its column in just that attitude of disjointed bemusement in which, any summer day, you may see amateur cameramen aiming themselves at the animal now.

It was a city of about 80,000 people, one of the biggest in Europe, and it was organized by parishes, each with its own strong character, its own social hierarchy, so that there was no rich quarter of town, and no poor. It was mostly built of wood, but its functional shape had already been evolved – that sensible, machine-like pattern which modern town-planners so admire. The waters all around it meant that it need not be circumvallated, but a wall protected the city on its seaward side, and the principal buildings were mostly defensive in style. This gave it a very *jagged* look: for besides the big pot-bellied chimney-pots which crowned every house, there were embattlements everywhere, and in particular a twin-pronged kind of merlonation, slightly oriental of cast, which seemed to run along the tops of everything, and pungently accentuated the exotic nature of the place.

In 1202 much of it was new. The first stone bridges had quite lately been built, the Piazza had been paved within living memory, the columns had not long been standing on the Piazzetta. The city plan, though, was immemorial, and was based then as now upon the Grand Canal, which bisected the city and was its principal thoroughfare. It ran in a big reversed S from one side of Venice to the other, and acted as a feeder highway for every part of the city: from it traffic fanned out through all the parishes by barge and boat on a myriad lesser canals, by horseback or porters' shoulders through a labyrinth of alleys.

The commercial centre of Venice was Rialto, halfway along the Grand Canal, where the single bridge that crossed the waterway provided an obvious fulcrum. Here the bankers had their stalls, the merchants their offices, the slavers their auction-yards, and here the barges from the mainland were moored in their hundreds for the transhipment of cargoes from ocean-going ships. The port of Venice was nearly everywhere, for if the Basin was the ceremonial harbour of the city, docks and wharves were scattered all over it, and deep-sea vessels found their way far into its urban heart. Most of the Grand Canal palaces, being the homes of successful merchants, had their own small docks in front, where cargoes were unloaded directly into their ground-floor warehouses, and there were shipyards up side canals, and chandlers in market squares, and ships' masts protruding among bell-towers, so that almost every part of the city had a dockside vigour and vivacity.

The centre of military power was in the east of the city: since 1104 Venice had possessed, in her famous Arsenal, the greatest of all shipyards, and probably the chief industrial undertaking in Europe. When Dante, descending into his Inferno, wanted images to express the awful turmoil and congestion of purgatory, he drew upon his memories of the Arsenal, for hardly less than the wonders of Venetian architecture and display, the shipyard captured the imagination of everyone: every old map, print and drawing shows it – fairly hazily as a rule, for security was tight, and draughtsmen with easels were hardly encouraged, I imagine, at its heavily battlemented gates.

Political power, though, was concentrated upon the Piazza San Marco, and this was still unmistakably an expatriated Byzantine forum. It was much its present shape and size, paved in herringbone brick, and the sides of the square were already arcaded; but scattered over it were the booths of trade guilds collecting dues, shipmasters recruiting crews and passengers, tourist entrepreneurs selling souvenirs, while at the entrance to the Merceria, the chief shopping street, there was a clump of elder trees to which citizens' horses were habitually tied. The buildings around the Piazza were a *mélange* of shops, offices and travellers' hospices, and the whole was dominated by the great red-brick tower of the Campanile at the corner, which was more or less flat-topped then, and served the simultaneous functions of a beacon-tower, a tocsin and a church belfry.

Around the corner, in the still unpaved Piazzetta, was the palace of the Doges. This was nothing very grand. It was rather like the palace of an Arab sheikh or African king, a jumble of buildings around a yard, some private, some public, with fortified towers forming part of the defences along the Riva degli Schiavoni. Its southern outlook, over the Basin, was magnificent even then; its eastward prospect, over the often muddy Piazzetta, gave the Doge a view of the public bakeries across the way, and the jumble of money-changers' stalls that clustered around the base of the Campanile.

Immediately next door was the Basilica of St Mark. The Patriarch of Venice, the bishop of the place, had his seat outside the city altogether, in the small town of Grado along the coast, but the true centre of the civic faith was this already remarkable church, in which had been deposited nearly four hundred years before the remains of St Mark himself. The third church on the site, it was officially the Doge's private chapel – he was its *patronus et gubernator*, its patron and its governor – but it had long since become a shrine of State and a focus of national emotion. In style it was pure Byzantine, its plan being based upon that of the Church of the Holy Apostles in Constantinople. Its domes were shallow in the Byzantine manner, giving to the brick exterior of the church a severe authority – only a few patches of coloured stone relieved it, and to the right of the main door a single lateen yard-arm protruded from the brickwork in token of some ancient victory at sea.

The devotions of the Venetians were distinctly eastern in temper: their style of singing was recognizably oriental, their priests wore golden vestments all their own and conducted peculiar offices – for instance, in the service of baptism they laid the child upon the baptistry floor during the singing of the *paternoster* to symbolize its coming into possession of the church. Over the years, to suit these ritual preferences, they had filled the Basilica with artifacts from the east, mosaics, reliquaries, marble columns, and the great screen called the Pala d'Oro which, beaten into its tremendous form by Byzantine goldsmiths, exquisitely ornamented by Byzantine jewellers, stood refulgently behind the high altar.

As for the people who thronged this extraordinary city, they were exotic too. For one thing there were always travellers from the east about: Slavs, Greeks, Arabs, Persians, pilgrims of every nation returning from the Holy Land; for another the Venetians themselves, from long association with eastern countries, had acquired something oriental in their temperament. They were more familiar with the east than any other Europeans. They had been trading for generations with the countries of the fertile crescent, with Egypt, and Persia, and Byzantium itself, and so strong was their taste for orientalia that a century before, the Doge Domenico Selvo had ordered every Venetian merchant ship returning from the east to bring back eastern substances and works of art for the embellishment of the city. The two columns of the Piazzetta were oriental booty. The agate-eyed lion of St Mark was a Syrian chimera. The Patriarchal throne was a super-annuated Muslim tombstone.

An eastern love of swank was already apparent in the Venetians, too, a penchant for display and flamboyant dignity, and for showing off in the Piazza – for if ever the Venetians needed a breath of air, if ever there was a rumour to be pursued or a spectacle witnessed, if they felt like a change of scene, or a bite to eat, or something to surprise them, or someone to slander – then as now, to the Piazza San Marco outside the great Basilica they instinctively made their way.

Imagine them, as we turn the corner by the Campanile, a sumptuous if motley assembly strolling up and down. There are not many women about, for they are hidden away at home as if in purdah, or alternatively busy plying their trade in the city's many brothels, but the men are colourful enough without them. With hats of ermine or damask and gowns heavy with brocade, with shoes with pointed toes, with multi-coloured tabards, with faces brownish often, or black, or even yellowish, perfumed with precious musk or sweaty from the galleys, talking in the thick Venetian dialect, or in Greek, or Arabic, or Persian – it is a city crowd unlike any other in Europe, looking always to the east, to the chances of Asia and the forms of Byzantium, for its pleasures as for its profits.

Within the atrium of the Basilica, mostly unnoticed by the tourists who clamorously pass in and out of the building, over-shadowed by the clutter of the souvenir stalls and generally cast in darkness anyway, there is set into the ground a small marble lozenge. It was already there in 1202, and it meant more to the Venetians then.

It marked the spot where, twenty-five years before, the Emperor Frederick Barbarossa, 'Redbeard', head of the western empire based in Germany, had been reconciled with the Pope Alexander III after a long and tangled squabble that had affected the whole of western Europe. They had settled their differences under the direct auspices of Venice, in circumstances highly gratifying to the Venetians. Prelates and potentates from all over

Europe had come to the city for the occasion, accompanied by armies of secretaries, acolytes, bodyguards and advisers, and when the Pope and the emperor met to sign their treaty of accord, it was as though the Piazza San Marco really was, as Venetians have always thought it, the centre of the world.

The Venetians loved to recall the story of the reconciliation, which had grown ever more satisfying with the years. We hear of the high throne outside the Basilica upon which the millionaire Doge Sebastiano Ziani, attended by the Patriarchs of Venice and Aquilea and flanked by a pair of gigantic Venetian flags, presided over the occasion. We are told that when the Pope mounted his horse after the ceremony, the emperor humbly held his stirrup for him: or alternatively that when, according to a more humiliating protocol, he was obliged to kiss the papal foot, he growled, 'Not for you but for St Peter,' to be hissed back at by His Holiness, *sotto voce*, 'For me *and* St Peter.'

That striking event, to be painted grandiloquently by Venetian painters, described ornately by Venetian chroniclers for generations to come, established Venice as a world power. She held the balances. She had forged her own particular relationships with the two empires, with the Papacy, with Islam. Barbarossa, before he left, recognized her uniqueness with special privileges all over his domains. The Pope blessed her with a whole paraphernalia of holy accoutrements, to accompany the Doge on special occasions ever after – a sword, a stool, a holy candle, an umbrella, a set of silver trumpets and eight richly embroidered flags. Venice was already Venice – 'subject', said one German commentator devoutly, having witnessed the Great Reconciliation for himself, 'only to God'.

All this only confirmed the Venetians in their native self-esteem. They often saw themselves as true successors to the Romans – the barbarians had never penetrated to these lagoons, and they believed themselves to preserve the Roman virtues unsullied. They liked to trace parallels between their institutions and those of ancient Rome. The noblemen of the Grand Council, in their flowing togas, seemed to them like reincarnations of the grave senators of old. The Doges were like so many Caesars.

Besides, the particular patronage of the Evangelist St Mark was

supposed to have given Venice some divine summons to greatness. Diverse legends assiduously associated St Mark with the
lagoon, and the presence of his body in the city was one of the
struts of Venetian pride. Everybody knew the famous tale of its
acquisition: how the brave Venetian merchants had snatched the
holy corpse from the infidels in Alexandria, conveying it to their
ship hidden beneath piles of pork to discourage inquisitive
Muslim customs men. Everyone knew too that it had been lost in
a great fire in the Basilica only eleven years before, but had
reappeared miraculously by bursting out of a pillar, when
appealed for by the combined prayers of Doge, Patriarch and
assembled populace. St Mark's patronage powerfully reinforced
the city's sense of separateness. The Venetians did not yet fly his
winged lion above their galleys, as they would to the wonder and
sometimes the terror of their rivals through so many centuries of
maritime history, but already the emblem was the talisman of
their state: carved above doorways, inserted into finials, exquisitely delineated in manuscripts and soon to give golden
franchise to one of the most commanding of all currencies, the
Venetian ducat – the Coin of the Doge.

The favourite daughter had come of age. Venice was clearly
destined to be something special among the nations, and her links
with her old Byzantine suzerains had long become anomalous.
Commercially she was still largely dependent upon them. The
Arabs were masters of the Levant, but much of the trade of the
east came through Constantinople, and like other European
nations, the Venetians maintained a permanent trading colony
there. But the relationship was full of ups and downs, fluctuating
from oaths of eternal loyalty to actual declarations of war. Now
we hear of a Venetian nobleman marrying, with every manifes-
tation of mutual esteem, the daughter of a Byzantine emperor.
Now we see a Negro slave, decked out in crude parody of the
imperial regalia, posed on the poop of a Venetian galley and
insultingly paraded before the Byzantine fleet. Sometimes the
Venetian merchants in Constantinople are honoured guests,
prominent at state functions and luxuriously accommodated.
Sometimes they are slaughtered. This year the Venetians might
have complete freedom to trade anywhere within the imperial

dominions. Next year they might find all their ships seized and their properties confiscated.

What was more, since 1054 Venice and Constantinople had been separated by a theological rift. The Great Schism had irreconcilably divided the Latin Church, based on Rome, from the Greek Orthodox with its headquarters in Constantinople, and Venice had stayed with the Papacy. This had dangerously exacerbated all the other differences, and many grudges were now cherished between the ageing despotism on the one side, the agile and ambitious republic on the other. The Venetians resented the continuing condescension of the Byzantine emperors, who tended to treat the Doges as their feudatories still, airily granting or withdrawing favours. The Byzantines disliked the Venetians for their fierce competitive powers, the hauteur with which they conducted themselves, even in Constantinople, and their notorious willingness, in the age of the Crusades, to do business with infidels.

As it happens, relations in 1202 were tranquil, a new treaty of cooperation having been signed in 1187. Venetian traders were making the most of their privileges throughout the empire. Venetian shipbuilders were rebuilding the Byzantine fleet. Nobody had been massacred in Constantinople for years. But the calm was illusory. The Emperor of Byzantium, Alexius III, had recently succeeded to the throne by blinding and imprisoning his brother Isaac II, and was half crazy. The Doge, Enrico Dandolo, had spent some years in Constantinople earlier in his career, and did not like it – it may have been there that, by accident or by malice, he had lost his sight.

Nor did this formidable old man think of his splendid republic as any kind of vassal. He thought of it as a Great Power in its own right – *La Dominante*, as the Venetians later learned to call it.

Venice, in short, was almost ready for empire. She was impelled by a fierce patriotism – perhaps the first proper national pride in Europe – and was a sort of overseas power already. The Byzantines themselves recognized her overlordship of the Adriatic, and had dubbed the Doge Duke of Dalmatia too: on the maps of the cartographer Abu Abdullah Mohammed ibn al-Idrisi, the finest of the day, the northern Adriatic was called the Gulf of Venice. Every Ascension Day the Doge sailed out to the open sea in his marvellous state barge, the gilded *bucintoro*, and with elaborate ceremonial threw a ring into the sea: it was supposed to symbolize this Venetian mastery of the Adriatic, but it had come to represent a marriage with the sea as a whole, and so aspirations to maritime supremacy everywhere.

Certainly Venice was already important throughout the eastern Mediterranean. Her agents all over the Near East gave her an incomparable intelligence service. Her merchants were immensely experienced in the affairs of the Levant. Her knowledge of the eastern trade routes, of Byzantium, of Islam, meant that already, when people in western Europe wished to learn about, travel to, plot against or do business with the peoples of the eastern Mediterranean, it was Venice that they were likely to consult. Many of her leading citizens had served their country in the east, as diplomats, sailors or soldiers, and many more had money bound up in eastern ventures. This was a merchant city, a city in which the ruling aristocracy was itself a commercial class: trade was its power, and trade, in Venice's particular geopolitical situation, meant a knowledge of the east.

This is how that knowledge was transmuted into imperialism. In 1197 the chivalry of France, encouraged by the Pope, Innocent III, determined to mount a new Crusade to liberate the Holy Land from Islam. They turned to Venice for help. The Venetians had the knowledge and the resources to convey a big army from Europe to the east, and they were particularly well-acquainted with Egypt, an old trading partner, which the Crusaders had chosen as their immediate target. It was true that the Venetians were by the nature of things reluctant Crusaders – they did not like antagonizing Muslim commercial colleagues, and they resented footholds gained in the Levant by rival European powers in the course of their pious campaigns. Moreover they were, it is believed, at that very moment negotiating with the Egyptians for even more profitable trading arrangements.

But they accepted the Crusaders' commission anyway, and undertook to supply a fleet to carry 20,000 men from Venice to Egypt. It was a mammoth undertaking for a state of 80,000 souls, but as they probably reasoned from the start, there was sure to be profit in it somewhere. Directly or indirectly the whole city was geared to the project. Even the conclusion of the agreement with the Crusaders was a civic function, for the six envoys of the Franks were invited to make their request to the people themselves, assembled in St Mark's. They were great men in their own countries, but they knelt humbly before the congregation, weeping tears for the Holy Land, and begging the help of Venice in the name of Christ: and when they had finished the Venetians raised their hands and cried as one man (so the chroniclers assure us), 'We consent! We consent!' – 'and there was so great a noise and tumult that it seemed as though the earth itself were falling to pieces'.

Later the Doge himself, in another tearful ceremony in the Basilica, announced that he himself would take the cross. 'I am a man old and feeble . . . but I see that no one could command and lead you like myself, who am your lord.' He knelt before the high altar there and then, and they sewed the cross on to a great cotton hat, and placed it on his head: and from that moment the destiny of the expedition was settled.

For old he was, but rascally. Enrico Dandolo's part in the Fourth Crusade has been debated ever since, but we may assume that, however moved his people were by the cause, he himself did nothing out of pure religious impulse. It is very unlikely that he ever intended to lead his ships to an assault on Egypt, as the Crusaders thought. Venetian trade with Egypt was extremely valuable to Venice, and some scholars suggest indeed that Dandolo told the Sultan of Egypt all about the Crusaders' plans.

The chances are that even as that great white hat was placed upon his head, Dandolo was planning to lead the Crusade to a very different destination: not an Islamic objective at all, but the greatest city of Christendom itself, Constantinople. The time had come to humble the arrogant emperors, and ensure once and for all Venetian commercial primacy in the east. In the meantime the Doge struck a properly Venetian bargain. In return for providing the fleet, and sailing it, Venice would be paid the enormous sum of 80,000 francs, and would be entitled to a share of any territory the Crusaders captured.

Everything then played into Dandolo's hands. The Crusaders began to arrive in Venice in the winter of 1201. They were mostly French, with some Germans, Belgians and Italians, and they were quartered on the island of Lido, well away from the city centre – for if there were, as the old historians were fond of saying, many good, worthy and holy men among them, there were many adventurers and vagabonds too. From the beginning they had difficulty in raising the necessary cash. To make a first deposit, enabling the Arsenal to start work upon new ships, their leaders borrowed 5,000 francs from the Venetian Jews. Then, when the army was already assembling, and the fleet was half-built, they were reduced to payment in kind – huge piles of precious objects were to be seen disappearing into the Doge's Palace, whence many of them would later reappear in the guise of another great Venetian coin, the silver grosso.

Almost at the same time there arrived in the west a plausible pretender to the imperial throne of Constantinople: Alexius, son of the blinded and imprisoned Isaac Angelus, and known as Young Alexius to distinguish him from his usurper uncle, the present emperor. He let it be known that if he ever gained the throne of Byzantium, he would not only be a munificent patron of Crusades, but would actually undertake to bring the Orthodox Church back within the fold of Rome.

Nothing could be handier for Dandolo than this combination of circumstances. When it became obvious that the Crusaders would never be able to pay their debt to Venice, he proposed that they commute it by stopping on their way to the east to subdue in the name of Venice a troublesome city on the Dalmatian shore, Zadar – Zara in those days – thus consolidating Venetian supremacy in the Adriatic. And when it was hinted that Young Alexius might be forcibly installed upon the throne of Constantinople, to end the Great Schism at last, why, Dandolo was doubtless the first to suggest that the Fourth Crusade, in its Venetian ships, might conveniently take him there.

So the Doge Dandolo manipulated the course of history, and laid the foundations of the Venetian Empire. He acted in collusion, no doubt, with some of the less scrupulous seigneurs of the Crusade, but the lesser knights, and the ordinary soldiers, were left in ignorance of these machinations, and thought they were still preparing for an assault on Alexandria. By the autumn of 1202 all was ready. The army had embarked from the Lido, the fleet was assembled on the lagoon. Then the belvedere of the Piazzetta saw its greatest spectacle of all, for nearly 500 ships were lying there. They filled that great water-stage, from the Basin itself to the distant shore of the Lido. 'Never did finer fleet,' wrote Geoffrey de Villehardouin, one of the principal Crusaders, 'sail from any port . . . Our armament could undertake the conquest of the world!' There were the fifty war-galleys of the naval escort, dominated by *Paradiso*, *Aquila* and *Pellegrina*, probably the most powerful vessels afloat: snake-like craft, very low in the water, with their long banks of oars like insects' legs, their lateen yard-arms drooping, at their sterns high canopied castles where their lordly captains, all in armour, strutted and postured as captains do. There were the 240 troopships, heavier and fatter in the water and square-sailed. There were seventy supply ships and 120 flat-bottomed cavalry transports, specially designed for amphibious war, with wide ports for the horses. And all around the hulls of these vessels, emblazoning the lagoon itself, were the crested shields of the knights-at-arms – Boniface of Montferrat and Baldwin of Flanders, Richard of Dampierre and Guy of Conflans, Count Berthold von Katzenellenbogen, the Castellan of Bruges and the Seneschal of Champagne.

Then there were all the hundreds of lesser craft that milled about the fleet, the pinnaces of the admirals and the generals, scudding from ship to ship, ship to shore – all the sightseeing craft too, no doubt, in which the citizens of Venice, as always, pottered inquisitively here and there, and fishing boats of the lagoon, still stoically at their work in clusters around the mudbanks, and gondolas, and market skiffs, and perhaps an astonished merchant ship or two, working their way through the Lido sea-gate to find that stunning armada crowding the roadsteads inside.

Trumpets blared; cymbals clashed; attended by senators and captains of Venice, counts and commanders of the Frankish chivalry, chaplains and aides and physicians, the blind Doge emerged from his palace and was led between the twin columns of the Piazzetta to his galley at the quay. The drums of the fleet struck up their rhythm. The bugles called from admiral to admiral. Hymns sounded from the waterfront. Vessel by vessel the great fleet followed the Doge's flagship out of the Basin, and gathering speed as the day wore on, disappeared past the eastern point of the city, and headed for the open sea.

By nightfall the Fourth Crusade was in mid-Adriatic, on its way (though so few of its soldiers knew it) to Constantinople: and there, squeamishly avoiding the assault on Zadar, a very blood-thirsty affair, and drawing a veil over the dissensions that arose when the rank-and-file Crusaders discovered that they were not, after all, going to rescue the Holy Places from the infidel – there, to the City of Cities, by the turn of a page we shall follow them.

O City, City!

*A great presence – the Crusade sails in – the
assault – the City – 'anger of the Lord' –
empire at a stroke – a hint of Venice*

'O CITY, CITY, THE eye of all cities!' So passionately exclaimed
Nicetas Chroniates, a contemporary Greek chronicler, writing of
the Fourth Crusade's expedition to Byzantium, and the cry may
echo in our minds now when, sailing out of the Sea of Marmara in
the wake of Dandolo's great fleet, we approach Constantinople as
the Crusaders approached it long ago.

O city, city! Nowhere on earth is more magnificently sited, or
greets the sea voyager with such a mighty sense of consequence –
not even Manhattan, when its tight-packed silhouette greets you
through the Narrows, or London when you first see the towers of
Westminster grave and heavy beyond its bridges. Constantinople
was built on a high narrow peninsula, the Marmara on one side,
the deeper-water inlet called the Golden Horn on the other,
commanding the narrow strait of the Bosphorus as it runs away
between hills towards the Black Sea. It is so tremendous a site, on
the very frontier between Europe and Asia, where the warm seas
meet the cold, that the ancient settlement of Chalcedon, on the
opposite shore of the Bosphorus, was said to have been called the
City of the Blind because its founders *must* have been myopic to
have settled so crassly in the wrong place.

Constantinople is called Istanbul now, and one's first distant
sight of it is misleading. It looks like simply another fold in
the hills, unimpressive beside the white-capped mountains of
Anatolia over the water to the east. But as the ship draws closer an
indefinable sense of excitement grows. The passing water-traffic

thickens, the pace quickens, and all of a sudden the peninsula is clarified, and you realize that it is not simply a protrusion of the landscape, but a solid mass of city. Nowadays its skyline is dominated by the domes and pinnacles of its mosques, one after the other along the ridge – a stupendous encrustation up there, huge hulks of buildings, dish-domed and buttressed all around, and transmitting like so many beams into the sky their fragile minarets. Below them the city spills away down the hillsides in a messy confusion, patternless, greyish, until at the water's edge it is bounded by the crumbled remains of a city wall, battlemented still. At the tip of the peninsula are the towers and gardens of a great palace: and as your ship steers beneath its walls, past the little castle which, standing on its island off-shore, looks like a toll-house for the passing vessels, abruptly to your left the Golden Horn runs away on the other side of the promontory, seven miles long, cast in shadow, spanned by two busy bridges and full of ships.

Everywhere is full of ships. 'You are accustomed to the Gondolas that slide among the palaces of St Mark,' wrote Alexander Kinglake in the 1840s, 'but here at Stamboul it is a hundred and twenty-gun ship that meets you in the street . . . the stormy bride of the Doge is the bowing slave of the Sultan.' It is true still. Ferry-boats push and manoeuvre crazily all about you, blowing their sirens, threshing their propellers, perilously keeling to their moorings as their passengers rush to the quayside rail. Caiques come chugging down the Horn, their masts laid flat for the passage of the bridges. A string of big liners is always moored along the waterfront, and perpetually off the city, never absent, never stopped, the deep-sea freighters pass up and down the Bosphorus. A constant rumble hangs on the air, as your own ship ties up, and wherever you look around you, pouring over the bridges and fly-overs, thronging the docksides, clambering up the steep sides of the peninsula, flooding down the cobbled streets on the other side of the Golden Horn – wherever you look the Turks are on the move, tireless, numberless and grey.

As you step ashore into the tumult of it all (fragrance of frying fish from the floating restaurants by the Galata Bridge, tinkle of brass bell from the water-seller outside the Egyptian Bazaar, swoop of dingy pigeons around the mosque of Yeni Cami) – as you edge your way into the crowd you know at once that you are entering a great presence, which displays even in its modern impotence the stance of old majesty.

If sailing to Byzantium feels like this today, imagine the sensations of the Crusaders as *they* sailed out of the Marmara on 24 June 1203, their purpose now revealed to them all! Istanbul is not even the capital of Turkey: Constantinople was the capital of half the world. It was also one of the supreme cities of the Christian faith: deep though the gulf was between the Latin and the Orthodox rites, Constantinople was a city to be reverenced even by Catholics. 'I can assure you,' says Villehardouin, 'those who had never seen Constantinople before gazed very intently at the city, having never imagined there could be so fine a place in all the world.'

There was no mistaking the historical impact of the occasion, or its beauty. 'It was something so beautiful as to be remembered all one's life.' The fleet, so Villhardouin thought, 'seemed as it were in flower', spread out in magnificent array across the Marmara under a cloudless sky: first the terrible war-galleys, rowed with a steady stroke, then the mass of tall transports, and then like a cloud behind, as far as the eye could see, all the small craft of the fleet-followers, the independent fortune-hunters, the hopeful entrepreneurs, the rogues and scavengers, who had attached themselves to the Crusade on its progress to the east.

To the soldiers from France, Belgium or Germany, Constantinople was more than just a city, it was a myth and a mystery. The Russians called it Tsarigrad, Caesar's City, the Vikings Mickle Garth, the Mighty Town, and it had long before entered the legends of the west. Young men grew up with a vision of it. The City on its seven hills, the grand repository of classical civilization – the greatest city of them all, rich beyond imagination, stuffed with treasures new and ancient, where the wonders of ancient learning were cherished in magnificent libraries, where the supreme church of Santa Sophia, the church of the Holy Wisdom, was more like a miracle than a work of man, where countless sacred relics were kept in a thousand lovely shrines, where the emperor of the Byzantines dressed himself in robes of gold and silver, surrounded himself with prodigies of art and crafts-manship, and lived in the greatest of all the palaces among the palaces of the earth, the Bucoleon. It was the City of the World's Desire. It was the God-Guarded city. It was the city of the Nicene Creed – 'Maker of heaven and earth, and of all things visible and invisible!'

For the worldly-wise Venetians the sight of the city doubtless provided *frissons* of another sort. It was not so strange to them. Many of the sailors had been there before. Countless others had relatives who had traded there or worked in the shipyards. There was a large Venetian colony in the city at that moment. To the Venetians, especially perhaps to the old Doge Dandolo as he scented the air of Byzantium upon his nostrils, it was not the sight of Constantinople that was exciting that day, but the circum-stances of this landfall. Never before had a Venetian fleet approached the city in such overwhelming force, carrying an army of the strongest and fiercest soldiers in Europe, and bringing with it too, as the Doge's particular puppet, a claimant to the imperial throne – Young Alexius, who had eagerly acquiesced in the plan for his future, and joined the fleet at Zadar.

Crusaders though they were, sailing to a Christian city, they made no attempt at a peaceful approach. When some of those fishing boats got in the way, they instantly attacked them; and when the fleet sailed, as we did, close under the walls of the city, the soldiers on deck were already cleaning their weapons for battle. It was the feast day of St John the Baptist, whose head was among the most precious of the relics enshrined in Byzantium: the ships flew all their flags in honour of the saint, and the noblemen hung out their decorated shields again all along the gunwales.

The people of Constantinople swarmed to the ramparts in their thousands to watch the fleet sail in. The soldiers looked back in awe at the walls towering above their ships. This was the most perfectly fortified city in the world. On its landward side, cutting off the peninsula from the mainland of Thrace, were the cele-brated walls built by Theodosius II in the fifth century: four and a half miles long, and elaborately constructed in four lines of defence – moat and three walls. Then all along the shoreline, enclosing the entire peninsula, a sea-wall protected the city

against amphibious attack. Some four hundred towers commanded these encircling defences, and behind them underground
reservoirs, granaries and innumerable windmills made the city
self-sufficient for months of siege. A huge chain, controlled by a
winch on a hill above, blocked the entrance to the Golden Horn.
The imperial army was concentrated within the capital, and at the
core of it was a formidable praetorian guard of Danish and
English mercenaries, the Varangian guard.

Nobody had ever cracked these defences. For a thousand years
they had kept the barbarians at bay. Six times Muslim armies had
been beaten back from them; Goths, Huns, Hungarians, Bulgars,
Serbs had all been repulsed. No wonder the Crusaders eyed the
walls of Constantinople thoughtfully as they sailed by. 'There
was indeed no man so brave and daring,' says Villehardouin
convincingly, 'that the flesh did not shudder at the sight . . .'

The fleet anchored on the other side of the Bosphorus, on the
Asian shore. The army encamped itself at Scutari, now Usküdar,
where Florence Nightingale had her hospital six centuries later
and where now, from the big turreted railway station on the
waterfront, the trains run away to Anatolia, Aleppo, Baghdad
and Teheran. The soldiers looted the surrounding countryside for
victuals and souvenirs: the leaders of the Crusade took over one of
the Byzantine Emperor's several country palaces. It was an
ominous scene from the battlements of Constantinople, across
the water. You can easily see from one shore to the other, and the
huge encampment on the foreshore there, its smoke in the
daytime, its lights at night, the forested riggings of its ships
off-shore, must have cast a chill in the heart. What was that great
host preparing? Was it merely passing by, or was it inexplicably,
beneath the banner of the Cross, about to attack this ancient
fortress of Christ?

The emperor did not wait to find out. His fleet, ramshackle in
the Golden Horn, was in no condition to tackle the Crusade, but
within a couple of days a squadron of his cavalry did ride down
upon the Scutari encampment, being humiliatingly driven off.
Two days later the Crusaders declared their purpose. They put
Young Alexius on the deck of a warship, and displayed him

below the walls of the city. They had come, they shouted, to place him upon the throne, since he was the true king and natural lord of Byzantium. 'The man you now obey as your lord rules over you with no just or fair claim to be your emperor, in defiance of God and the right. Here is your rightful lord and master. If you rally to his side you will be doing as you ought, but if you hold back, we will do to you the very worst that we can.'

These were specious arguments (long-winded, too, to be yelled into the wind from the deck of a galley) and the people's predominant response, as they looked down at the Young Alexius, was 'Never heard of him!' Succession by coup or revolution had always been a feature of the Byzantine monarchy, and it was the accepted form for the populace to transfer their loyalties to a new emperor, however bloodily he had come to power. There was no suggestion that the people of Constantinople thought of Alexius III as an unlawful usurper. Hardly a single citizen defected from the imperial cause to join the pretender, just as nobody tried to rescue his blinded father Isaac, now old and derelict, from the dungeons in which he had so long been immured.

So it had to be done by force. On 5 July 1203, the first assault ships crossed the Bosphorus, each galley towing a transport, and made for the mouth of the Golden Horn. Most previous assaults on Constantinople had been from the landward side, the attacking armies beating themselves vainly against Theodosius's tremendous walls. Dandolo knew that the weakest part of the defences was the sea-wall along the Goiden Horn. The Horn was unbridged in those days, and on its northern bank, opposite Constantinople proper, was the foreign quarter of Galata, where the trading colonies were settled, and the envoys of the powers were all obliged to live. Halfway up its hill stood the massive Galata Tower, and from it ran the chain across the entrance to the Golden Horn: it was 1,500 feet long, with links the length of a man's forearm, and it was suspended a few feet above the surface of the water.

Once through this chain, and the Crusaders would be under the lee of the city on its weakest side. The walls along its northern shore were feeble compared to the others, without moats or *enceintes*, and made difficult to defend by the steep streets running

directly down the hills behind them. Dandolo, the tactician of
the assault, accordingly ordered the first landing to be made on the
Galata shore. There was no resistance. At the first sight of the
Norman knights on their armoured horses, led by grooms out of
the sally-ports of the assault craft, the Greek forces fled from the
waterfront, and in no time a bridgehead was established. Next
day they captured the Galata Tower, after a stiff fight, and
winched down the chain across the Horn. In sailed the warships,
led by the mighty *Aquila*, into the crowded waterway, storming
and burning whatever ships they found there: and so by 6 July the
flank of the city was turned, and they were ready to storm it.

From the middle of the Ataturk Bridge, the higher of the two
bridges that now span the Golden Horn, one may see almost
exactly the view the soldiers saw, as they planned their assault
from the decks of their warships. This is visibly the city's soft
side. It has none of the piled, phalanx look that characterizes
Constantinople from the Sea of Marmara. Here all the muddled
bazaars, speckled with small mosques and splashed here and there
with green, give the place a rather helpless look, and the great
buildings along the skyline, which look so forbidding from the
sea, seem almost avuncular from the Golden Horn.

   Along the shoreline you can make out the remains of fortifications. It is a sleazy shore there, a slum of small warehouses and
factories, old houses crumbled into squalor, small boatyards
where the caiques are caulked, tanneries and tyre depots. Big
ships do not moor here, only grubby coasters from the Anatolian
islands, their masts shipped, their crews wearing cloth caps and
eating fried fish sandwiches out of carrier bags. But not quite
obliterated by the confusion, still just distinguishable against the
warren of streets on the hillside behind, turrets stand shadowy,
and city gates reveal themselves. In 1203 this line of walls was
complete, and joined the Theodosian walls at the head of the
Golden Horn. Its turrets were manned all along the water's edge,
and there was no way of turning it. This was the one place,
though, where the defences of Constantinople might be broken –
by the skills not of soldiers, who had invariably failed to take this
city, but of sailors, who had never tried before.

For it was the Venetians themselves who mounted the assault here, on 17 July 1203. The French decided to march to the head of the Horn, along its northern bank, and attack the Theodosian walls at the point where they joined the sea-wall on the water-front. The Venetians resolved simply to hurl themselves across the Horn, a very Dandolan device. The point that they chose as the fulcrum of their attack can be identified. It is a rotted mass of masonry still called the Petrion Gate, immediately below the modest residence of the Greek Orthodox Patriarch, the Pope of eastern Christendom, who still lives in somewhat prickly cir-cumstances in this Muslim and less than philhellene city. If you run your eye along the line of the waterfront buildings, you may identify almost exactly the site of the first landing: a small grubby square, with a struggling tree or two, beside the remains of the gateway at the water's edge.

In the small hours of every morning they open the Ataturk Bridge to let the ships go through, and then, with the flashing of the lights, the beat of the engines, the slow movement of the vessels down the waterway in the dark, you can best imagine the Venetians preparing for their assault before the dawn of the battle. The fleet's room for manoeuvre was awkwardly small. The Horn is only half a mile wide there, the tide runs fast, and somehow several score ships had to be navigated across this narrow channel simultaneously. The waterway was jammed full with their threshing oars and creaking hulls, and the later Venetian artists, when they came to recall this epic moment in the idealized historical reconstructions they were fond of, rendered it con-fusedly. In an excitable version I have before me now, for instance, the Golden Horn seems to be one solid mass of warships, all ropes, masts, spars, oars and ladders, and one peers along the walls of Constantinople through a curtain of arrows and plunging missiles. Sailors clutch yard-arms, arrows plunge into knightly shields, axemen hack each other, men-at-arms fall upside-down into what little can be seen of the water.

But serenely dominating the picture, armoured on the foredeck of his flagship, is old blind Dandolo, holding a flag and pointing firmly towards Santa Sophia. This, it seems, is perfectly just, for he really did lead the assault. If he could not actually see the walls,

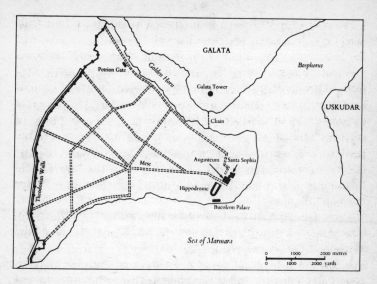

Constantinople, 1203

at least he had them in his mind's eye, and at his inspiration the Venetians had devised a particular mechanism for attacking the high towers from the water. Using the lateen yard-arms of their ships, they contrived a series of gangplanks which protruded from the prows of their galleys at a steep angle, like ladders to the tops of the ramparts. Covered with awnings of leather, to protect the assaulters against fire and arrows, these were jammed hard against the battlements by the impetus of the ships' grounding.

Supported by 250 shipboard catapults, up these precarious contraptions crawled the assault force, beneath a storm of stones and arrows, and presently the first of the towers was in Venetian hands. Instantly grappling ladders were thrown against the walls below, and the main body of the army swarmed up to the ramparts. The fight did not last long. Inspired by the frail but militant figure of their Doge, sword in hand on the strand below, the Venetians cleared the battlements tower by tower – twenty-five in all, in a single hour's fighting – and by afternoon the city seemed to be won. The news went home to Venice, we are told, by carrier pigeon across the Balkans.

*

'O city, city!' To disembark in Constantinople thus must have been a traumatic experience for the more sensitive of the Venetians. This was a holy city, after all. Constantine, its founder, had set up his capital here after the vision which, on the hills outside Rome, had converted him to Christianity, and he conceived it from the start as a divine city: asked how far he proposed to go, as he first marked out its limits, he is supposed to have replied, 'Until He stops who goes before me.' His successor Justinian too, when he built the matchless shrine of Santa Sophia, felt he was fulfilling a sacred destiny. 'Now at last,' legend had him saying as he entered its gigantic nave for the first time, 'I have outbuilt Solomon.'

Even the glitter of Venice paled somewhat beside this marvel. The shape of the place was strictly functional. Through the Theodosian walls two roads entered the city, one from the west through the Adrianople Gate, one from the south through the ceremonial entrance called the Golden Gate. They met on the spine of the ridge, then proceeded the triumphal way called the Mēsē through a succession of forums, each the pride of a different emperor, to the complex of state buildings, memorials and open spaces that was the heart of the city.

It was a city of marvellous statues. Lysippus was supposed to have created the great bronze Hercules, whose thumb was as big as a man's waist, Phidias had made the image of Athene Promachos, Athene the Champion, that had been brought here from the Acropolis in Athens. The bronze group of Romulus, Remus and the she-wolf had come from Rome at the foundation of the city; the wooden statue of Athene was supposed to have been removed by Aeneas from Troy; the lovely marble figure of Hera was from the isle of Samos. Bellerophon riding Pegasus was so big that ten herons had made their nests between the crupper and the horse's head. A huge bronze ox-head from Pergamon gave its name to the Forum of the Ox, and here is how Nicetas described the statue of Helen of Troy: 'Fairer than the evening air, clad in the beauty of a thousand stars . . . all harmony, grace and elegance.'

It was a city of columns, too. There was a column whose elaborate frieze, if you read it right, supposedly foretold the future. There was a column with hermits living on the top. There was a column one of whose trap-doors flew open every hour, to announce the time of day. There was a column into whose base had allegedly been inserted the crosses of the two thieves at the Crucifixion, St Mary Magdalene's alabaster jar and the basket of the miraculous loaves. There was a column carrying an equestrian figure of Justinian, and another with the Empress Helena, and another with a bronze woman, Servant of the Winds, swinging with the prevailing breezes. There was Constantine's Pillar sheathed all in copper. There was an Egyptian obelisk. There was a sinister and beautiful object, called the Column of the Three Serpents, which had come from the oracle at Delphi.

It was a city of churches, strewn across every quarter of it – more than one hundred dedicated to the Virgin alone, at one time or another, and thirty-five to the Baptist. At one extreme there was Santa Sophia, which seemed to have been lowered into place from heaven itself, which was served by 600 clergy and illuminated at night by lanterns, flickering from each arch of its dome, to be seen like a vision far out at sea. At the other extreme there were the myriad tiny shrines and hermitages which were hidden away in back-alleys, in the purlieus of palaces or the crannies of bazaars, or the scores of monasteries and nunneries which were embedded unobtrusively in the fabric of the place.

The churches of Constantinople were built in the sweet symmetry, at once innocent and commanding, which was the essence of Byzantine architecture, and was to find its way across the western world in successive adaptations of the Romanesque. They were decorated with the mosaics, frescoes and woodwork which only Byzantine artists could create. They were crammed with holy objects: fragments of the True Cross or the Virgin's veil, heads of St Stephen or the Baptist, the lance that pierced the Saviour's side, St Thomas's doubting finger, arms and legs of holy martyrs, and, most revered of all, the wonder-working Nikopoeia Madonna, painted by St Luke himself, an icon of victory which was carried into action in the van of the imperial armies, and whose sheltering veil, every Friday morning, was miraculously parted as a pledge of the divine favour.

Then there were the kaleidoscopic bazaars of the city, which made even the markets of Rialto look ordinary. They were a labyrinth of lanes, ordered trade by trade, commodity by commodity, and in them cultures and continents met. If there were always buyers from Greece and Italy, there were always sellers from Persia, Afghanistan, India, Russia. Slavs, Armenians, Syrians, Negroes, Jews all frequented these stalls, and you could buy Siberian furs and skins there, honey from Turkestan, amber from the distant Baltic, cottons and sugar from the Levant, ivories, silks, spices, carpets and *objets d'art* from India, Tibet and China. There were no restrictions on imports to Constantinople: it was the whole world's bazaar.

In the heart of all these wonders lay the Augusteum, the great open place outside Santa Sophia which was the focus of the capital. Here was the Hippodrome, the huge arena which was not only the empire's sporting centre, but its great place of public assembly: criminals were executed there, triumphs were celebrated, and there the two national factions of old, the Blues and the Greens, had fought out their differences and proclaimed their emperors. Dynasties had risen and toppled in the Hippodrome. In the centre of it stood the serpent column, the Egyptian obelisk, and a whole parade of curious blocks, pillars and pyramidal objects; all around were heroic bronze figures of famous charioteers, with their horses, commissioned by the heroes themselves in self-esteem, or sometimes by their supporters in tribute. And mounted magnificently on the emperor's box at the head of the stadium, more lovely than nature itself, stood the four golden horses of Constantinople, the most famous animal figures ever made by man, nostrils elegantly flared, forelegs raised in postures of gentle but masterly power – cast from some alloy no man could analyse, brought from some source no man could remember, created long before by some genius whose name was forgotten.

Immediately beside the Hippodrome, immediately opposite Santa Sophia, stood the Bucoleon, the Great Palace, just as the Doge's Palace stood beside the Piazza and the Basilica (the church for God, it used to be said, the palace for the emperor, the arena for the people). It was like an inner city of its own, spilling down the hillside in a complex of pavilions, courtyards, churches, barracks and gardens to its water-gate on the Marmara shore. It was the palace of palaces, full of astonishments. The Imperial Silk Factory occupied only a small corner of its space; in the imperial chapel even the nails and hinges were made of silver; the palace lighthouse was a signal station too, and its flashes kept the emperor in touch with his officials far away in Asia Minor. The very complexity of the place, corridor leading into gallery, hall opening only into anteroom, was designed to overawe the princes and ambassadors of lesser powers, while the core of it all, the audience chamber of the emperor himself, seemed to simple visitors actually magic. Mechanical birds twittered on enamelled branches as one entered it. Automatic lions roared, beating the ground with their tails. The towering blonde Varangians, like creatures from another planet, stood perpetually on guard with their battle-axes. When at last one reached the imperial presence, the emperor was discovered sitting on a sumptuous throne of gold and diamonds dressed in robes of many colours: but even as one made one's obeisances, to a peal of organs he was whisked into the air and out of sight, descending a moment later still on his throne but in a yet more dazzling change of costume.

Such was the city, part art, part mysticism, part sleight-of-hand, part shambled orientalism, that awaited the Venetians that morning. It remains The City still to thousands of Greeks all over the eastern Mediterranean, and some of it survives. Constantinople coincided exactly with that part of Istanbul known today as Stamboul, and you can still follow the course of that triumphal way along its spine, from the Theodosian walls to Constantine's original forum – thick with traffic now, and enlivened by the exuberant freelance minibuses which, packed to the doors, and announcing their destinations with raucous shouts from the young conductors hanging to their steps, are proper successors to the racing chariots. You can see the stump of the serpent column, still eerily suggestive in the centre of the Hippodrome. Santa Sophia has been a mosque and is now a museum, and down at the seashore you may find, neglected behind a car park, the ragged water-gate of the Great Palace. The domes of the Church of St Irene still show above the trees of the Topkapi Palace. The mighty Mosque of Fateh occupies the site of the Church of the Holy Apostles, the model of St Mark's. A few last lovely mosaics smile down at us from the Christian past. A pillar here, an obelisk there, attest to the pride of the old emperors.

All the life has gone, though, from old Byzantium: too many layers of history have been piled on top.

In the event this was not the Fall of Constantinople – not yet. The Venetians were obliged to withdraw again, the French, faced by the tough Varangians, having failed to break the defences in their sector of the attack. But that same night Alexius III fled anyway, disappearing into Thrace, and the Crusaders were free to put their own nominee upon the throne without violence. Having rescued the poor blinded Isaac from his dungeon, from which he emerged trembling and disturbed, they set up the two of them, father and son, as joint rulers of the empire, and withdrew the armies to the Galata shore once more.

This was not a success, as Dandolo probably foresaw. The father was senile, the son presumptuous, and nobody was pleased. Young Alexius miserably failed to meet his commitments to the Crusade – 'You stupid youth,' Dandolo is reported to have said to him, 'we pulled you out of the dung, and we'll soon put you back there' – and before long another contender to the throne arose. He was the court grand-chamberlain, Alexius Ducas, nicknamed Murzuphlus, 'bushy-browed', because his eyebrows met in the middle. Under his leadership the people rejected Young Alexius absolutely. Chaos fell upon Constantinople. The mob furiously destroyed Phidias' great figure of Athene because, they said, it was her beckoning shield, flashing out to sea, which had brought the Crusade so calamitously upon them. Fires started by drunken soldiers destroyed whole areas of the city. Fighting broke out between the factions. Murzuphlus had himself crowned in Santa Sophia, assumed the livery of the emperor and stormed about the city on a white horse. Poor old Isaac died at last. At the end of 1203 Young Alexius was found strangled in his palace, and in the spring of 1204 the Crusaders, stimulated as always by the Venetians, were obliged to storm Constantinople all over again.

This time they did it with a vengeance. Now the enmities were cut-and-dried, and the rough laws of war applied. The riff-raff

Crusaders could indulge their lust for blood and loot. The Venetians could revenge all the humiliations of the past. It was Holy Week, but this did not deter the warriors of Christ. In three days of half-crazed rape, looting and destruction the soldiers sacked Byzantium once and for all, almost obliterating its heritage of splendour and sanctity. The booty was supposed to be fairly shared among the armies, but when the time came there was no controlling the soldiery.

Everywhere they smashed, stole and ravaged. No woman was safe on the streets, and no church was sacrosanct. The greatest treasures of classical times were wantonly destroyed. Lysippus' Hercules was melted for its bronze; so was Bellerophon on his flying horse; the Servant of the Winds was wrenched from her pillar, and all the copper sheathing was stripped from Constantine's column. The she-wolf of Rome, the ox-head of Pergamon, were thrown into the cauldron for their metals, and Nicetas' Helen of Troy, that heavenly relic of the Golden Age, was never seen again.

The myriad holy relics of the city were ruthlessly stripped from their shrines, to find their way to churches, monasteries and castles all over Europe. The toys of the Great Palace were taken apart. The precious Greek manuscripts of the libraries were burned as so much wastepaper. The tombs of the emperors were rifled. The mosaics, tapestries and reliquaries of Santa Sophia were ripped from their settings, its altar was broken into pieces, and on the patriarch's throne in the centre of the nave the drunken soldiers seated a painted whore in mockery – like a scene from Bosch, the harlot preening and screaming with laughter on the throne, the horde of drunken soldiers, brandishing swords, chalices, icons, bottles, swathes of precious silk or obscene mementoes of their lust, dancing heavy-booted round the nave.

'Since the beginning of the world,' wrote the Marshal of Champagne, 'never was so much riches seen collected in a single city.' There was more wealth in Constantinople, reported his colleague the Count of Flanders, than in all the rest of Europe put together. The great barons of France were no doubt shrewd enough in their choice of booty – Louis IX was later to build the Sainte Chapelle in Paris specifically to house the Crown of Thorns. The Venetians, though, were the most organized looters. They alone maintained the discipline of their forces, and looted methodically, under orders, for the glory of their nation.

They knew exactly what they wanted. They took the head of St Stephen, to go with the martyr's feet already enshrined in the monastery of San Giorgio at home, and a multitude of lesser sacred relics, with the prodigious gold, silver and enamelled reliquaries which the Byzantine craftsmen had made for them: shared out among the Venetian churches, these would vastly increase the profitable allure of the city as a pilgrim port. They took a series of exquisite enamelled cameos from the Pantokrator Monastery, to make the Pala d'Oro even more magnificent, and a pair of great carved doors to make the entrance to the Basilica still more impressive. They took a pair of marble columns, floridly decorated, to enrich the Piazzetta. They took a quartet of little porphyry knights, probably Roman tetrarchs, to embellish a corner of St Mark's. They took stones and panels from all over Constantinople, classical fragments, plinths of lost statues, streaked slabs of alabaster, to be shipped home as ballast and built into the texture of Venice.

Most deliberately of all, they snatched two supreme treasures of The City which would for ever afterwards be associated with their own power and providence. The first was the miraculous icon of the Nikopoeia, the Victory-worker: this they spirited away from the Church of the Virgin, where it made its weekly revelation, to be enshrined in a new chapel within the Basilica, and brought forth in glory or in supplication whenever a victory had been won, or a disaster was to be averted. The second was that grand quadriga of horses from the emperor's box at the Hippodrome: from these they removed the harnesses, and they were to be associated always with the independence of Venice from Constantinople as from all other suzerains, never to be bridled again, but to stand side by side until the end of the Republic, surveying the Piazza from their platform on the façade of St Mark's – whinnying sometimes in the dusk, imaginative visitors were always to think, and displaying in the very ripple of their muscles or the toss of their noble heads, the spirit of proud liberty.

Venice became, from that day to this, the chief repository of Byzantine art and craftsmanship. Constantinople was left stripped of its glories. 'Oh city, city, eye of all cities,' mourned Nicetas. 'Thou hast drunk to the dregs the cup of the anger of the Lord.'

Even the bold Murzuphlus fled before these horrors, and this time the leaders of the Fourth Crusade decided to take the empire for themselves. Count Baldwin of Flanders was crowned first Latin Emperor of Byzantium in Santa Sophia. Dandolo had declined the honour, but to balance the authority a Venetian of well-known family, Tommaso Morosini, was made Latin Patriarch of Constantinople, with the undertaking that all Patriarchs there-after would be Venetians too (Morosini was only a sub-deacon at the time, but they made him a deacon at once, a priest two weeks later, a bishop next day and a patriarch as soon as he arrived in Constantinople).

In the end, of course, it was the Venetians who gained most from the fall of Byzantium. When it came to splitting up the Byzantine territories, they acquired an empire at a stroke. Dandolo did not want great mainland possessions for the Repub-lic, and willingly agreed to the fragmentation of Greece among the various Frankish barons – all he demanded was free trade for Venice, and as little trade as possible for her competitors. It was along the trade routes that he built his dominion.

He took, for a start, the best part of Constantinople itself, the district around Santa Sophia, seat of the Patriarchate, running down to the Golden Horn. He then demanded a chain of islands, fortresses and coastal strips, from the Dardanelles all the way back to the Adriatic, which would provide permanent security and convenience for Venetian shipping. Only the Venetians, among the negotiating parties, knew these waters well, and they chose their acquisitions carefully. When all was sorted out they were to include most of the Aegean islands, strongpoints dotted around the coast of Greece, the Ionian Islands at the mouth of the Adriatic, and Crete, which commanded the approaches to the Levant. Most of the best harbours of the Byzantine Empire became Venetian.

The rest of the Byzantine dominions presently degenerated into a welter of feudal principalities and conflicting invaders. The Bulgars seized part of it, the exiled Greek emperors re-established themselves in another. The Frankish barons of the Crusade turned Greece into a patchwork of feudal states, the Principality of Achaia, the Duchy of Athens, Burgundians in one place, Normans in another – Italians too, later in history, and Greeks again, and Catalans from Spain, until at last the Turkish conquerors, in their slow advance through the Middle Ages, swept the petty dynasties aside and made it all a part of Islam.

The Venetians, unable with their small resources to handle all their new territories, left one or two claims in abeyance, and handed other acquisitions to individual Venetian nobles, to be governed as feudal fiefs: but the backbone of their new territories, the train of strongpoints leading back from the Levant to the lagoon, they took firmly into their own hands. The Republic became an imperial power, and the Doge added to his titles the most sonorous of them all: 'Lord of a Quarter and a Half-Quarter of the Roman Empire' – which was to say, in less stately mathematical terms, rather more than three-eighths of old Byzantium.

This was Dandolo's moment of fulfilment. It was an astonishing thing that the ruler of Venice should actually be on the spot, in the field, for this seminal moment of Venetian history, and the terrible old man made the most of it. He assumed yet another title, that of Despot, and hobbled around the city, we are told, wearing the scarlet buskins of an emperor of himself. He was the true hero of the hour, the strategist of the expedition, the inspiration of the assault, the disposer of the spoils – *Blind old Dandolo!* as Byron was to apostrophize him. *Th'octogenarian chief, Byzantium's conquering foe!*

At this moment, in his nineties by now and in the plenitude of his triumph, in 1205 he died. He had never gone home to Venice again, but of all the Doges of Venice, he remains the best-known to this day – a supreme champion to the Venetians, a supreme rogue to all philhellenes. They interred him, of course, in Santa Sophia, in a pillared sarcophagus on the south balcony. Nobody quite knows what happened to his bones when, two centuries later, Constantinople fell into the hands of the Turks, and the cathedral was turned into a mosque. Some say they were thrown to the dogs, others suggest that when in 1479 the Venetian painter Gentile Bellini was fulfilling a commission from the Sultan of Turkey in Constantinople, he was allowed to take the old warrior's remains home to Venice, together with his sword and helmet.

Anyway, his tombstone remains in Santa Sophia still, a plain oblong slab carved crudely with his name. I mentioned once to a Byzantine specialist of my acquaintance that hardly anybody seemed to visit the stone these days, on their circuit of the great building. The scholar snorted. 'I visit it,' he said. 'I go to spit on it.'

It is true that Dandolo and his Venetians, more absolutely than anyone else, had destroyed the Byzantine civilization. The Latin Empire did not last long. Though Murzuphlus returned to Constantinople only as a blinded prisoner, and was made to jump to his death from one of its columns ('because it was felt that an act of justice so notable should be seen by the whole world'), other Greek emperors were restored to the throne within half a century, and presided over a late revival of the Byzantine genius. But the city and its empire were never the same again. The spirit had gone, the heritage was dispersed, and in the fifteenth century, when the Turks took it in their turn, they found it half-ruined still.

Greeks everywhere never forgave the Venetians, whom they regarded as the instigators of this tragedy. The Venetians themselves actually considered moving their capital to Constantinople – 'truly our city', is how an official document described it – but lost their share of sovereignty there, and their Patriarchate too, when the Greek emperors came back in 1261. They were not finished with the city, however. They maintained a trading colony there for two centuries more, and were to fight battles in its waters, against one enemy or another, on and off until the seventeenth century. But they left no monuments on the peninsula above the Golden Horn. The Venetian quarter that Dandolo acquired left no trace. The covered bazaar now called the Egyptian Market, or the Spice Bazaar, is on the site of the

Venetian market, but not a sprocket is left, not a machicolation, to show that they were even there.

Sometimes though, by some trick of climate or association, some alchemy of setting, in Istanbul to this day I feel a hint of Venice in the air. In the early morning especially, when a thin mist still hangs over the Golden Horn and the ships feel their way through a sea-haze towards the Bosphorus, when the clamour of caiques and ferry-boats is just beginning to stir the waters, and the bazaars are coming to life with coffee-smells and truck-rumbles – sometimes then, as the sun catches the tips of the minarets on the high ridge of Stamboul, I see in the eye of fancy that other city far away, where the golden horses of the Hippodrome are stabled now, and the little light burns, within the recesses of the Basilica, night and day before the Victory-worker.

Aegeanics

*In the Archipelago – Duke's island –
tumultuous princelings – a show-place –
colonial life – the fall of Euboea – on admirals
– slow retreat and last stronghold – surrender*

HUMPED AND SPECKLED, lush or rocky, hefty or insubstantial, littering the waters between the Dardanelles and the Sea of Crete are the islands of the Aegean Sea. You are never out of sight of them, and as one by one they slide past your ship's prow, blue or grey or golden in the evening – as Patmos fades into the haze astern, Amorgos looms over the horizon ahead, so one myth follows another too, and the distant rocks are peopled in your mind with the gods, nymphs, heroes and sea-kings of the Aegean legend.

The Venetians called them generically 'The Archipelago', and cared little for their pagan echoes. Their importance to the Republic was strictly military, as potential strongpoints or havens along the shipping routes. Venetian merchantmen had been sailing these waters for centuries, generally just passing through, sometimes stopping to pick up fruit, salt or sweet wine from the islands. Their navigations, though, had always been hazardous. In times of war every island was potentially a hostile base, and even in peacetime passage among them was risky. The Aegean was a corsair's paradise. From the landlocked bays of Lesbos; from the fine wide anchorage of Cos; from hidden havens in uninhabited islets; from a thousand unflushable lairs the pirates sprang, sometimes in hazy causes of national or religious purposes, more often for private gain.

Byzantium had been the suzerain of these waters, and to a sea-people like the Venetians, whose welfare depended so largely upon the trade routes to the Dardanelles, complete mastery of the Aegean might have been one of the greatest prizes to be snatched from the fall of Constantinople. They never achieved it, though. Their rivals the Genoese got Chios, off the Turkish coast, which they made into a great trading mart and naval base. The Knights of St John got Rhodes. Other islands were tossed down the years from proprietor to proprietor, from Frankish lord to Greek freebooter, from transient pirate to passing admiral. The Greek islanders generally detested the Venetians for their part in the Crusade, and often encouraged their enemies. The Turks, from bases in Asia Minor, made their positions in the islands progressively more precarious.

In one way and another, however, the Venetians did achieve a lasting overlordship in Euboea, the biggest of the off-shore islands on the Greek side of the sea, and in the scattered islands of the Cyclades. They earned few revenues from their possession of these places, and they spent fortunes in preserving them; but with the support of their naval bases in Crete and on the Greek mainland, for the next five centuries they maintained a presence there, until the banner of St Mark was lowered from the last island fortress, the hilltop city of Exombourgo on Tinos, in 1715.

The division of the Byzantine Empire by the Crusaders was, of course, a paper division – in many of the imperial possessions Byzantine officials were still in control. In 1205 the new Doge Pietro Ziani, considering how best to handle Venice's own share of the spoils, decided to offer the Cyclades to free enterprise. Any Venetian citizens with enough ships, men and temerity might take the islands for themselves as feudal chiefs, on the assumption that they would remain in some sense clients of the Republic. It was no chance, perhaps, that the first to accept the challenge was a nephew of Enrico Dandolo, Marin Sanudo, who had followed his uncle to Constantinople. He was serving as a judge in the Venetian courts there, but he resigned his office at once, mustered a scratch force of adventurers, equipped eight fighting galleys, and sailing south through the Dardanelles into the enchanted seas, seized the Cyclades and declared himself their duke.

In theory his duchy became a fief of the Latin empire in

Constantinople, but the Venetianness of it was never in doubt, and over the years it provided many imperial agents and governors in the east. The dukes, officially regarded by the Venetians as the premier dukes of Christendom, remained Venetian citizens. Venetian law obtained and the Venetian dialect of Italian was the official language. Sanudo handed over some of his two hundred islands as sub-fiefs to his comrades, and so some of the most celebrated Venetian clans became associated with the Cyclades. If one nephew of Enrico Dandolo was the duke himself, another was master of Andros. A Foscolo took Anafi, a Barozzi took Thira, Stampalia went to one of the Querinis, the Ghisi brothers took Tinos and Mykonos, a Giustinian helped to rule Kea. These were names destined to figure again and again in the annals of the Republic: and the distant island of Kithira, to the south of the Peloponnese, went to Marco Venier specifically *because* of his name – it was the birthplace of Venus, and the Veniers had always claimed that, as their patronymic demonstrated, they were direct descendants of that goddess. ——

Sanudo himself chose as his headquarters the island of Naxos. It was the place where Ariadne, having saved Theseus from the Minotaur in Crete, was abandoned by the hero on his way home to Athens. It was also the birthplace of Dionysos, god of wine, whom she married instead, and was one of the greenest and most cheerful islands in the whole Aegean. It did not fall easily to Sanudo and his cutthroats when, in 1207, their galleys appeared off the little village capital out of the Paros Channel, and sailing past the tall temple of Apollo on its islet, beached themselves upon the shore. The Genoese had got there first, and fought back so fiercely that in a gesture familiar enough to chroniclers of these seas, Sanudo ordered his galleys to be burned, to encourage the faint-hearts in his ranks. Inspirited thus, they stormed the Genoese positions at last and proclaimed Sanudo Duke Marco I of the Archipelago. A Catholic archbishop was promptly dispatched to the island by the Pope, and Apollo's temple served as a quarry for the construction of a twelve-towered citadel, the seat of dukely government.

The remains of this stronghold are what we first see, as we sail in the wake of the galleys into the harbour of the island capital, the

Chora ('chief town', in Greek). Some of its buildings have lately been restored, and from a distance it looks remarkably sheer and massive on its hillock in the middle of the town, like a miniature Potala. When we disembark, though, and begin our climb from the waterfront up its flanks, it is revealed as a more inhibited kind of fort. Throughout the centuries of their occupation the Venetians of Naxos remained aliens, if only because they were the Catholic rulers of a Greek Orthodox population, and so their headquarters on the hill, set as it is in the heart of the island's chief town, has a curiously inbred or introspective feel to it.

We approach it through a labyrinth of steep and crooked streets, the homes in Venetian times of the Greek shopkeepers, fishermen, sailors, craftsmen, who soon came to live around the slopes of the citadel. Up we go, leaving the harbour and its life behind us, the polyglot clamour of the waterfront cafés, where the back-pack travellers gather, the splutter of rented motorbikes, the hoot of the approaching ferry, the thump of the hi-fi, perhaps, from the corner disco – up through the flowered and cat-frequented alleys until almost at the summit of the hill we pass beneath a grave fortified gateway (iron-studded door, black-shadowed archway) to find ourselves in the Kastro, the core of the ancient duchy.

Even now, so long after the departure of the Sanudos and their successors, it remains a Catholic enclave in an Orthodox comity. Silent and empty its streets run within its walls, and the es-cutcheons of the Venetian nobility stand haughty above its door-ways still. In the central square of the Kastro are the remains of the ducal palace, and in the little Catholic cathedral next door, heavy with the crests and tombs of the duchy, on Sunday mornings you may still see, stooped and blackly gowned, late representatives of the Venetian feudalists worshipping in their hereditary style. They live in houses built into the ramparts of the citadel, and from one of their enviable rooftops, eating an omelette and Greek salad, perhaps, or drinking a glass of the island's particular liqueur, a powerful embodiment of Dionysian traditions made from island lemons – established thus upon one of these eyries of the con-querors, looking down upon the alleys, cafés and fishing-vessels of the Greeks, and the solitary tall archway that alone remains of

Apollo's temple, it is easy enough to feel the old *hubris* of empire still.

Certainly the arrogance of the Venetians has never been forgotten by the Greeks – who, established here in Homeric times long before Venice existed, have out-stayed all successive rulers to remain as Greek as ever. Until the land reforms in Greece after World War II the Catholic descendants of the Venetians, with their Latinized local associates, remained overwhelmingly the landlords of Naxos. Embittered locals used to say that the war had not been won at all until the Catholics of the Kastro had been dispossessed. Seven and a half centuries after the arrival of Sanudo and his young men, the lifestyles of the island remained recognizably those of conquerors and conquered: even in the 1950s, there used to be at least one family of the Kastro which, loading its necessary comforts upon strings of mules, set out each spring beneath parasols, attended by servants and household pets, seigneurially through the dusty suburbs for the annual migration to its summer estates in the interior of the island, held by right of conquest since the beaching of Marco's galleys.

A tumultuous line of princelings governed the Venetian Aegean under the watchful, often baffled and sometimes infuriated eye of the Serenissima. The chronicles of the Archipelago are confused and very bloody, and the only constant thread linking the feuds and the dynasties is the shadowy presence of Venice in the background, the knowledge of her war-galleys over the horizon and the stern if not invariably effective supervision of Doge and Grand Council far away. Sometimes the intervention of Venice was resented by her subjects on the spot, but sometimes it was devoutly welcomed: 'They look upon our Admiral,' reported a Venetian diplomat of one particularly tormented community, 'as the Messiah.'

Sanudo, his colleagues and his successors behaved, as often as not, with a reckless impropriety. Sometimes they were absentee landlords – for years the lord of Andros governed it from his palace in Venice – but more frequently they lived life as a sort of game in their sunlit and storm-swept fiefs. All their islands were fortified, and they frequently went to war with each other, their petty navies fighting it out between the headlands, their minuscule armies hurling themselves at each other's citadels. The Lady of Mykonos was abducted once by the Duke of Naxos, while Syros and Tinos once went to war over the ownership of a donkey.

For the Signory itself Aegean suzerainty must sometimes have seemed more trouble than it was worth, especially when problems of succession arose, and the judgement of Venice was called for. When in 1361, for instance, the reigning Duke of Naxos died without an heir, the Republic had to make sure that his daughter, who was young and beautiful, found herself a husband sufficiently compliant to Venetian interests. So uncooperative was she, and so unsuitable were the candidates for her hand, that in the end the Venetians sent a commando force to Naxos to kidnap her. They took her away to Crete, where they confronted her with a fiancé of *their* choice, a bold military man nicknamed 'The Host Disperser': fortunately she fell instantly in love with him, so we are assured, married him splendidly in Venice and lived with him happily ever after in the citadel on the hill.

Or there was the problem of the Duke Niccolò III. He was so ungrateful a vassal that he actually tried to steal Euboea from the Republic, and antagonized his Venetian peers as much as he oppressed his Greek subjects. He was conveniently murdered by a rival claimant to the dukedom, Francesco Crespi. Crespi seized the Kastro and proclaimed himself Francesco I, and the Venetians, who saw no contradiction between criminal tendencies and a talent for government, promptly and gratefully recognized him.

Then there was Giovanni III, at the end of the fifteenth century. Everyone loathed him, too. He encouraged pirates to use Naxos as their base. He taxed his people disgracefully. He affronted the Turks unnecessarily and took no notice of the Venetians. The Archbishop of Naxos himself appealed to Venice for his removal, but once again they were saved the trouble, for the Naxians themselves assassinated him.

There was Niccolò Adoldo, Lord of Serifos. This tyrant generally lived in Venice, but finding himself paid insufficient taxes by his subjects, in 1397 he went out to his island with a band of Cretan brigands, seized a number of island notables and shut them up in his castle. There they were tortured to make them disclose where they hid their money, but the plan failing (perhaps they *had* no money) they were thrown off the castle ramparts to their deaths. This was too much even for the pragmatic Republic. Adoldo was imprisoned for two years, deprived of his island and forbidden ever to visit it (but he died in the sanctity of old age, and was buried with every sign of respect in the church of Santi Simeone e Giuda, which he had prudently endowed).

Or finally there was Francesco III, the Mad Duke of the Archipelago. He was a direct protégé of the Signory, but unfortunately turned out to be a homicidal maniac. He murdered his wife by stabbing her in the stomach with a sword. He tried to kill his eleven-year-old son. He criminally assaulted his aunt the Lady of Nio. The Venetians whisked him away to Crete, where he died under restraint, but his son, growing up to succeed him, proved almost as difficult as his father, once getting himself captured by the Turks, and once forcibly occupying the island of Paros against the wishes of Venice: it did not matter much, however, for within half a century the dynasty was extinct anyway and the Duchy of the Archipelago was a Venetian ward no longer, but was held in fief by a Jewish financier, Joseph Nasi, under the patronage of the Ottoman Sultan, Selim the Sot.

So went the history of the Aegean, in the days of the *Pax Venetica*. There were few islands that did not at one time or another fall under the influence of the winged lion. So close was the association of Venice with this sea that for years the very sponge itself, that inescapable familiar of the Aegean waterfront, was known as the *enetikos*, the Venetian. The free-booting feudalists spread themselves, by skulduggery, matrimony or insinuation, from Tenedos to Karpathos. The merchant-venturers nosed in their cobs from port to port. The war-galleys glided into petty harbours, with awful oar-strokes and intimidating standards, like visitations from on high. Sometimes the Republic took an island peacefully under its protection, sometimes an island was seized in the exigencies of war, and wherever you wander now among those wine-dark waters, traces of Venice show.

Within the Dardanelles themselves Venetian castles stand at the water's edge, while far in the south at Thira you may still fancy, in the thin line of white houses along the volcano's ridge, the Venetian town that stood there until nineteenth-century earthquakes rattled it into oblivion. In Syros, the hub of the Cyclades, the Venetian citadel stands obdurate and cathedral-crowned on one conical hump, while the Greek Orthodox cathedral and its community stands slightly lower on another. Crumbled small castles on Andros or Paros, harbour moles and ornamental dovecotes, a Catholic bishopric surviving here, an antique snobbery somewhere else, escutcheoned doorways and pronged merlons – all these are the mark of Venice, and the exquisite little row of gimcrack houses on the waterfront at Mykonos, perhaps the most famous and familiar structure in the whole Aegean, is called Enetika to this day.

Much the greatest of the Venetian possessions was Euboea, which the Greeks call Evvoia nowadays, but which was known to the Venetians as Negroponte, Black Bridge. It is only just an island. About 120 miles long, 35 miles wide at its widest part, it lies so close to the Greek mainland of Boeotia that at one point the intervening channel, the Euripos, is only 130 feet across, and has been spanned since classical times by a bridge.

Beside the Euripos stood a town, which the Venetians called Negroponte too, but which is now Khalkis. It was of obvious importance to the Republic. It was not only a useful outlet for trade on the Greek mainland, but was also an invaluable staging point for shipping moving in and out of the Dardanelles, and a naval base commanding the whole of the Aegean. Khalkis itself became Venetian in the division of the crusaders' spoils: later, by successive stratagems the Venetians acquired the rest of the island too, and made it a bastion of their maritime strength, with castles all over it, and a Bailie who was their most important official in the Aegean. To the courts and offices of Euboea came appeals, complaints or disputes from the other islands: from its harbours the galleys sailed out to keep the troublesome feudatories in order. When the Greek emperors returned to Constantinople in 1261, ending the Latin empire, the Catholic Patriarch transferred his see to Khalkis, and so it became a kind of spiritual pro-consulate too.

Khalkis was the show-place of the Venetian Aegean, and in old

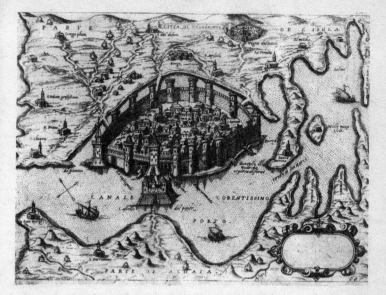

Negroponte, today's Khalkis, on Euboea

prints it is drawn bristling with towers and turrets, surrounded entirely by moat and sea-wall, and tight-stacked upon the water's edge. Its site remains extraordinary. The Euripos is one of the world's enigmas, for through it there rush, as through a mighty funnel, as many as fourteen powerful tides a day, in alternate directions. This is a weird spectacle. So narrow is the channel there, so immense is the weight of water rushing through, with the force and pace of a mountain torrent, that it feels as though all the water of the Aegean is being pumped that way. Nobody seems quite sure even now why it happens, and tradition says that Aristotle, infuriated by his failure to explain the mystery of the Euripos, drowned himself in it. The Venetians built actually on top of the channel, in the middle of a double drawbridge, a fortified tower that marked their imperial frontier. It was a romantic, Rhenish-looking construction, if we are to believe the old pictures, and so remarkable was the place, so suggestive the movement of the waters beneath it, that local rumour held it to be an enchanted castle, guarded by fairies or demons.

Beyond this magic tower Venetian Khalkis thrived. Besides its

Venetian rulers and its Greek indigenes, it attracted sizeable communities of Italians, Albanians and Jews, while a colony of gypsies made their base beneath its walls. The banking-house of Andrea Ferro, transferred here from Venice, did a booming business throughout Frankish Greece, while the Jewish financiers of Khalkis were advisers and money-lenders to improvident barons and prodigal princelings from Thebes to Thira. The patriarch became a great figure, with huge estates in the island countryside, and hundreds of serfs. The church of St Mark, the cathedral of the town, was handsomely endowed by the monastery–church of San Giorgio Maggiore, beside the Basin at Venice. Khalkis was powerfully fortified at the expense of the Jews and had two deep-water harbours, one on each side of the Euripos.

Through the thirteenth, fourteenth and fifteenth centuries Euboea was to figure constantly in the annals of the Republic. The job of Bailie went to men of great stature in the state, and the colony's flag was one of those that flew on ceremonial occasions from the bronze flagstaffs before the Basilica of St Mark. But even as it reached the climax of its success, and the Venetian empire itself approached some kind of apogee, the luck of Khalkis changed. By then the Ottoman Turks had advanced far into Europe, around the northern flank of Greece. In 1453 they took Constantinople, and soon they were pressing into Greece itself, destroying the ramshackle Frankish kingdoms one by one. It was only a matter of time before they turned their attention to Euboea. Already their corsairs were brazenly raiding the island in search of Greek slaves and booty, and life in the remoter country parts was becoming so hazardous that some islanders actually petitioned the Bailie for permission to go over to the Turkish side.

In 1458 the Sultan of Turkey himself, the magnificent but predatory Mohammed II, sent notice to the Bailie of Khalkis that he would like to visit the town. This was an ominous announcement, and the Venetians awaited his arrival nervously. When he came, he came in character. With a great train of attendants and a thousand cavalry, he appeared on the high mainland ridge of Boeotia that looks down upon the Euripos, and sent a courteous message to the Bailie to announce his impending entry: but first he spent a quarter of an hour up there on the ridge, making a careful survey of the scene.

The view from there is dramatic. Euboea, which is wild and mountainous, hardly looks like an island at all, but bounds the whole horizon like another country, while from north to south the strait narrows almost ridiculously into the funnel of the Euripos far below. Though Khalkis is no longer a great port, its southern roadstead is crowded with laid-up shipping, row after row of rusty freighter and abandoned tanker, and this gives to the prospect even now a spurious sense of consequence, and enables the modern traveller to see, if only through half-closed eyes, the view that Mohammed saw that day – the war-fleets of the Venetians beneath the towering walls, the smoke of the busy town, its spires and towers and pinnacles clustered there within the ramparts, the merchant cobs with bellied sails sweeping in and out.

The Venetians hastened out to meet the Sultan, and fulsomely conducted him across the bridge. He did not stay long, leaving again later the same day with urbane expressions of gratitude: but he took the opportunity to inspect the fortifications of the place, and twelve years later he was to make a second visit.

A storm was gathering, but never mind, in their scattered fiefs and colonies the Venetians generally managed to make the best of things. Balls and festivities, we are told, greeted admirals and ambassadors when they toured the islands, 'at which there was no lack of polished and gracious ladies', and even as the power of the Turks spread westward across the Aegean, life among the colonists proceeded much as before.

Let us go back to Naxos now, and follow those families of the Kastro on their summer migration to the countryside, for in Naxos more than anywhere one can still see how the Venetians and their clients lived, in the heyday of their Aegean dominion. It is a surprisingly tropical kind of island – it lies on the same degree of latitude as Algiers – and this gives it a suggestively colonial feel. There are palm trees about, and prickly pears. The high wind-barriers of bamboo which protect the coastal fields and pastures are oddly reminiscent of sugar-cane and slave-plantation. And the lush valley of the Tragea which lies athwart the island is a true oasis, its declivity filled with rich green olive trees like groves of dates, its old tower-houses like fortresses in Oman and Aden. The scattered hamlets are almost lost in the green of it, and on a high peak far above, looking seawards towards Turks and pirates, landwards towards rebellion, the Venetian fortress called Apano Kastro stands in vigilant dereliction.

Venetian remains are scattered all over this idyllic countryside. The most suggestive of them, I think, are the fortified monasteries, six of them in all, for there not merely an empire, but a faith stands to arms. There is one on the escarpment immediately behind the Chora, painted white and inhabited only by a clutch of nuns, which looks astonishingly like some defiant frontier stronghold east of Suez, stamped about by sentries and pebbled with regimental crests. There is another, at the head of its own valley on the eastern coast, which though all in ruins now seems to bristle with the bellicosity of its Latin monks in this Orthodox landscape, its battlemented walls blocking the head of the gulley as though ready still to shower it with arrows or flood it with boiling oil.

But the most evocative of the memorials are the country houses. These are fortified too, and are mostly tower-houses, called *pirgoi* by the Greeks, heavily merlonated in the Venetian manner, and rising solid and thick-walled above their olive groves. Many of them, though, remain genial and gentlemanly despite their battlements, and speak seductively of hedonist days, and licentious nights, in the duchy long ago. One such country house, surrounded by its properties, lies in its own fold in the hills ten or twelve miles behind Naxos, and there is nowhere better in the Aegean to dream a few hours away in the sage-brush of the hillside, or beside the sedgy stream that runs along the bottom of the valley, imagining the Venetian imperialists at their ease.

Behind the house Apano Kastro stands upon its peaks, and beyond rises the mass of Mount Zas, at 3,000 feet or so the highest mountain in the Cyclades. Set against so grand a backcloth, the house seems to lie gratefully in its hollow. It is a ruin now, inhabited only by cattle and scrabbling hens, but it retains its poise delightfully. It is built of roughly dressed stone, and is drawn, so to speak, with a gifted but bucolic hand – a simple house, but stylish too, like a good country wine. Its tower is low and unaggressive, though conventionally battlemented, and a little terrace, almost like a private piazzetta, gives to its front door a nicely ceremonial look. Above the door there lingers the ghost of an escutcheon, undecipherable now, and inside a faint air of squiredom survives. Ruined rooms still show their fine proportions, and shattered casements look out across the muddy farmyard to feudal hectares beyond.

Orchards attend this fortunate house – lemons, oranges, almonds, apples. Gnarled fig trees grapple with its garden walls. Lizards twitch about the place. Across the valley doves still fly around the family pigeoncote, and on a ridge a little way behind the house a small family chapel, its plaster peeling, its walls a little askew, flickers with the candles kept alight, year after year, by the descendants of the serfs.

But while those *pirgoi* mellowed in the sunshine, Mohammed went back to Khalkis, and this time he brought an army of 100,000 men, with twenty-one guns, using 45-pound charges to fire balls 26 inches across, and a fleet so vast that it looked, so one Venetian galley captain thought, 'like a pine forest on the sea'. There ensued a great Venetian tragedy – 250 years after the Fourth Crusade, a terrible token of things to come.

For as the fall of Singapore was to the British in 1941, the fall of Euboea was to the Venetians in 1470 – the first grim warning that empires never last. The island was the cornerstone of Venice's position in the Aegean, and its loss to the Muslims would be a mortification to all Christendom: yet its fall seems to have been ordained and inevitable. Everybody knew what was about to happen. The Sultan had made his reconnaissance. The huge Turkish fleet was made ready in Constantinople. The Ottoman army was embarked. The tragedy assembled itself slowly, inexorably, but nobody came to help. 'The princes of Christendom,' we are told, 'looked on as if in a theatre.'

On 15 June 1470, the Turkish fleet appeared off Khalkis, and landed an army on the island shore just outside the city. Three days later a second force appeared over the mainland hills, led by the Sultan himself, and wound its way down the hillside to the shore of the Euripos. Mohammed did not try to take the castle over the channel, behind its open drawbridge, but instead threw two bridges of boats across the strait, north and south, and so got his whole force on to the island. Khalkis was surrounded. There were 2,500 souls inside the city, at least 100,000 encamped outside, but when the Sultan summoned the city to surrender, promising its inhabitants exemption from all taxes for ten years, he got a tart response. The Bailie, Paolo Erizzo, replied that he proposed to burn the Turkish fleet and root up all the Turkish tents, while the men of the garrison told the Sultan to go and eat pork. The bombardment began that evening, and 3,000 Greeks rounded up in the countryside around were slaughtered below the walls of the city, *pour encourager les autres*.

The Venetians were hardly less savage in their resistance. When they discovered a traitor in the city, a captain of artillery who had been giving intelligence to the Turks, they hung him by one foot in the town piazza before cutting his body into pieces and firing it out of guns into the Turkish camp. The information he had sent the enemy was then exploited to lure them into especially strongly defended sectors of the defence, where they were massacred. Successive Turkish assaults were beaten off, the morale of the defenders was high, and on 11 July the city seemed to be saved when the lookouts reported that a fleet of seventy-one Venetian warships was approaching down the strait from the north.

This was the fleet of Admiral Niccolò da Canale, Captain-General of the Sea, sailing in from Crete, and when he heard of its arrival the Sultan, so it is said, burst into tears of thwarted rage. If Canale broke the boat-bridges, the Turkish army would be isolated on the island. But inexplicably Canale anchored his ships six miles north of the Euripos, and there he stayed. He ignored all signals from the garrison. He refused requests from his own officers to ram the bridges. Perhaps, like all navigators, he was baffled by the tides of the channel: perhaps he was just frightened, or indecisive; whatever the reason, he hesitated too long, and next day the Turks, hardly believing their luck, took the city of Khalkis.

They had filled the moat with rubbish and corpses, and across this stinking causeway stormed the landward walls. The garrison still fought desperately back. Barricades were erected street by street. From the rooftops women threw pots, pans and boiling water on the Turks below. Hour by hour, nevertheless, the Turks forced their way into the central piazza, and by noon on 12 July the fighting had ended. Canale, seeing the Turkish flag rise above the walls, sailed away to sea: every male person in the city over eight years old was butchered; the women and small children were enslaved. The Sultan himself rode through the streets, sword in hand, looking for skulkers, and the heads of the slaughtered garrison were piled in a huge bleeding heap in front of the Patriarch's palace.

Erizzo the Bailie, with a group of women and children, had escaped from the town by a tunnel, and taken refuge in the tower on the Euripos bridge, hoping that Canale would at least send a ship to take them off. He was soon forced out of it. His companions were summarily executed. He himself was promised that his head would be spared, and so it was, for the Turks placed him upon planks and sawed him in half. The smoking city lay desolate at the water's edge, and the Sultan, leaving a garrison behind, departed for Constantinople again. The Turkish fleet, too, loaded with spoils and captives, soon sailed for the Dardanelles. Canale's ships did not interfere with its withdrawal, but escorted it on its homeward voyage, so the Turkish admiral sarcastically reported, with every courtesy. 'You can tell the Doge,' said the Grand Vizier to the Venetian envoy in Constantinople, 'that he can leave off marrying the sea. It is our turn now.'

Not much is left of Venetian Khalkis. The tower on the bridge was wantonly destroyed when a new swing bridge was built in the nineteenth century: only its base survives, with a tall tide indicator mounted on it. The famous walls of the city, upon which the Sultan looked down that day from the ridge above, still stood in Victorian times, when John Murray's *Handbook to Greece* reported that the streets behind them were littered with the cannon-balls of the siege, but gradually collapsed, subsided or were demolished over the years. One by one the winged lions disappeared from the ramparts, as Venetian rule gave way to Turkish, Turkish to Greek, slowly the shape of the place was blurred, and in 1940 the Germans, dive-bombing the shipping in the harbour, where the Venetian warships used to lie, and herding the retreating British army to the water's edge as the Turks had forced their captives to the galleys, destroyed what was left of the old fortifications, and erased all but the bitter memory of Negroponte.

Venice was appalled at the news from Khalkis, the worst that had ever reached the Republic. 'Our grandeur was abased,' wrote a contemporary historian, 'our pride was extinguished.' The Captain-General of the Sea was sent home in chains to stand trial for his timidity: he was banished from Venice for ever, and his back-pay was forfeited to ransom some of the more important captives carried away to Constantinople.

Poor Canale! If he was scarcely a Nelsonic sailor, he was a man of culture and discrimination, a scholar, an experienced diplomat. In this he was not unusual among the admirals of the Venetian fleet. The Venetian system of oligarchic responsibility meant that while the Republic's sea-commanders were always noblemen, they were not always professional seamen, and although this led sometimes to humiliation, it produced also, over the centuries, some very remarkable captains to lead the flotillas of Venice through the eastern seas. Let us, while we recover from the horrors of Khalkis, and try to forget the disjuncture of poor Erizzo on his planks, take a look at a few of them.

Another eminent amateur was Antonio Grimani, Captain-General later in the fifteenth century. He was a highly successful financier and a skilled negotiator, the father of a Cardinal and a great man in Venice, but like Canale, no genius as an admiral. Having lost a particularly crucial engagement against the Turks, he too was sent home in irons (one of them fastened to his leg, as a special favour, by his own son). In Venice he was greeted as a traitor, lampooned in popular ballads as 'the ruin of the Christians', and exiled for life to the Dalmatian island of Cres, but he arranged matters better than Canale. He escaped to Rome, and so cannily organized his reconciliation with Venice that in 1521 he was elected to the Dogeship, eighty-five years old, and officially described, so many years after his disgrace at sea, as serene, excellent, virtuous, worthy, and giving great hope for the welfare and preservation of the state.

Vettore Pisani, on the other hand, Captain-General during the fourteenth-century wars against Genoa, was everybody's idea of a sea-dog, beloved of his men, contemptuous of authority, always ready for a fight. He was 'the chief and father of all the seamen of Venice'. Arrested and charged after a defeat at Pola, in Istria, in 1379, he was spending six months in the dungeons when the Genoese took Chioggia, at the southern edge of the lagoon, and threatened Venice herself. The seamen of Venice declined to fight without him, and 400 men arriving from the lagoon towns specifically to serve under him threw down their banners and went home again – using, so their chronicler says, language too dreadful to record. So they let Pisani out. '*Viva* Messer Vettore!' cried the adoring crowd as he emerged from the prisons, but he stopped them. 'Enough of that, my sons,' he said, 'shout instead *Viva* the Good Evangelist San Marco!' – and so he went to sea again, and rallied the fleet, and beat the Genoese, and saved Venice, and died in action like the hero he was.

His great peer and contemporary was Carlo Zeno, a very different character. Intellectual, statesman, fighting man, a knowledgeable scientist, a devoted classical scholar, a buccaneer and a showman, Zeno played a multitude of roles in a life full of excitement. We see him as a theological student at Padua, a young curé at Patras in Greece, a merchant on the Golden Horn, Bailie of Euboea. We see him as the most dazzling of galley commanders: burning Genoese ships all over the eastern Mediterranean, sending whole cargoes of loot to be auctioned in Crete, seizing in Rhodes harbour the greatest prize of all, the *Richignona*, the largest Genoese ship afloat, with a cargo worth half-a-million ducats and a complement of 160 rich and highly ransomable merchants.

Finally we see him, in the theatrical way he loved, appearing with his fleet before Chioggia just in time to join Pisani in the salvation of Venice from the Genoese. Zeno was imprisoned for conspiracy once, and once failed by only a handful of votes to become Doge of the Republic. He was scarred all over from his innumerable sea-battles, but he kept his eyesight until the end, never wearing spectacles in his life. They buried him, as was proper, near the Arsenal that built his ships for him, and somewhere there, lost under new dockyard buildings down the years, his grand old bones still rot.

Vittore Cappello, in the fifteenth century, was so disturbed by a series of reverses in Grecian waters that he was not seen to smile for five months, and died of a broken heart. Benedetto Pesaro, in the sixteenth century, kept a mistress on board his flagship until he was well into his seventies, and habitually beheaded insubordinate officers of his fleet, while his kinsman Jacopo Pesaro was not only an admiral, but Bishop of Paphos too. Cristofero da Canale wrote a book about naval administration in the form of an elaborate imaginary dialogue and took his four-year-old son to sea with him, claiming to have weaned him on ship's biscuit. Francesco Morosini, whom we shall meet again, dressed always in red from top to toe and never went into action without his cat beside him on the poop.

Such were the remarkable characters who commanded the fleets of Venice. They lost battles almost as often as they won them, they could be cowardly as well as heroic, venal as well as high-minded. Few of them, though, sound ordinary men, and it must have made pulses beat a little faster, brought history itself a little closer, when one of these magnificos swept into harbour beneath his gold-embroidered standard, and stepped ashore upon the modest waterfront of Mykonos or Kea.

But even the admirals could not hold the Aegean for Venice. The loss of Euboea did not mean, as Cassandras forecast at the time, the loss of the whole empire, Cyclades to Istria, but it did deprive Venice of her chief base in the Aegean, and one by one the other islands fell to the Turks.

It was a slow and awful process, extended over 200 years. Sometimes the squeeze was squalid – the demand for protection money, for example, collected by implacable Turkish captains island by island. More often it was horrific. For generations the Aegean was terrorized by Turkish raiders: ports were repeatedly burned, islanders were seized in their thousands for slavery or concubinage, whole populations had to shut themselves up each night within fortress walls. The terrible corsair Khayr ad-Din, 'Barbarossa', when he raided an island, killed all the Catholics for a start. He then slaughtered all the old Greeks, took the young men as galley-slaves and packed away the boys to Constantinople. Finally, making the women dance before him, he chose the best-looking for his harem, sharing out the rest among his men according to rank, until the ugliest and oldest of them all were handed over to the soldiery.

The Aegean islands were the most exposed outposts of Christianity against the advance of Islam, but by the sixteenth century Venice was clearly powerless to save them, and the other powers of Europe would do nothing to help. Duke Giovanni IV of Naxos appealed directly to the Pope, the Emperor Charles V, Ferdinand King of the Romans, François I of France 'and all the other Christian kings and princes', but it did no good, and he became virtually a puppet of the Turks.

Desolation crept over the islands, and the more remote of them were almost empty of life. There were virtually no men at all, reported a fifteenth-century traveller, on the island of Sifnos; at Serifos the people lived 'like brutes', terrified night and day of Turkish raiders; the islanders of Syros lived only on carobs and goat flesh, while at Ios the farmers did not dare to leave the castle ramparts until old women had crept out in the dawn to make sure there were no Turks about. The lights faded in the *pirgoi*, the choirs no longer sang in the little island cathedrals, and one by one, almost organically, by assault or default the Venetian possessions of the Aegean dropped into the hands of the Turk.

By the last years of the seventeenth century everything was lost, except only the island of Tinos in the Cyclades. The Greek islanders had often betrayed their Catholic masters to the Turks, but this was one place where many of them had been converted to Catholicism themselves – other Greeks called it 'the Pope's island'. They were intensely loyal to the Signory, and so it was that when Euboea had been Turkish for 250 years, when the Duchy of the Archipelago was no more than a romantic memory, little Tinos, all 200 square miles of it, still bravely flew the flag.

The Republic could not take much credit for this, for it had neglected the island disgracefully. Tinos had come under direct Venetian government in 1390 by the bequest of its feudal lord, descendant of one of Sanudo's men, but the Venetians were not anxious to be saddled with it. They auctioned a lease on it at first. Later they acceded to the appeals of its inhabitants, who had suffered greatly from their feudal masters (one of them had tried to deport them all to another underpopulated island he happened to possess), and who declared in a petition to the Signory that 'no lordship under heaven is as just and good as that of Venice'. For three centuries a Venetian Rector governed the island, and the Venetian fleet intermittently protected it.

Intermittently, because here as everywhere they never did succeed in keeping Turkish raiders off. Time after time ferocious Muslim generals landed on the Tinos foreshore, burning villages and killing everyone in sight. They seldom stayed for long, though, and were often sent off in ignominy. Once a passing Turkish admiral sent a message to the Rector demanding the instant payment of a heavy tribute, in default of which the entire island would be laid waste by fire. The Rector replied that the Pasha had only to come and get it, but when the Turkish galleys entered the port, instantly their crews were fallen upon by a thousand Tiniots, led by the Rector in person, and humiliatingly beaten back to their ships. Tinos acquired a reputation for unwavering resolution, and was much praised in the reports and chronicles of the Venetians – 'a rose among thorns', as one writer picturesquely put it, surveying the ever pricklier prospect of the Aegean. (Besides, they very much liked its onions, which were eaten raw, like apples, and which were claimed to be odourless.)

The Tiniots themselves were no less proud of their loyalty, and to this day Tinos remains one of the most Catholic islands of the Greek archipelagos. This is piquant, for it is also the Lourdes of Greek Orthodoxy. In 1824 a miraculous icon of the Virgin was found buried beneath a chapel on the island, and a powerful cult grew up around it, with popular pilgrimages twice each year. Thousands of people come out for the day from Athens, and hundreds of sick are brought to be cured. On the Feast of the Assumption in 1940, when the place was crowded with pilgrims, the Greek cruiser *Helle* was torpedoed in the harbour, presumably by an Italian submarine, and this tragedy has become curiously interwoven with the story of the icon itself, so that models of the warship (which was built in America for the Chinese navy) are sold everywhere among the *ex votos* and holy pictures, arousing a powerfully emotional association of ideas.

At first, then, even on an ordinary weekday, Tinos feels

anything but Venetian. The big white pilgrimage church above
the town is patrolled by bearded tall-hatted priests. Crowds of
black-shawled women move in and out of the shrine. Through
the open doors of the icon's chapel you may glimpse that mystery
of candles, incense, gleaming silver things, swarthy ecstatic faces,
shadows and resplendences that is the essence of the Orthodox
style. The long, wide highway to the church is lined with booths
and pilgrim hostels, and every other souvenir is stamped, somehow or other, with the image of the icon. Attended by these holy
events, busy always with the ferry-steamers, the motor-caiques,
the speedboats, the visiting yachts and the rumbling motor-
gunboats of the Hellenic seas, Tinos town is pure, almost archetypically Greek. Only the fancifully decorated dovecotes on the
edge of town, like so many pastry-houses, remind one that the
Venetians, with their taste for the frivolous and the extravagant,
were ever here at all.

It is in the countryside behind that you can still get in touch with
them. The Catholic archbishop, successor to a long line of
Venetian incumbents, tactfully has his palace in the inland village
of Xynara, well away from the holy icon, and the Venetians
themselves, in their days of power, established their headquarters
away from the water's edge. From a boat off-shore you can see the
pattern of their settlement. To the left of the modern port a mole
and a couple of ruins mark the site of their harbour; inland, white
villages with Italianate campaniles speckle the countryside like
exiles from the Veneto; and over the shoulder of the town,
clinging to the sides of an almost conical mountain peak, you can
just make out the remains of the Venetian colonial capital, their
very last foothold in the Aegean Sea, Exombourgo.

Not much is left of it. In its great days it was something of a
wonder, and the old prints, prone to licence though they are,
suggest its spectacular character. The peak, which is actually
1,700 feet high, looks excessively tall, steep and sudden in these
high-spirited old versions, and towers like an Everest over the
island: and perched dizzily on its summit, like an outcrop of the
rock itself, the fortress of Santa Elena stands in a positive eruption
of towers, walls and flags. Apparently impregnable ramparts
circle the peak, and below it the island seems to lie trustful and

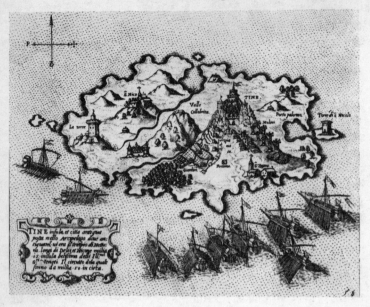

Tinos

secure, characterized by benign farmsteads and peacefully anchored ships.

It is not like that now. The remains on top of the hill still gloriously command the island landscape and the seas around, westward to Kea, northward to Andros, eastward to Chios and Irakia, southward to Paros and Naxos of the dukes. They are scarcely more than piles of stones, though, hardly recognizable as a fortress at all but for the steep steps that lead up the crag to them, the fortified gateway in the ramparts, and the little chapel which survives, fresh-painted and candle-lit, in the lee of the mountain below.

Besides, if the drama is there, the glory is gone, for in the end the Venetians themselves tamely surrendered the Rose of the Aegean, and brought their long suzerainty in these waters to an ignoble conclusion.

It was a famous scandal. By the end of the seventeenth century the island's defences were in a shameful state. The Rector might still row about the place with his fourteen-oar galley, and the Venetian gentry still lived in some style in their mansions on the mountain. But the fortress was held, so a French visitor reported in 1700, only by 'fourteen ragged soldiers, seven of whom are French deserters'. There were some 500 houses within the walls of Exombourgo then, but grand though their situation seemed to imaginative cartographers, on the spot it was not so enviable. Tinos was traditionally the home of Aeolus, Lord of the Winds: the cutting north winds of the Aegean swept through those stony houses as it chills the ruins today, and the office of Rector in this comfortless and perilous outpost of empire was looked upon by likely appointees, so the Frenchman says, as a mortification.

Huddled here then at daybreak on 5 June 1715, the last of the Venetian rulers of the Aegean saw, far in the bay below them, a Turkish fleet off-shore. A lonely moment! There were forty-five warships down there, and transports enough to carry an army of 25,000 men. The islanders rushed up to Exombourgo for safety, taking their weapons with them. The Turks advanced inland with artillery, mortars and scaling-ladders and, surrounding the mountain, began a bombardment of the fortress. At first the garrison fought back strongly, and Turkish casualties were heavy. There was plenty of food and ammunition up there, and the Greeks, we are told, were perfectly ready to fight it out to the end. It was the Venetians who surrendered. They are thought to have been bribed, and certainly the terms they arranged were disgraceful. Every Venetian on the island would be allowed to leave. Every Greek must remain. The Rector, Bernardo Balbi, agreed without argument, and he and his men were allowed to march out of the fortress with all the honours of war. They sailed away unharmed, leaving all their subjects, the most faithful they ever had, to the mercy of the Turks.

So the long Venetian presence in the sea of legend ended miserably, not at all as Dandolo, Sanudo and their bravos could have foreseen. Balbi, returning shamefaced to Venice, was accused of accepting bribes from the Turks, and imprisoned for life. His officers are said to have been punished for their venality by having hot silver poured over their bodies. The Turks blew up most of Exombourgo, and shipped the loyal Greeks of Tinos away to slavery in Africa.

The Great Island

*The nature of Crete – the imperial system –
troubles – two memories – ironic benefits –
mixed masonries – the siege – 'time to go'*

AT THE SOUTHERN end of the Aegean, like a breakwater, stands
the isle of Crete. It is another world. I first set eyes on Crete from a
ship's deck at the end of World War II, and it seemed to me then,
as we lay off-shore in the dark bay of Soudha, to be positively
smouldering with the furies of the battle just concluded. In the
years since then tourism has penetrated every last cove of the
Grecian seas, and ancient lifestyles have been tempered from
Lemnos to Corfu: but Crete, we shall find as we sail in from the
airy Cyclades, is smouldering still – not just at the moment with
the embers of any particular conflict, but with its native intensity
of temperament, its terrifying landscapes and its always ferocious
memories.

It is the fourth largest island in the Mediterranean – the Greeks
call it simply 'The Great Island' – and it is like no other. It rises in
wild mountain ranges directly from the sea, scoured often by
savage winds, and nearly half of it is uncultivatable. It is not really
very large – 160 miles long, never more than 36 miles wide – but
its presence is gigantic. The mass of it is hacked all about with
ravines, twisted this way and that, and the deep shadows scored in
its mountain flanks seem to double the size of it, and make it all
terrific. It is the very opposite of, say, Mauritius, which Darwin
once defined as an 'elegantly constructed island'. Crete is brutally
built and full of portent – the birth-place of Zeus, the lair of the
Minotaur.

Even in sunshine this is a landscape daunting and suggestive.

During the bitter winter it can be magnificently awful. Then the clouds which hang so often round the mountain summits spread over the whole island, swirling above the passes in mists and rainstorms, and sometimes then, when the driven vapours are tinged with sudden sunshine too, the place looks all afire. Crimson clouds scud by! The winds rush up those valleys like jets, and if it thunders the crash of it sounds among the highlands as though caves are there and then being split in the rocks.

Cretan history has matched its look, and its legend. The Minoan civilization of pre-history was destroyed by some suitably appalling catastrophe, and was followed by centuries of alien occupation – Roman, Arab, Byzantine. In the Cyclades one feels that the pagan gods survive all that geopolitics can do to them, and may easily be out there sunbathing, or twanging guitars on the upper decks of ferry-boats. Crete is not that kind of place. It is an island charged with power, but without *tingle*. I once went up to the birthplace of Zeus, the cavern called Idheon on the slopes of Mount Ida, when the dusk was falling on a grey winter evening, and found it a disturbingly sterile site. The mountain is very lonely up there, and the tipple of goats' feet somewhere was the only sound upon the silence, but it was not the desertion of the scene that chilled me, or the ashen colour of it. It was the feeling that, though it had once been the holiest of holy places, where if not a god, at least a grand idea was born, not a shred of emotion lingered there. There was no numen to it, no magic. The Cretan wind had swept it all away, and the cave was just a hole in the mountain face.

This awesome island inevitably became Venetian after the Fourth Crusade. It was allotted to Boniface of Montferrat but the Venetians bought the rights to it, cheaply enough, in an agreement resonantly entitled *Refutatio Cretae*. They had to dislodge the Genoese, though, who had already seized part of the island, and it was another decade before they were truly masters of it. Crete was called Candia then, and it became, especially after the loss of Euboea, the centrepiece of their eastern empire, to which their scattered settlements might look for protection, judgement or intervention, and through whose ports all their traffic to Egypt and the Levant might pass. Many another possession was considered ancillary to the Great Island, and the thirteenth-century Doge Renier Zeno declared that the whole strength of the Venetian Empire lay in its possession.

Crete is one of the world's junctions, equidistant from Europe, Asia and Africa. Even now, though it is an administrative region of Greece, it has an exotic feel, and parts of the capital, Iraklion, seem less like a European city than a bazaar town of Islam. Herb-scented, carcass-hung, brass-shining, hammer-ringing are the tumultuous alleys of its markets. Sizzling are the shish-kebabs of its backstreet restaurants. The haggle, the false retreat, even here and there the regurgitive hubble-bubble – all these symptoms of the east permeate the town, and give to its seedy lanes a consoling sense of caravanserai.

Life in the countryside, too, is sometimes more oriental than Hellenic. Consider the little procession stumbling down the rocky track towards us now. It might be stumbling down from Damascus. First, like scouts, come the purposeful dogs, then the herdsman on his fine donkey, wearing a black beaded turban and swishing a stick. The wife comes next on her rather less majestic ass, half-veiled with a black scarf around her chin, and cluttered with pans, bags and baskets. A myriad sheep and goats mill all around, tousled and blunt-faced, frequently stopping to butt each other, or nibble something by the track, or simply stand stock-still to sniff the air. Finally the sheep-boy strides along behind, with two or three cows in tow too, and a crook over his shoulders, and a fine high wave of the hand that seems to come straight from the black tents of the desert.

On a hot still day on the southern coast you may fancy you see dustclouds of Africa, sullenly blowing out of the Libyan Sea. Perhaps you do. It is only 200 miles from Crete to the African coast, and when the Romans built on the island they grouped it as a province with Cyrenaica. Bananas grow in Crete. Egyptians ruled it in the nineteenth century, and when in 1940 the Germans invaded the island thousands of Greek and British soldiers got away in small boats to Alexandria.

The Venetians well realized the geographical importance of the island. No impetuous nephews would be allowed to rule this great possession. It must be a proper colony of the Republic, governed directly from Venice, settled by Venetian families, organized by Venetian administrators and given a complete system of government based upon the Signory itself – the first properly imperial government of the *Stato da Mar*.

Crete was to be Venice translated. At the head of the colony there was a duke, the shadow of the Doge, appointed from Venice for a two-year term of office. With him came two councillors, and these three formed the local Signory. Beneath them was a Grand Council of Venetian noblemen, which elected from its own members a standing council to advise the duke. The island was divided into six administrative regions, corresponding to the six city districts of Venice, and bearing the same names – San Marco, Cannaregio, Dorsoduro, Castello, San Polo, Santa Croce: so exact was the analogy intended to be that settlers for the Cretan districts were encouraged to come from their Venetian namesakes. Below these *sestieri* the island was split into 200 fiefs, mostly held by colonists from Venice in return for military duties to the Republic.

Each fief had its own corps of serfs, generally Arab by origin, who were tied to the land, and could be mustered for military service, and the prospect of feudal grandeur in Crete appealed to many ambitious young Venetians. Some of the greatest Venetian families took up lands in Crete, as they had grabbed islands in the Aegean, and names like Faliero, Foscari, Grimani, Contarini and Morosini gave an aristocratic shine to the settler community: in 1383 twelve noblemen had to be sent to Crete to escort home to Venice one member of a settler family, Antonio Venier, because he had just been elected Doge of the Republic.

Control from Venice was rigid, at least in theory, despite the three weeks it took the average vessel to sail from the lagoon to Crete. The organization of government was specified in every detail by the Signory, and teams of inspectors saw the rules were obeyed. A particular body of specialists, the *Sapientes* or Wise Men, came each year to inspect the maritime affairs of the island, and all-powerful *proveditori*, superintendents, periodically arrived to reorganize everything all over again.

The administration was purely self-interested, and not very edifying. Crete was governed simply for the benefit of Venice. The Cretans were shamelessly exploited, driven to forced labour or conscripted for the wars against the Turks: 'Many Cretans were killed in the last war,' reported a Venetian official blandly in 1573, 'but in a few years the gap will be filled, for there are many children between the ages of ten and fifteen . . .' Wine was the chief export, but when in 1584 there was a glut on the international market, all the Cretan vines were torn up. Sugar was introduced, but was worked chiefly by slaves – Circassians, Armenians, Russians, sold by Tartars to Venetian shippers on the Black Sea or the Sea of Azov: the profits of the plantations went to Venice, or at least to Venetians. Wheat, barley, oil, cheeses, cotton, silk, timber for ship-building – all went into the Venetian commercial maw, and helped to make Venetian fortunes. Corruption was rife: one of the duke's two professional councillors was imprisoned for taking bribes in 1431 – 'What do fish care about law?' demanded the outraged if prejudiced Pope Pius II. 'As among brute beasts aquatic creatures have the least intelligence, so among human beings the Venetians are the least just and least capable of humanity . . .'

Over the years the Venetians fortified the island strongly. They walled its three towns – Iraklion, Khania, Rethimnon, which all stood on its northern coast. They built protective sea-castles on three off-shore islands, Gramvousa, Soudha and Spinalonga, and they covered the countryside with lesser strongholds. They established their capital in Iraklion, the easternmost of the three towns, which they confusingly called Candia too, and turned what had been a petty village, founded by Arabs long before, into an impressive colonial centre. Here the two-year duke lived, the expatriate nobility met to sustain their dignities, and here the Venetians tried to re-create some of the grandeurs of the mother city.

You could not call Iraklion very grand now. The Venetians might enjoy those oriental evocations of its backstreets, but they would be horrified by its discordant concrete blocks and grubby thoroughfares. Nevertheless you can still discover in the shape of the town the pattern of their old authority, deliberately symbol-

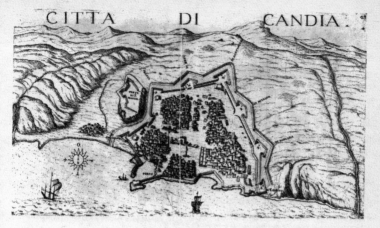

The city of Candia, today's Heraklion

ized in architecture. The centre of the town was a miniature replica of the imperial headquarters in Venice. It is called Venezelou Square now, and is a shambles of congested traffic, but through the hubbub its design is recognizable still. On its north side was the duke's palace, now obliterated by shops and offices, except for a few arcades, once towered and merlonated in direct imitation of its great original. On the west was the Basilica of St Mark, the duke's private chapel here as in Venice: this is still there, in use as a public hall, but has lost its presiding winged lion, its three great flagpoles and its campanile. Around the corner is the Armoury, now the city hall, and nearby, recently reconstructed, there still stands the elegant Loggia, a nobleman's club, a centre of social power, from whose balconies heralds made announcements, and dukes watched festive processions. Grouped around, though vanished now, were the houses of the military and naval commanders, and the big block of the state warehouse, where grain was stored for emergencies.

A little way down the street was the cathedral of St Titus. This had been an Orthodox cathedral under the Byzantines, but the Venetians took it over, made it the see of a Latin archbishop, and later shipped away to Venice its most precious relic, St Titus's head. The flag of St Mark flew always from its bell-tower, to proclaim it the church of state; in its graveyard bishops, dukes and generals were interred. At Christmas and Easter, and on the feast days of Saints Mark and Titus, the settler feudarchs were obliged by the terms of their fiefs to pray for the Doges of Venice in the cathedral, and outside it all the sacred ceremonials of state were conducted. St Titus's was replaced by a mosque under the Turks in 1872, but this in its turn has been converted into an Orthodox cathedral again, and in 1966, all imperial instincts gone, the Venetians returned to it the head of its eponym, still in its original reliquary.

From this official nucleus the city's main street, a true imperial way, ran as it runs still directly to the harbour, and the whole was surrounded by a ring road. Outside it the life of the town fell away in diminishing circles of consequence. There were the barracks of St George, for the soldiers of the city garrison; there were the many monasteries and nunneries; there was the Jewish ghetto; and filling in the gaps were the markets, shops, bazaars and dwelling-places of the Greeks. Even now the people of Iraklion seem to be inhabiting the interstices between the buildings of authority, and even now too they are clamped within the circuit of walls with which, in the sixteenth century, the Venetians enclosed their capital.

They are magnificent walls, engineered by the great Michele Sanmicheli, and more or less complete still, though here and there poor people have settled within their *encientes*, and there are ramshackle huts blocking embrasures, and tethered goats nibbling in moats. Birds in their thousands nest in the more sheltered stretches, skimming in and out of their crevices, whirling around the silent turrets, and lizards scuttle here and there from arrow-slit to gun-port.

As you tramp the round of them, the elaboration of these imperial defences gradually unfolds: the strategic inner circle of roads, like a fire-break among the houses; the mighty defensive gateways, St George's Gate, the Gate of Jesus, the Gate of the Pantokrator; the hidden magazines and barrack halls; the complex angles and protrusions of the walls themselves; until, reaching the northern side of the town, and looking out across the sea, you find the harbour of Iraklion within its own protective mole below you. On its quays the humpback sheds of the Venetian ship-wrights stand, and at the end of the mole rises the isolated fortress of La Rocca al Mare, the postern of Crete: squat, strong, forbidding, with the winged lion still gigantic above its gateway, and its battlements facing all ways, inwards to the subject Cretans, outwards to Turks, Greeks, Genoese and other perils of the sea.

All their defences faced both ways, outwards and inwards too, because from the very start the Cretans detested Venetian rule. They are people of formidable self-reliance, and throughout their history their response to foreign interference has been one of irreconcilable violence. Death and cruelty are familiars of Crete, and a constant theme of Cretan life has been a dilemma of blood and fear, the choice between liberty and a quiet life, self-respect or survival.

> Weep not for the eagle
> Who must fly in the rain:
> Keep your tears for a bird
> That has no wings.

So ran one of the Cretan folk-songs, and it was apposite. The Cretans lived harshly in their challenging landscapes, but they bore themselves heroically. They flew through thunderstorms, when required. Their system of resistance to unwanted authority was part guile, part brute force, part comradeship. The word 'Cretize', says the *Oxford Dictionary*, means 'to play the Cretan, to lie, cheat': but the word 'syncretize', from the same root, means to unite in the face of a common enemy. To this day, when you see a group of Cretans doing something communally, threshing perhaps, or treading the strange steps of their bewitched circle dances, half jig, half saraband, they can seem invincible in their bond of origin. This indomitable manner they greatly cherish. They have a word for their ideal hero, that moustachioed and cummerbunded swaggerer, heavy with bandoliers, so often to be seen immortalized in prints and village monuments. They call him the *palikare*, a bully-boy for freedom, and they honour him in the sagas of all their heroes down the ages.

For the first two centuries of Venetian rule there was nothing but rebellion in Crete, and the *palikare* became a figure all too well known to the Venetians, one of whom described him generically as having big moustaches, big boots, lots of weapons and a strong smell of goat. The Venetians were fond of quoting St Paul on the Cretans – 'liars, evil beasts, slow bellies' – and newcomers to the island were warned that if a bite from a Cretan woman's teeth was automatically fatal, the pox of her favours was pretty lethal too. Almost the moment the Venetians arrived, the islanders rebelled, obliging the very first duke to escape from Iraklion disguised as a woman, and within half a century a Venetian chronicler was frankly recognizing the Cretans as irreconcilable – 'they have always held ill feelings towards Venice, never accepting their subordination to it'. So contagious was the island spirit, too, that by the end of the century some of the Venetian colonists were themselves rebelling against the Republic: they resented their exclusion from the top government jobs, and, like the British settlers in Africa, chafed under the interference of the distant central authority – what the Rhodesians used to call 'the imperial factor'.

The Cretans had been intensely loyal to Byzantium and its church. The leading island families bore celebrated Byzantine names. The church was devoutedly Byzantine in ritual and belief. The all-powerful priests hated everything Latin. So tremendously did Constantinople loom in the imaginations of the people that for another six centuries the bards would sing of a return to The City, and the expulsion of its usurping rulers. No wonder the arrival of the Venetians, the debasers of Byzantium, was hardly welcome. Revolutions and repressions dismally followed each other, and the stories of Venetian Crete are full of horror.

Once there was a plot to murder all the Venetian officials on a single day: it was betrayed to the Doge and all the plotters were strangled. Once a rebel Cretan was invited to negotiate: when he arrived at the duke's palace he was tortured, sewn into a sack and thrown in the sea – reprimanded for doing all this in secrecy, the Doge replied that he had wanted to spare the feelings of the deceased's family. Once a Cretan leader, like Shakespeare's Antony, finding his particular insurrection lost, ordered his servant to kill him (which, unlike Eros, he did). Among the

Cretans, political terrorism, brigandage and vendetta overlapped: among the Venetians, insecurity repeatedly led to spitefulness. Villages were burned, hostages were executed or deported in their hundreds. Sometimes rebels were persuaded to hunt each other, being rewarded with pardons when an insurrectionary head was brought in to Iraklion: but by the sixteenth century the rule was that a rebel would only be forgiven if the head was of a comrade who had murdered more victims than he had himself – by the nature of the arrangement, two at least.

The most serious rebellion of all took place in 1362, when some of the leading settlers occupied Iraklion, deposed the duke, announced their conversion to the Orthodox faith and threw off their allegiance to the Republic. With the enthusiastic support of the Cretans they then elected a duke of their own and proclaimed the brand-new island republic of St Titus. A mercenary army was raised in Italy to deal with them, troops were rushed from Naxos and Euboea, the Pope declared it a holy war, but only after protracted and terrible fighting was the rule of Venice restored.

The poet Petrarch was in Venice during this affair, as a guest of the Signory. The news from the island was being followed there with distress – there had never been an imperial crisis so serious, and the involvement of so many Venetian families in the revolt profoundly disturbed the city. One morning, Petrarch says, he was standing at the window of the house he had been given on the Riva degli Schiavoni, looking out across the lagoon, when a galley sailed into the Basin garlanded all over with flowers, its crew crowding the decks waving flags and shouting. At its stern the ensigns of a defeated enemy were trailing in the water. Vast crowds rushed to the Piazzetta to greet this ship of victory, 'and when the ambassador steps off the vessel, the facts are speedily known. The enemy has been conquered, slain, captured, put to flight; the citizens of the Republic have been rescued; the cities have returned to obedience, the yoke has been riveted on Crete once more.'

The city threw itself into celebration. There were three days of games and pageantry in the Piazza. Mock battles were fought. Grand banquets were held. The King of Cyprus, who was passing through Venice, took part in the jousting. No such spectacle had ever been seen, wrote Petrarch delightedly, within the memory of man. Far away the isle of Crete lay desolate, and the rebels had all been executed, every one.

In the Cretan mind the old antagonism has long been blurred, and the Venetians are muddled in the folk-memory with later adversaries, Turks, Egyptians, Germans. But there remain some sad legacies, here and there in the consciousness of the people, of the long fight against the Serenissima. Here are two of them.

The first is a story. It is the tragic allegory of George Kandanoleon, one of the boldest of the *palikares* – part fiction, perhaps, for it has been embellished by generations of Cretan story-tellers, but told so often that it has acquired a truth of its own. It concerns one of the last of the revolts, in the first decade of the sixteenth century. The people of mountainous western Crete then refused to pay any taxes, threw out the Republic's officials, and set up their own revolutionary government under Kandanoleon. He formed a true administration, not just a guerilla command, and was supported by some of the great men of Crete, members of those ancient Byzantine clans which had been powerful in the island before the Venetians came. Taxes were collected, local government was organized, and much of western Crete became in effect an independent state.

Kandanoleon (so the story goes) now conceived the idea of marrying the two rival authorities – literally, for he proposed that his son Petros should wed the daughter of one of the great Venetian nobles, Francesco Molino of Alikianos. He took the fearful risk, in fact, of crossing into Venetian-held territory to put the proposal face to face to Molino. The Venetian unexpectedly consented to this startling match. Rings were exchanged, and the marriage was fixed for the next Sunday but one. It would, both sides agreed, be a quiet wedding, in the country castle at Alikianos. The Molinos would invite a few friends from Iraklion: Kandanoleon would bring not more than 500 of his comrades and relations from the mountains.

The day dawned fine, as they say in these tales. Kandanoleon and Petros arrived in high fettle, with 350 guerillas and about 100 women, to find that the wedding feast was already prepared. A hundred sheep were turning on their spits, barrels of strong Cretan wine were being broached. The marriage contract was signed; the pact was concluded; the company relaxed. They danced, especially the Cretans. They drank as Cretans do. They ate all the spitted meat. By nightfall the guests were left sleeping it off around the great hall of the castle, and in the yard outside.

But it was all a ruse, and what starts as an allegory of reconciliation ends as a figure of betrayal. Molino had alerted the military command in Iraklion, and during the night the troops arrived. One company came by road from the capital, another landed from galleys on the beach, until nearly 2,000 men surrounded the castle. Signal rockets went up from the troops; they were answered from the castle tower; the place was stormed, the Cretans were seized, and Kandanoleon was taken in chains to Iraklion. They hanged him from a tree, with his son the bridegroom, and all the other prisoners were shot, hanged or sent to the galleys. Their villages were razed to the ground. 'Men of faith,' reported a Venetian official, 'who respected their God and their leaders, were comforted and consoled.'

The second memory concerns a place. Lassithi is a high mountain plateau, six miles across and almost circular, which stands some twenty-five miles south-east of Iraklion. It is like a volcanic crater, 1,300 feet high and surrounded by harsh peaks on every side. The road there twists dramatically away from the coast into the heaps of slag, shale and limestone that are the Cretan highlands, the air getting rarer and cooler as you climb, the stones sharper, the road more precarious at its edges, until suddenly you see before you, standing in disconcerting sentinel across the lip of a pass, a line of squat stone forms. They straddle the road, and wait at intervals up the hillside on either side. Are they megaliths? Are they forts? Are they Minoan totems?

They are windmills, immensely old and distinctly malevolent, some merely turrets now, some with the remnants of arms hanging derelict from their snouts; and when you cross the pass, and run down the gentler hill on the other side, towards the symmetrical green plateau that lies like an arena below, you discover that they are, so to speak, only the sentinels of their kind. Massed in the plain behind, wherever your eye turns, in every field, above every hut, there stand the 10,000 iron windmills of Lassithi, silent and motionless on a winter morning, clanking, whirring, flapping and groaning when the summer breezes freshen off the hills.

Each is an ironic memorial to Venice. The people of the Lassithi plateau were a particularly prickly and independent community even by Cretan standards. Their fertile home, rich in corn, fruit and vegetables, was shut off from everywhere else by the high mountains all around it, but had been inhabited continuously since pagan times, and was littered with ancient sites and associations. It was a hive of Cretan feeling, and became a natural centre of resistance to the Venetians. From its great pit in the hills raiding parties of *palikares* repeatedly harassed the shores below, and they played an important part in the great rising of 1362.

In retribution the duke in Iraklion, Paolo Loredan, ordered that the entire Lassithi plateau should be laid waste. Every single inhabitant was made to leave. The fruit trees were uprooted, the fields devastated, the villages burned. Cultivation of the plateau, even grazing of cattle on the surrounding mountain slopes, was punishable by the loss of a foot. By these means, Loredan reported to Venice, Crete 'is for ever rendered incapable of further revolt'. Lassithi became a dead place, and for a century remained utterly deserted. Its fields were hidden in weeds and undergrowth, and dense forests sprang up in its cultivated foothills. The plateau was scorched brown in summer, while in winter the rains turned it into a lake, and only the *agrimi*, the great wild ibex of Crete, roamed its acres undisturbed. Among generations of Cretans the very name of Lassithi inspired grim fancies and cruel traditions.

Crete, though, was a granary for Venice, and in 1463, when food was short, the Venetians were obliged to bring Lassithi to life again. Technicians from Venice criss-crossed it all with a huge grid of drainage ditches, each square marked with a stone pillar in the classic style of the irrigation engineers. The scrub was cleared, the first of the windmills were erected, and gradually Lassithi's fertility was restored. It was then leased out in plots, a third of its harvest to go to the state. Most of the new tenants were descendants of the original inhabitants, but for generations they would not live in the haunted plateau, but merely camped there on their fields in the summer months, like nomads.

So Lassithi remains an ambiguous reminder of the Venetian empire. Any large-scale map shows the rectilinear grid of the imperial surveyors, and on the ground their ditches and marker stones, still standing here and there, are oddly suggestive of the Brenta marshes, or the further reaches of the Venetian lagoon itself. To this day the Lassithi villages bear the names of their tenants under Venice – Tzermiadho the pitch of the Tzermia family, Farsaro the lease of the Farsaris. And even now, when the windmills are silent in their fields, in the heat of the afternoon perhaps, or early on a winter morning, Lassithi still looks like a dead place, its scattered hamlets abandoned as they were during the years of its anathema, and only the goats and ghosts at large.

Yet the Venetian impact on Crete was not all harsh. In some respects it was fructifying. By a happy paradox, if the Venetians oppressed the body temporal, they sheltered the body spiritual and artistic, and allowed the imagination of the Byzantines to flower once more under their anomalous aegis.

The Venetians began their imperial career in a mood of ritual intolerance. Morosini, the first trumped-up Patriarch of Constantinople, pointedly swaggered around the city shaven, a deliberate affront to Orthodox convictions, while wearing, so one of the Greek chroniclers reported, 'a robe so tight that it seemed to have been sewn to his skin'. The first Latin priests of the Aegean islands did their best to discredit the Orthodox rite, and scandalized the islanders with their worldly behaviour. To many Greeks, the religion of the Venetian was, if anything, more repugnant than the religion of the Turks – the Turks generally left the churches alone, and did not try to proselytize.

When the Venetians first came to Crete they seized all the churches, tried to ban the Greek language in church rituals, threw out the Greek bishops and made the Orthodox clergy subject to their own Latin prelates. The three towns were allowed only one Orthodox church apiece. But the fervour did not last. In some parts of the empire the antipathies were sustained to the end, but in Crete, if only theologically, the Venetians mellowed.

For one thing their attempts to squeeze out Orthodoxy abysmally failed, the people resolutely declining to shift their loyalties. For another the Venetian settlers became increasingly Hellenized themselves. Many of them married into Orthodox families, and many joined the Greek church. At the same time some of the Cretan nobles, though they remained Orthodox in faith, became increasingly Latinized in style, bringing the two classes of landed gentry ever closer together. Gradually attitudes were tempered. By 1403 we find the Captain of Iraklion, the military commander of the capital, actually taking Greek lessons, and in the countryside churches were now sometimes dedicated to *both* rites, the Latins worshipping in one half, the Greeks in the other. By the sixteenth century the tables were turned entirely: all the country priests were Orthodox again, and the only Catholics were in the Venetian quarters of the towns.

Orthodoxy flowered, and with it art. The exquisite painted churches of Crete are almost all protégés of Venice. Tucked away in unexpected valleys, perched gaily on hillocks, sprawled in the middle of villages, with their amalgam of landscape, sweet architecture and dazzling colour they form almost an art form in themselves. Outside they are domed, whitewashed and innocent: inside they glow with the grandeur of their Byzantine frescoes, given a particular dimension, a rustic frankness, which is unique to Crete. In colours bright but often peeling, in images striking but often defaced by time or bigotry, all the Christian ideas are given expression – the grand cycle of the Christian story, nativity to ascension, the terrible conceptions of heaven and hell, miracles and resurrections, angels and archangels, saints, martyrs, massacres and second comings – all are lavished upon these little country churches, as though a huge sacred book has been torn into fragments and scattered through the island.

The artists were often refugees. When the Greek emperors returned to Constantinople in 1261 there was a revival of Byzantine art and craftsmanship: when the city fell again in 1453, this time irrevocably to the Muslims, it was ironically to Venetian Crete, where the indigenes struggled so restlessly for their independence, that many of the best artists, writers, artisans and scholars brought their gifts. The Great Island, secure if scarcely happy under the protection of Venice, became for a time the cultural centre of the whole Greek world: Venice, which had helped to destroy Byzantium, now cherished its survivors. The refugees who came to Crete were mostly destitute and often terrified:

> Where are you from, ship, where have you come from?
> I come from the curse and the heavy dark,
> From the stormy hail and lightning, the dizzy wind,
> I come from the City burnt by the thunderbolt.

Learned and gifted men as they often were, they were coming to an island where the Greek population was largely illiterate, where there were few schools and no universities. But the presence of Venice ensured an element of educated sympathy, and so they flourished there, whatever the *palikares* might think, under the banner of St Mark.

Many of the Greek scholars and their pupils moved on from Crete to the imperial capital, and so made Venice in its turn the chief repository of classical learning. The great Aldine Press, which printed the whole catalogue of Greek classical literature, depended upon Cretan scholars, editors and craftsmen. A Cretan in Venice established the Kalergis Press, and published the celebrated *Etymologia Magnum*, a Greek dictionary of seminal importance. Cretan icon-painters founded their own Venetian guild: Cretans established the Scuola di S. Niccolò dei Greci in Venice, with its own church. The painter Michael Damaskinos, who went from Crete to Venice in 1574, created a whole new manner of icon painting, combining Venetian techniques of chiaroscuro with the ancient Byzantine traditions.

The Cretan painter Domenico Theotokopoulos went further still to synthesize the arts of east and west. He migrated to Venice in his youth; studied with Titian, and presently went on to Rome and Spain: and strangely blending his Cretan background with the skills and styles he had learned upon his travels, became known to the world as El Greco.

★

The Venetians transformed the face of Crete, during their four centuries upon the island. Not only did they change its landscapes, by denuding them of their great cypress forests, but they built in every corner of it. Even in the deepest recesses of the Samaria Gorge, one of the geographical wonders of Europe, a gloomy defile ten miles long, 1,800 feet deep and sometimes only ten feet wide, silent but for the sheep-bells, the clatter of falling stones and the shrieks of raucous birds – even in the depths of this unnerving phenomenon there stands, deserted now except for the passing trekkers, the Venetian hamlet of Santa Maria which gave the declivity its name.

Some of their monuments are great fun, oddly enough, and bring a rare touch of gaiety to the sombre Cretan scene. Fountains especially splash their greetings with an anomalous *brio*. In the village square at Spili, near the south coast, nineteen curly-maned stone lions spout their water into the village fountain with the authentic fizz of the baroque, all the more exhilarating in that rocky and goitresque environment. In the Orthodox monastery of Vrondisi, high on the flank of a bare mountain, a fountain is presided over with lovely incongruity by a now headless couple from the Garden of Eden, a plump but accommodating Eve, a skinny but virile Adam. In Rethimnon the Arimondi fountain has Corinthian columns and three lions' heads, and is a delightful plashy structure in the middle of town, where old ladies still go to collect water in buckets in the morning, and the sound of the running water agreeably alleviates the traffic din; while in the very centre of the old Venetian capital, in Venezilou Square, stands the exuberant fountain which Duke Francesco Morosini built in 1628, supported by grimacing lions, covered all over with mythological reliefs, and supplied with water by its own aqueduct, twelve miles long, from the mountain slopes behind the town.

Arkhadi, the most famous monastery in all Crete, is another blithe surprise from Venetian times. It was blown up by the Abbot and his monks during a revolution in 1866, to prevent its capture by the Turks, and is now a national monument, a Valhalla of the *palikares*: it still has a slightly detonated feel, standing alone on a bare plateau, attended by an ossuary of heroes and a few funerary cypresses. But though it looks gloomy from the outside, when you enter its central doorway, passing through its deep shadows into the courtyard, a marvellous fantasy awaits you: for there in the middle of a fairly ramshackle yard stands a church so gay and entertaining, so elaborate of invention, that it might easily stand, an undiscovered prodigy, in one of the lesser-known squares of Venice itself. Arkhadi was built in 1657, almost at the end of the Venetian empire in Crete, and with its merry *mélange* of fancies classical and baroque, forms the happiest monument of all to the Venetian presence – a structure altogether Italianate, dedicated from the start to the rituals of Greekness.

These are only grace-notes, though. The great walls, the castle towers, the keeps and the barrack blocks – alas, these are truer reflections of the long occupation. The three towns of Crete are all recognizably Venetian still, and are all instinct with the nervous inhibitions of the regime. The best of them is Khania, in the west. It is one of the most delightful towns in Greece, but retains its slightly neurotic air. Behind the town the bare ridges of the White Mountains, often snow-covered, stand in threatening mystery, and the houses of the town seem to cluster around the little harbour for comfort, as though they wish they could embark. Stout sheds of the old Venetian arsenal line the waterfront still, disguised now as fish restaurants; a Venetian lighthouse guards the harbour entrance; the bollards of the mole, which look from a distance like charred or petrified tree-stumps, are actually captured guns embedded there by the Venetians. The city walls are robust, and emblazoned ever and again with the lion of St Mark, but if you look down from them into the heart of the little town, you will see that they are only an outer protection for the Venetians who lived there: for in the middle of the place, with its own convenient water-gate to the harbour and the get-away ships, there stands an inner fort, the Castello, where the town Rector lived, and his chief officials, and where the local archives were kept. It is elevated slightly above the general level of the town, is pretty now with window boxes and indolent with pampered pets, but gives an ineradicable impression still of an élite embattled against all contingencies. NULLUS PARVUS EST CENSUS QUI MAGNUS EST ANIMUS, it says to this day on the façade of the Venetian loggia, in the heart of it – 'He is not poor in wealth who is great of soul.'

The most compelling Venetian structure of all, I think, is a small fortress called Frangocastello, which stands on a desolate tract of shore on the southern coast. It is less desolate than it used to be indeed, now that the tourist trade is bringing surfaced roads and seaside chalets to the remotest corners of Crete, but it is still a chill and comfortless place, especially in the winter. At this point, where a narrow shaly plain separates the mountains from the sea, a dramatic gorge opens to split the highland mass in two, like an earthquake fault, or the effect of some stupendous lightning: directly in front, silhouetted on the empty shore, stands the castle.

This was always an especially violent part of Crete. Its inhabitants, the Sfakiots, were among the most troublesome of all the islanders, brigands and rebels almost to a man, given to piracy at sea, unremitting vendetta on land. Cut off by high mountains from the Venetian towns in the north, the coastline was also vulnerable to the corsairs of Genoa, the Turks and the Barbary emirs, who frequently stormed ashore here to seize slaves for their galleys or their harems. Frangocastello was built at the anxious request of the Venetian colonists of the district, and must have been an undesirable billet from the start.

It is not a very beautiful work, except for its honey colour, but it is immensely suggestive. It stands at the water's edge heavy, square and uncompromising on a bleak expanse of turf, like a tidal meadow. Its outer walls are sturdy still, and emboldened by a sculptured lion, but inside all is empty ruin. The ground is muddy after rain, hard as wood in the hot dry summer. Through the shattered windows you can see, across the flatland, that grim gash in the hills behind. It is a sinister spot, and is attended by a famous superstition. It is said that once a year, on 17 May, a host of dead warriors is to be seen on the turf outside Frangocastello – in the small hours, when the dew is shimmering and cobwebby on the grass. Some are on foot, some are on horseback, and they are led by a huge spectral *palikare*, shimmering sword in hand. The Cretans call them the *dhrosoulites* – the dew shades. They are the ghosts of liberty, or alternatively of revenge.

★

The time came, of course, when the Turks demanded Crete. The time came to most Venetian colonies, sooner or later. By the end of the sixteenth century the island was showing every symptom of imperial degeneracy. The worst of the rebellions were over, it is true, but only from sheer exhaustion, and the place was in a cruel condition. The old feudal system had more or less collapsed. The peasants lived miserably, 'the women dressed in rags', as one Venetian inspector reported, 'the children naked, the men half-naked'. Press-gangs constantly raided the villages to carry men off for the galleys. Already many Cretans were defecting to the Turkish service, and in 1597 a group of Rethimnon citizens actually invited the Turks to intervene.

For by then the Turks were looming large over the Great Island. They were the masters of the Arab world. They had occupied the Balkans from Constantinople to northern Hungary, and stood at the gates of Vienna: they had even turned the flank of Venice itself, and sent their advance forces into the plain of Friuli, between the lagoons and the Dolomites – the smoke of their camp fires was seen from the Campanile in the Piazza San Marco. The Aegean was almost all theirs, and so was Cyprus. But they had been thwarted in their attempts to gain complete sea-control of the Mediterranean. In 1537 they had failed to take Corfu. In 1565 they had been driven away from Malta. In 1571 they were beaten by the Christian fleet in the great sea-battle of Lepanto. They came to see the island of Crete, lying there massively athwart the sea-routes from Constantinople, as a maddening obstacle to their success, and in 1645, after years of hit-and-run raiding, they attacked it in force.

The Venetian Republic was enfeebled and outclassed by then, but still it took the Ottoman fleets and armies, first to last, almost a quarter of a century to drive the Venetians out of Crete. The island was the last big Christian stronghold in the eastern Mediterranean, and so the struggle became, as it were, a contest of champions, between the warriors of Mohammed and the knights of Christ. All Europe watched the spectacle in fascination, and the Turks threw their armies into the island with a fanatic disregard of losses, and an implacable resolve. As for the Venetians themselves, their record of government in Crete was not much to boast about, but at least when the great crisis came their fighting spirit rallied. The long defence of the island acquired an epic quality. The siege of Iraklion was one of the longest in history, and went into the Venetian language as an image of intransigent resistance – *una vera guerra di Candia*, a regular war of Crete.

Sieges are sieges always, and the dogged defence of Iraklion, as it is remembered by the Venetian historians, has much in common with Troy, Lucknow, the Alamo, or even Leningrad. The same heroics are recorded, the same horrors – the roasting of rats and the stewing of dogs, the unremitting bombardments, the bestial living in ruined houses or holes in the ground. Here, as always, the women are pictured by the epicists passing ammunition or selflessly tending the wounded. Here, as usual, tattered flag flies upon half-demolished battlement, attended by commander with drawn sword among his smoke-blackened, heavily-bandaged but still indomitable soldiery.

What makes the siege of Iraklion different from the others is the fact that it lasted for twenty-two years. A whole generation was born and grew up during the siege of Iraklion. The whole of European history moved on. Commanders came and went, soldiers grew grey in the service of St Mark, drummer-boys matured into sergeant-majors, veterans died of sheer old age. Observers came out from Europe to analyse the progress of military techniques. Kings died, governments rose and fell, dynasties were established, frontiers shifted, and still the Turks besieged Iraklion.

They had easily taken the other Cretan towns. The defenders of Khania soon made use of that convenient water-gate, while Rethimnon, the most powerfully fortified of the three and reputedly the strongest town in the Venetian empire, fell in just three days. The Venetians threw everything, though, into the defence of Iraklion. They appointed one of their most impressive fighting nobles, Francesco Morosini, to the command of the town; the admiral with the cat and the red outfit, he was the son of the Duke of Crete who had erected that jolly fountain in the central square. They raided Turkish islands in the Aegean, as distractions, and tried to force the Dardanelles to attack Constantinople itself. They fell upon Turkish convoys making for Crete.

They instituted taxes in Venice specifically to pay for the defence of the town, and even sold membership of the nobility to help finance the struggle. Through it all the Venetian fleet kept the supply lines open from the lagoons: but still the Turks besieged Iraklion.

They appealed to the rest of Christendom, and the Kings of Sweden and Savoy, the Elector of Bavaria, the Prince-Bishop of Fürstenberg, the Emperor Leopold and the Knights of St John all sent contingents to help. The Protector Cromwell of England would have sent soldiers too, if the Levant Company had not persuaded him otherwise in the interests of commerce. In 1669 7,000 Frenchmen arrived, led by the swaggering Dukes of Beaufort and Noailles, 'mightily satisfied with themselves'. Bells pealed to greet them when they ran the blockade of the city, guns were fired in the harbour, red banners of welcome were displayed upon the ramparts. They made one gallant sortie from the Gate of St George, lost the Duke of Beaufort in a panicky retreat, refused to attack again unless the Venetians went first, and after two months sailed home to France again. Still the Turks besieged Iraklion.

By the autumn of 1669 there were less than 3,000 Venetians fit to fight within the city. Some 30,000 had been killed or wounded. They had made ninety-six sorties over the years, used 53,000 tons of powder, fired 276,000 cannon-balls. The foreign volunteers, party by party, sailed for home: the Knights of St John were the last to go, 'and I lose more by their departure', said Morosini, 'than by that of all the others'. At last, on 5 September 1669, the city was surrendered to the Turks. The Venetians were given twelve days to leave the city, after ruling it for 459 years.

A strange hush fell over Iraklion, an eye-witness tells us, after so many years of carnage. The soldiers could leave their pickets at last, and the enemies met without malice, 'speaking to each other about the accidents and adventures of the war, as though there had never been differences between them . . .' Almost the entire community of Iraklion left the city. Only some priests, a few Greeks and three Jews elected to remain. The Turkish army entered through the wrecked walls of the St Andreas bastion, in the west, and as they did so the last of the Venetian soldiers, 2,500 sick and ragged men, marched down to the harbour and boarded the galleys for home.

Under the treaty that followed the Turks allowed the Venetians to retain sovereignty over the three islands which they had fortified so long before off the northern coast of Crete. It was only in 1715, the year Tinos fell, that the Republic surrendered these last strongholds, and their castles still stand. Gramvousa is remote and inaccessible in the north-west. Soudha guards the entrance to Soudha Bay and the warships of the western alliance still steam beneath its ramparts to their base beneath the mountains. Spinalonga is in the east, in the land-locked and fiord-like bay of Elounda.

This is tourist country nowadays, whose shores sprout with hotels, and whose waters stir in summer to the scud of speed-boat and water-ski. Nevertheless Spinalonga is the best place to contemplate the last years of Venetian rule in this, the most difficult of all their colonies. It was, as it happens, the place where their first troops landed, when they arrived to drive the Genoese away in the first decade of the thirteenth century. During the half-century after the fall of Iraklion it became a haven of Crete, as Venetian Crete had been a haven of Constantinople: the sight of the old saintly banner flying there from its turrets, only a mile or two from the Muslim mainland, was a token of hope to the Christians of Crete, who escaped there in their hundreds.

The Venetians had named it for the island, at home in Venice, which was then called Long Spine and is now Giudecca; they stacked its mass with barracks and fortress walls, a fine house for the governor, a church for the garrison, and they armed it, in its later years, with thirty-five heavy guns. Its bristling presence must have been very galling to the Turks on the main island. They stomached the affront for half a century, but eventually repudiated their agreement of 1669 and laid siege to all three island castles. The Venetians, to whom by now the forts can scarcely have been of more than symbolic value, did not resist for long, and in 1715 the garrison was removed from Spinalonga by sea, and taken away to Corfu. The island remained a Turkish fortress until 1898, providing in its turn a refuge for Muslims against insurrectionary Christians, and then became a leper colony.

Nobody lives there now, though heaps of tourists visit it in the summer, and when one November afternoon I persuaded a boatman from Elounda to take me there, I found not a soul upon the island. 'Be back in half an hour,' the boatman told me darkly as we parted at the jetty, 'or there will be problems': and so I set off rather nervously among the remains. Some are Venetian, grand and military, some are sad huts and derelict wards from the leper settlement. All seemed bitterly haunted and oppressive. I climbed up the steep lanes, though, past the Dona Rampart, through Mocenigo Square, beyond the Grimani Curtain, until I reached the little redoubt on the summit called the Castello degli Spiriti, the Castle of the Spirits: and there suddenly a grand excitement seized me. It was as though the island had sprung to life again – and I saw the trireme galleys foaming past the island, and heard trumpets from the redan below, and felt the very slap of the rope on the flagstaff above my head, where the winged lion streaked still, all afire in the sunshine, in the dry hard Cretan wind.

'Time to go!' cried a voice far below me. 'Time to go!'

The Bitter–Sweet Island

*Black Cyprus – Queen and Colony – a rotten
government – a peculiar possession – the
Turks come – breathing space – Grand
Guignol – reprise*

TO SAIL FROM Venetian Crete to Venetian Cyprus is to sail out of
epic into Grand Guignol – or novelette. The ghosts that stalk the
Cretan hills are ghosts of war and fury. The spirits of Cyprus are
altogether more lubricious. Here you are on the very edge of Asia.
The high white mountains of Anatolia shimmer to the north, the
mountains we saw as we sailed into Byzantium with Dandolo
long ago, and not far away, you feel, watchers on the Syrian shore
have their eyes upon you – it was from Beirut, sixty miles to the
east, that James Elroy Flecker saw his old ships sail:

> . . . dipping deep
> For Famagusta and the hidden sun
> That rings black Cyprus with a lake of fire . . .

The chief deity of Cyprus is Aphrodite, goddess of love and
dalliance, and the legends of the island are shot through with
licence and intrigue, the passions of women, the loves of kings.

> Oh for Cyprus [Euripedes wrote]
> Island of Aphrodite!
> There go the Loves
> In fields familiar:
> They who beguile
> Man's heart awhile
> On his road to death.

The Venetians had known Cyprus since the earliest days of their
trading with the east, and perhaps felt spiritually proprietorial

towards it because Mark the Evangelist had learned his trade there, but they did not acquire it at the division of the Crusader spoils because it was not then part of the Byzantine empire. Its peasantry was Greekish, and Greek Byzantium had ruled it for a time, but it was really a *mélange* island, tinged by strains Assyrian, Persian, Phoenician, Arab, Egyptian, Turkish and many more. Since 1192 it had been an independent kingdom governed by Crusader grandees, and by the last decades of the fifteenth century indeed, when the Venetians first seriously considered getting hold of it, it was the only Crusader kingdom left, the only survivor of the brave if preposterous feudal entities, gaudy with the chivalry of the west, which the holy wars had established in the eastern Mediterranean.

It was ruled by kings of the Lusignan dynasty, of French descent. Though they paid an annual tribute to the Sultan of Turkey, by way of protection money, they called themselves Kings of Jerusalem and Armenia too, and were habitually surrounded in their capital of Nicosia by a colourful, brilliant and feline court. The kingdom was wealthy – Cyprus was the great mart of the eastern Mediterranean – and under the Lusignans architecture, literature and philosophy flourished. All the great trading countries had agents and warehouses on the island, all the religious orders had houses there. Famagusta, the chief port, was claimed in its prime to be the richest town on earth, where courtesans lived like great ladies, drugs were sold 'as openly as bread', and young bloods rode about on horses with orange–dyed tails. Not surprisingly, the history of the Lusignans was charged with coups and counter-coups, politic marriages and ill-explained deaths. Their kingdom was, said one acerbic contemporary, the place where French pride, Syrian effeminacy and Greek fraud were all combined.

The Venetians were concerned above all with the military value of the island. Euboea had just been lost, the Aegean islands were on the brink, Crete was in its usual condition of stifled dissent, and the security of their eastern routes was threatened once again. Cyprus was the easternmost island of the Mediterranean, and its loss to any hostile power would be a disaster. The fripperies of the Lusignan court were not at all the Venetians' style, their own pageantries being of a much more calculated kind, and they viewed the island unromantically. For a figurative introduction to their attitudes we can hardly do better, the moment we arrive in Aphrodite's island, than take a car and drive to one of the ruined castles which, high on pinnacled vantage points along the mountain range of Kyrenia, stand like so many eagles' roosts above the northern coast.

The Crusaders built these marvellous forts, in lofty windswept places, scoured by sun and sea-breeze, drifted about by clouds, so improbable that they might be sets for some dream of Camelot or Ruritania. They are haunted by old tales, of mythic treasures, of fairy queens, of demons, enchanted gardens, bewitched peasants, of Aphrodite herself. Sweet smells and suggestions of the Mediterranean linger around them – the sage and the dry grass, the tinkle of the goat-bells, the whisper of nymphs and the grunts of satyrs. Fringed with surf the coastline runs away to Kormakiti and Cape Andreas; the wooded Troodos mountains stand far to the west; to the south the wide brown Nicosia plain, the central plain of Cyprus, lies at your mercy.

Such are the fancy emotions, and purple passages, those castles arouse in suggestible visitors. The Venetians, taking a more realistic look at them, realized that they had lost any serious purpose since the invention of gunpowder, and blew them all up.

Nevertheless Cyprus came into Venetian hands in circumstances of high romance – the novelette element. There was a powerful clan in Venice, the Cornaro (or Corner) family, which had been connected with Cyprus for generations. Since the 1360s the Cornaros had held in mortgage from the Lusignan kings the peninsula of Episkopi, in the south of the island, and by skilful irrigation works, and malleable slave labour, they had developed so profitable a sugar plantation that they had become the richest family of the whole Republic. They were as grand in Cyprus as they were in Venice, and they reached a summit of their ambitions when in 1468 Caterina Cornaro, daughter of Marco Cornaro and granddaughter of one of the Dukes of Naxos, was betrothed to James II, Lusignan King of Cyprus and Jerusalem. She had never met him, having lived in Venice all her life, and she was fourteen years old.

From the start the Signory watched this match with a crafty eye. The king was a bastard. He had been helped to his throne by Venetian intrigue, and his right to it was hotly disputed by his half-sister Carlotta, who was married to the Duke of Savoy. Caterina accordingly became Queen of Cyprus as a personal ward of the Republic. She was solemnly adopted as a 'daughter of St Mark' ('never knew he was married', commented the cynical Bishop of Turin) in an arcane ritual, especially invented for the occasion, before the high altar of the Basilica. The Doge acted as a kind of godfather. Caterina formally abandoned her family name, becoming Caterina Veneta instead, and the Serenissima solemnly vowed to act *in loco parentis* towards her. There was method to this madness: by acquiring the queen as a daughter the Republic acquired a claim to Cyprus itself, if the queen outlived her husband and died without heirs.

The betrothal lasted four years and then Caterina sailed from Venice to meet her husband and accept her crown. This was a moment delightful to the Venetians of the time, and vivid to their descendants ever after: it is likely that Carpaccio, who was a boy then, based upon his memories of the event his picture of St Ursula sailing away from Britain with all her virgins. Legend says, of course, that Caterina was a girl of surpassing beauty: later portraits show her to be more *interesting* than beautiful, but at least in 1472 she had the vivacity of youth, and presumably the glow of bridal and regal prospects. Anyway, Venice bade her farewell in the high old style. The *bucintoro*, the Doge's luxurious official galley, was rowed stately up the Grand Canal to the steps of her palace, loaded deep with all the great men of the Republic, and down to the Basin they took her in glorious progress, flags and bunting all the way, to board the galley that took her to her kingdom.

In the very next year King James died, and it was a common assumption that the Venetians had poisoned him. ('We shall treat your kingdom,' the Venetian envoy told him just before he died in words that might have been more tactfully chosen, 'as if it were our own.') Two months later his baby son, James III, was born to Caterina, but he died too before his first birthday. The queen was left heir- and husband-less, and nobody was surprised when the

Venetians, like wicked stepfathers, promptly moved into the palace. Three councillors were sent to Cyprus to advise the queen in her bereavement. A corps of Venetian crossbowmen landed in the island. One of the Serenissima's magnificent admirals, Pietro Mocenigo, Captain-General of the Sea, looked in at Famagusta with a fleet of sixty galleys. In no time Caterina was a puppet queen. The councillors were instructed to involve her in all their actions, 'so that everything may appear to proceed from her', but in fact her views were disregarded, and she was shamelessly bullied in the name of her adoptive parent, the Republic itself.

The Venetians had good reasons for this, too. Carlotta's faction was still powerful in the island. Cliques and caucuses revolved around the court, weaving melodramatic plots, and always there lurked in the surrounding seas, only waiting for a moment of weakness, the predatory Turks. Hardly had the king died, indeed, than there was a rebellion against the queen, plotted by the Archbishop of Nicosia with the King of Naples, and two of her close relatives, stabbed to death one night, were left as rotting corpses outside her window.

The Republic preserved her, and tightened its grip. The Captain-General was a frequent visitor now. Cretan soldiers replaced the unreliable Cypriots at the gates of Famagusta. Official posts of State were gradually filled by Venetian expatriates or nominees. Carlotta and her family were deported to Venice, and all possible claimants to the throne were exiled or shut up in convents. For nearly fifteen years Caterina was virtually a prisoner in her own palace, and when in 1487 a new Venetian ambassador was sent to Constantinople, his instructions were that if he were asked about Cyprus, he should say that it had really been Venetian for many years, 'and we have dominion over it and all its fortresses, and send our rector and proveditor hither, who rule over, govern and guard the island as our own, just as they do for all other places belonging to our state'.

In the end, inevitably, they did become its rulers, and rid themselves of its queen. By 1488 they had several plausible pretexts for her removal. They had heard that the Sultan of Egypt might be planning to seize the island. The Turkish threat seemed more menacing than ever. There was yet another plot to subvert

Venetian control, this time by marrying Caterina to Alfonso of Naples. An ambassador was sent from Venice to demand her abdication. 'We fully authorize you,' he was told, 'to bow her to our will, with or without her own consent . . . by wise, circumspect, cautious and secure means, you are to get the queen on board a galley and bring her here to us at Venice.' Poor Caterina complained in vain. 'Is it not enough,' she cried, 'that Venice shall inherit when I am gone?' But she was only thirty-four still, and Venice could not wait.

They insisted that she undergo a ceremony of abdication in every Cypriot town, to elucidate the shift in power. *Te Deums* were sung in the piazzas, the Lusignan flag was lowered, the banner of St Mark was unfurled, and, surrounded by Venetian advisers, guards and officials, the queen was ritually de-crowned – the same ceremony everywhere, town by town across the island, the solemn removal of the crown from her head, the discarding of her regal vestments, until not a soul in Cyprus could be unaware of the fact that their queen was un-throned, and Venice was their ruler. Caterina sailed for Venice in March, 1489, and never saw Cyprus again. She was no Aphrodite perhaps, but she left many sympathizers behind.

For the next eighty-two years the Venetian government of Cyprus, so cynically established, cynically proceeded with its duties. It was a rotten government. Its system was based on Crete's, though the head of the administration was called the Lieutenant, with his capital at Famagusta, and the Grand Council consisted mainly of Cypriot noblemen, of Crusader and Byzantine origin. The Venetians never tried to make Cyprus a proxy Venice, though, as they had Crete, and they stamped upon its life none of the hierarchical splendours of the Serenissima. No great proconsuls are remembered from their years of rule. The only administrator history recalls is Cristoforo Moro, after whom a tower in the fortifications of Famagusta is still named: he was the original of Othello, and it was probably because of his name (shared by so many swarthy Welsh Morrises) that Shakespeare assumed him to be a blackamoor.

They exploited the island, of course, as thoroughly as they

could. Grain was the chief export, and whenever Venice ran short, ships arrived in Famagusta for extra supplies. Salt was shipped home under a government monopoly. Strong Cyprus wine became popular in Venice – three million gallons went to the lagoon in one year. So did *beccaficos* – pickled black-caps, which are rather like wagtails, and which were sold in their thousands in the markets of Rialto. The Cornaro sugar plantation flourished still, and cotton became so valuable a crop, cultivated as it was by serfs and sold at enormous profits, they called it 'the plant of gold'.

But none of this benefited the islanders much, least of all the Greek peasantry: it paid for the sumptuous houses of the capitalists in Nicosia, or went home to the coffers of the Signory. The rich became richer, and more great Venetian magnates established themselves in the island: for instance Caterina's own nephew Marco, who had become a Cardinal at the age of eighteen, and who was not only titular Latin Patriarch of Constantinople (a peripatetic dignity now that Khalkis was lost), but also, as Grand Commander of the Order of St John in Cyprus, the largest land-owner in the island. The Venetians did little to encourage indigenous industry or agriculture: there were virtually no schools, and hardly any doctors. The Greek merchants, financiers and craftsmen who had thrived under the fecund if febrile regime of the Lusignans, drifted away from the island, to Venice, to Greece and even to Turkey.

A German visitor to the island in 1508 reported that the ordinary people were 'slaves to Venice . . . so flayed and pillaged that they hardly have the wherewithal to keep soul and body together'. The law was frequently corrupt. Petty officials were tyrannous. Taxes were very heavy. The serfs, forming more than half the population, were so cripplingly poor that when in 1516 the 26,000 villeins on the royal domains were offered their freedom for a fifty-ducat fee, only one had enough money to pay. Church benefices, Latin and Greek, were sold shamelessly to the highest bidders, but the Latin archbishops of Nicosia, who were always Venetian, seldom bothered to live in Cyprus anyway. By 1560 the Augustinian monks of Bella Paise, the lovely monastery outside Kyrenia, had adapted so thoroughly to the times that they nearly all had wives, sometimes more than one apiece, and restricted the novitiate to their own children. When the Venetian Signory intervened in these affairs, as it did from time to time, disgraceful things were brought publicly to light: one official in Paphos was charged with sixty separate offences, including ill-treating the poor, condemning people without evidence, torturing accused persons unjustifiably, illegally dealing in salt and associating with pirates.

A monument to Venetian motives is the city of Nicosia, which stands almost in the centre of the island, dominating its central plain. This had been the capital of the Lusignan monarchs, and was by all accounts one of the liveliest and most fascinating cities in Europe. When the Venetians arrived, we are told, it had been a city of 50,000 people, a marvellously mixed population of Greeks, Italians, Frenchmen, Armenians, Arabs and even Abyssinians. It was a scattered place of gardens, squares and flowered palaces, with 250 churches, a fine cathedral in the centre of town, and a magnificent royal monastery, San Domenico, where the kings, queens, patriarchs, archbishops and bishops of the island lay buried, together with their constables, marshals and seneschals.

In the 1560s, when a Turkish attack seemed imminent, the Venetians determined to turn this richly cultured city into a fortress. The scheme of fortification they devised, based upon the recently built walls of Iraklion, entailed the destruction of old Nicosia. Everything was to be subordinated to fire-power and defensive strength. A huge circuit earthwork was built, five miles around with a wide ditch in front of it, and nothing was allowed to stand in its way. The engineers destroyed everything that blocked its field of fire or obstructed its approaches, and a huge uninhabited swathe was created all around. Nothing was spared. Churches were blown up. Palaces were pulled down. Thousands of people were evicted from their homes. The monastery of San Domenico, the most precious building in Cyprus, disappeared with all its royal tombs, and its timbers were used for gun-carriages. The city was bound tight into a fortified circle, guarded by seven bastions, and symbolically in the centre of it stood the granite column, with the winged lion on top, that was the emblem of Venetian power everywhere in the empire (and which had been taken, like so many more, from a conveniently handy classical ruin – Salamis).

You can see it all still, and sense to this day the singleness of purpose with which the Venetians developed, wrecked or adapted their colonial possessions. Even the column of dominion still stands near the government offices in the city's central square, though its lion has been replaced by later imperialists with an iron bell and Queen Victoria's royal cipher. The walls have been pierced here and there for new roads, but are still complete in circuit, and still overlook in many places the wasteland of that field of fire. From the air, as on the map, Nicosia still looks like a military machine – which is, more or less, what the Venetians made of it.

(The disciplined unity of the city has been lost, though, for slap across the middle of Nicosia now another wall has been built. It separates the Turks of northern Nicosia from the Greeks of the south, and it slashes through the pattern of the city streets as ruthlessly as any Venetian fosse. Soldiers stand guard here and there along it, toting their automatic rifles, and a tristesse of no man's land, very apposite to our tale, hangs heavily around its purlieus.)

'Who built these walls?' I asked a passer-by once. He shrugged his shoulders. Franks? Arabs? Greeks? Turks? British? It might have been anybody, down the complex years of Cypriot history: and in fact the Venetians were the least likely constructors, for their stay in Cyprus was brief and infertile, and many intelligent Cypriots now are unaware that they were ever there.

It was not at all like Crete. The Cypriots suffered, by and large, in silence, and nothing much happened. The island languished down the years, only awaiting, it seemed, the moment when the Turks fell upon it at last: throughout the Venetian dominion of Cyprus, the galleys and corsairs of the Turks prowled around it threateningly, their diplomats huffed and their agents intrigued, and though the Venetians paid a tribute to the Sultan as the Lusignans had before them, nevertheless they nervously prepared themselves for the day of reckoning.

In Venice the Signory became preoccupied with the island's

fate, constantly trying to interest the Christian powers in its survival, sending mission after mission to report on its affairs. They got little comfort, and the Cypriots themselves gave them no encouragement. Most of the Greeks actually looked forward to the arrival of the Turks, while the mixed population of Levantines was considered so unreliable that plans for the defence of Nicosia included the immediate internment of all Jews, Copts, Maronites, Syrians and Armenians. The flinty, dangerous tinge to the air of Cyprus, so inescapable in our own times, was potent then too, and the Venetians hung on to the island tensely, always looking over their shoulders.

It was, on the whole, the most peculiar of their possessions. Many languages were spoken in Cyprus – Latin, Italian, French, Greek, Albanian, Arabic – and every valley, it seemed, had its own customs, traditions and secrets. A great gulf divided the sophisticated rulers from their simple subjects; a mesh of legend and superstition helped to blunt the inquiries of government inspectors, or baffle the intentions of landowners.

The passive resistance of the islanders was enshrined in their particular version of the Orthodox faith, and this was esoteric enough to mystify anybody. The island was full of wonders. Here was the Monastery of the Snake-Hunting Cats, here the Monastery Built-Without-Hands, which had been brought over prefabricated by the Virgin herself from Asia Minor. Lazarus had been the first Bishop of Cyprus, it was claimed, while the Cross of Tokhori, brought to the island by St Helena, could raise tempests and defy fires, and had cured the dumbness of the Lusignan Queen Alice, when she lost the power of speech upon entering a monastery forbidden to women. St Theostios of Melandra was revered for his ability to blind crows in the interests of agriculture; St Mamas of Morphou was beloved because he had refused to pay taxes, and when ordered to the royal palace in Nicosia to explain why, rode there on a lion with a lamb in his arms.

At Nicosia they kept the body of St John de Montfort; this had been mutilated by a besotted German lady, who in the intensity of her devotions had bitten a slice out of its shoulders, but when she was apprehended and it was replaced, the flesh miraculously grew back into place again. At Kŏuka they preserved a small box of the sawdust which dropped from the Cross when it was sawn into pieces. At Ayios Georgios the villagers ground down the fossil bones of pygmy hippopotamuses, common in the area, and drank them as medicine, believing them to be the bones of St George.

It was all very confusing. What with the Maronites of Cyprus, who held their services in Syriac, and the Nestorians, who held theirs in Chaldean, and the black Copts from Africa, who held theirs in Ge'ez and owed allegiance to the Patriarch of Alexandria, it is no wonder that the Venetians were somewhat dazed by the subtlety, the stubbornness and the secrecy of this island; but like all the other rulers who ever governed the place, they failed utterly to do anything about it.

Then the Turks came. The Sultan Selim II, Selim the Sot, formally demanded Cyprus from Venice in 1570. It is said that he was egged on to it by his financial adviser and confidant, Joseph Nasi. This formidable Jew had become, as we saw in the Aegean, Duke of Naxos, though he never visited the island. Now he wanted to establish a Jewish colony in Cyprus: he himself would be king of the island, and he already had its royal arms carved on the walls of his house in Constantinople.

Throughout the 1560s the Turks had waged a war of nerves against the island. Corsairs harassed shipping bound for Cyprus. There were repeated rumours of warlike armadas being fitted out at the Golden Horn. In 1561 the Turks were implicated in an attempted coup in which thousands of Cypriots were involved (though when two Cypriots arrived in Constantinople to enlist Turkish help in the liberation of the serfs, the Grand Vizier found their particular cause insufficiently attractive, and handed them over to the Venetian ambassador: neither of them was ever seen or heard of again).

In 1569 the Arsenal of Venice, still the source of all the empire's naval power, was damaged by fire. The hand of Nasi was seen in this too, and certainly the accident, which was greatly exaggerated by rumour, encouraged the Sultan to take Cyprus by force. Officially he ordered the assault because the island was legally his: the Venetians had paid tribute to the Porte, and this, said the Turkish apologists, clearly implied that the Sultan was sovereign there. Besides, the Venetians had been using the island to raid Turkish shipping, and so they did not deserve to keep it.

In any case the absorption of Cyprus into the Turkish empire was inevitable. Then as now, the anomalous situation of Cyprus, the eastern outrider of western society, meant that it could never find peace for long. Europe was alerted to the danger at last, and the Holy League, combining the forces of Spain, the Papal States and Venice, was formed specifically to check the Turks: but it was too late to keep them out of Cyprus, and on 1 July 1570 a Turkish army landed at Larnaca, on the southern coast of the island. The Greek population, far from resisting, welcomed its soldiers fulsomely: the Venetians of Larnaca surrendered at once, and the Turkish army, in the heavy heat of summer, crossed the parched central plain to cut off Nicosia from Famagusta.

Nicosia was commanded by a general of a famous family, Niccolò Dandolo. For all the charisma of his name, though, for all its mighty walls and ditches, it resisted feebly enough, and after seven weeks the Turks captured it. Few of the Greeks helped with the defence, and it was a Greek who hauled down the banner of St Mark and hoisted the crescent flag in its place. The Venetians and their Italian mercenary soldiers were driven into the central square, beside the column of St Mark, and like the garrison of Khalkis before them, slaughtered. 'The victors,' wrote one Venetian eye-witness, 'kept cutting off the heads of old women.' They frequently cut off people's arms too, or split skulls when the whim took them, and in all it is said that 20,000 Christians died.

In the middle of Nicosia stood the Latin cathedral of Santa Sophia, a thirteenth-century building of great magnificence. Here it was that the Venetian Bishop of Paphos, Francesco Contarini, on the very eve of the city's fall tried to raise the hearts of his people: '. . . inasmuch as you, freemen and scions of a noble and illustrious race, are called upon to contend with slaves, an ignoble and unwarlike rabble!' Help would certainly be arriving from Venice soon, he assured his congregation, but until then 'you will have time and cause to praise, honour and glorify the Most High God who, with singular kindness showing you the appearance only of his anger through the rage of this Ottoman barbarian, has been pleased to provide for the safety of your souls and for the

The city of Nicosia under Turkish siege

obtaining of the heavenly riches, and at the same time for the protection of your lives, your native land and property . . .'

It is a disquieting experience now, to read those fighting words in the porch of Santa Sophia, because for the past 400 years the old cathedral has been used as a mosque. It stands in the Turkish part of Nicosia, and is now the chief centre of the Islamic faith on the island. All its Gothic elaborations have been severely whitewashed, its stained glass is gone, and its high altar: instead a mihrab faces Mecca, and there are always Muslims meditating cross-legged on its carpets, or reciting the Koran to themselves in the shadow of its pillars.

Its doors are usually wide open to the street outside, and on the stillness of the old building market cries and blaring motor-horns intrude, and the buzzing of cicadas. Sitting in the narthex, beneath the great carved angels who still swing their censers above the main door, one can see the scene as it was in Bishop Contarini's day. Beside Santa Sophia stood the domed Orthodox cathedral – Gothic arch beside Byzantine curve, the Latin out-facing the

Greek – and in front the busy cathedral piazza was surrounded by handsome houses of the nobility, with the meandering city markets just around the corner. It was a very European scene, the very image indeed of the Christian presence in Cyprus, temporal and secular too. But when the Turks came, the day after the Bishop's sermon, it proved that the Divine Providence had neglected to preserve either the lives or the property of his congregation, and as the houses of the rich were looted all around, Bishop Contarini was among the first to die.

As for Niccolò Dandolo, his head was sent along the road to Famagusta, in a basin carried by a peasant, and presented to the Venetian commander there as a *memento mori*.

A breathing space amid these miseries – for there is worse to come – to sit for a moment on the castle walls at Kyrenia, on the northern coast, where the high barrier of the mountains over-looks the sea, and those obsolete castles of the Crusaders vaguely show, like lumps of crumbled granite, on their high summits, The Turks did not destroy Kyrenia, for it was not defended – its commander took the hint when a Venetian officer from Nicosia arrived in chains on horseback, with the heads of two Venetian generals hanging from his saddle-bow. The fortifications, part Crusader, part Venetian, are much as they were in the sixteenth century. Having taken the city from the Venetians, and kept it for four centuries, the Turks were to lose it first to the British, then to the Greeks, but since 1974 they have been back there again, and Kyrenia today is entirely Turkish. A bust of Ataturk stands outside the military headquarters on the waterfront. Turkish motor-gunboats lie at their moorings beneath the castle. Twice a week a hydrofoil streaks away from the mole, jammed to the gunwales with stocky Turkish peasants and close-cropped Turkish soldiers, for the port of Tasucu in Anatolia.

For me Kyrenia is Venetian still. With its neat little rounded waterfront, its customs house upon the quay, the bulk of its castle looming powerfully but genially over the harbour, it has the true tang of Venice to it. But it feels like Venice in enclave, hemmed about and subtly distorted. The smell is wrong for a start – too oily, too southern. The light is wrong, too – too dry and uncompromising. There is a special suggestion to the air of Cyprus which is particularly un-Italian – something sly perhaps, which springs I think out of the conspiratorial history of the place, its bare landscapes and its incestuous legends. The Venetians were seldom happy in Cyprus, and the Signory so far recognized the uncongeniality of the island that they often banished people there: for example, a convicted sodomite once, an uncelibate prioress, a man who spoke malignantly about the Republic, two who tried to introduce a law giving money to the poor, and one who made a fellow Grand Councillor's nose bleed.

Almost nobody wanted to serve in Cyprus. They had extreme difficulty even in getting a chaplain to take the services in Nicosia Cathedral, and the Senate once officially declared itself sick to death of people refusing to become Captains of Famagusta. Efforts to induce Venetians to settle there, to make it a Venetian colony like Crete, were hardly more successful, though free passages were offered, and any Venetian who stayed in the island for five years, and 'practised no mechanical arts', was eligible to join the Cyprus Grand Council as a member of the local nobility. It was not an easy island for Venetians: the local people mostly hated them, while earthquakes, droughts, lethal epidemics and plagues of locusts all occurred during the eighty-odd years of their occupation. Besides, throughout their stay the Venetians were in dread of a Turkish attack: the most common reason for refusing an appointment to the island was perfectly frank: '*Because of the Turks*'.

Ineffective though it was, the control of the home government was a constant irritation to the men on the spot. Here are some of the instructions given to a Captain of Cyprus, John Contarini, when he was posted to the island in 1538. He is to take eight servants at his own expense, and keep eight horses. He is strictly forbidden to engage in trade. Once during his term of office he is to ride throughout the island inspecting its fortresses (ten bezants a day to be allowed for his expenses): otherwise, except in emergencies, he is never to sleep out of Famagusta. He is not to wear mourning except for father, mother, child or wife, and that only for eight days, and with no mantle. In handing over to his successor at the end of his term, he is to say only, 'I consign this government to you in the name of the most illustrious Signory of Venice'; penalty for saying more or less, 500 lire and loss of office.

So Kyrenia, with its restrictions and its half-reminders, must have been a homesick place. If you sit up on the walls there alone on a summer evening, when the stars hang resplendently over the mountain behind you, and the little town has gone to sleep, then the slap, slap of the water on the rocks below may remind you naggingly of the water-noises of the Serenissima, and the feel of the old stone, slightly rotted, is like the feel of a garden wall beside the lagoon on Giudecca, and for a moment you may feel yourself at one with those poor Venetians who, loathing the island exile, watching the dark sea anxiously for the splash of the corsairs' oars, wished themselves safely home and happy beneath the bright lights of San Marco.

The news of the fall of Nicosia reached Venice in seventeen days and the Signory was plunged in despair. Still, all was not lost. The combined fleet of the Holy League was at that moment assembling for a trial of strength against the Turks. The Arsenal, far from being crippled by the fire, had turned out one hundred new ships in the past year. And the defences of Famagusta, the Turks' next objective in Cyprus, were said to be the strongest in the world – the apogee of Renaissance military architecture.

All its walls still stand, with their two gates. The Sea Gate has a great winged lion upon it, and a couple of demi-lions recumbent inside, one so crumbled as to be anatomically unrecognizable, the other badly gnawed away by time around the haunches. The Land Gate stands astride the road to Nicosia, with a powerful ravelin above. Between the two is the main bastion of the defences, the Martinengo Bastion, almost a mile square, and at the water's edge is the Citadel, only a shell now, romantically called Othello's Tower, but in Venetian times a formidable structure with four towers and its own moat. The two gates, the bastion and the citadel are joined by a tremendous wall, generally fifty feet high and often more than twenty-five feet thick: a ditch surrounds the town on three sides, and on the fourth side is the sea.

Within these works there is an air, nowadays, of shattered resignation. Famagusta has seen terrible things even in our own

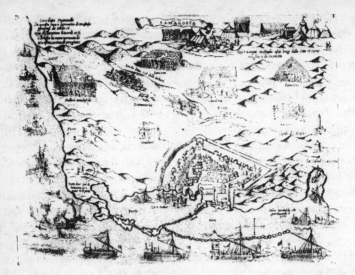

Famagusta under siege

time – it was bitterly fought for in 1974, when the Turks kept it from the Greeks. In the north-west corner of the town, immediately beneath the walls, a sort of urban wilderness extends, like a bomb site or an unfrequented car park, and amid its emptiness stand the hulks of three churches, all in a row – ruins every one, very old, very sad, and pungently suggestive of lost consequence. The cathedral square in the middle of the town, now a hangdog provincial kind of place, where policemen pick their teeth on street-corners in the heat and shopkeepers loll the hours away sitting backwards on their pavement chairs – the cathedral square is a forlorn shadow of the days when it was the centre of Venetian power in Cyprus.

Although the town may be broken and shabby, it is well-proportioned still and somehow commanding, like some stout old dowager gone down in the world. The cathedral of St Nicolas is still there, with its great rose window, though it was long ago turned into a mosque; its façade is lopsided now because the Turks put a minaret upon its north tower, and most of its windows have been filled in with arabesque patterns of plaster of Paris, but it is still recognizably descended from Rheims or Amiens.

Directly opposite, across the dusty square, rises the grand façade, all that is left, of the Venetian Lieutenant's palace. It has been badly knocked about in one war and another, and is now all mixed up with the adjacent police station, whose trucks are parked in its shattered courtyard, and whose trembling detainees are sometimes to be seen briskly escorted towards the cells. A pile of Turkish cannon-balls gives it a martial flavour still, and above its precarious central arch you can make out the arms of the Venetian nobleman, Giovanni Renier, who governed Cyprus during its construction.

There is a ruined Franciscan church just in sight beyond the square, bits and pieces of Venetian stonework lie here and there, and when a gust of wind blows up, dust from old Venetian masonries still swirls upon the air. Down the road to the south Othello's Tower, only a few hundred yards away, marks the presence of the sea. Beside the cathedral stand two grand old pillars, doubtless filched from Salamis too, which were the symbols of Venetian sovereignty.

We are looking at the scene of the grand tragedy which, in 1571, marked the end of Venetian rule in Cyprus, and gave a famous martyr to the Republic. Here was Grand Guignol. Famagusta bravely resisted the Turks for ten months, long after the rest of Cyprus was lost. It was an allegorical kind of siege. The Turks were commanded by a general known to history only as Mustapha Pasha, a sort of generic Islamic commander. The Venetians were led by Marco Antonio Bragadino, Captain of Cyprus and a member, as they preferred, of one of their oldest noble families. Even the style of fighting fitted. Sometimes there were single combats between champions, watched by crowds of soldiers and citizens, and often messages of threat or defiance were exchanged between the combatants, as jousting knights might exchange courtly abuse between charges.

The Venetians fought with great spirit. Once they pretended to have abandoned the city, and when the Turks moved in for the capture, mowed them down with gunfire and slashed them about with cavalry charges. Once they recaptured one of their own standards, taken by the Turks at Nicosia. They made daring sorties, they scattered poisoned nails outside the walls, to disable the enemy cavalry. The Turks, for their part, invested the city with their usual massive determination, appallingly wasteful of lives and money, but true to their own code of moral and national duty. They had at least 200,000 men to invest some 8,000 defenders, and fresh troops kept pouring in from Syria to keep their army up to strength. The Pasha was advised by a Spanish military engineer, until he was killed by a mine, and his corps of 40,000 Armenian sappers dug an enormous mesh of deep trenches all around the town – so big that the whole army, it was said, could be concealed within them, and so deep that tents were pitched inside, and cavalry could move about unseen. At the head of these subterranean approaches they filled in the town ditch and built two forts, of oak and earth, which towered castle-like above Famagusta, so that they could bombard it constantly and at almost point-blank range.

Bragadino was undeterred. One day, he told Mustapha after another of the Pasha's repeated calls for surrender, the Venetian fleet would arrive to relieve the city and destroy the Turkish army: 'Then I shall make you walk before my horse and clear away on your back the earth you have filled our ditch with.' He lived to regret this choice of threat. A Venetian squadron did fight its way in after a brilliant little action, but it sailed away again to Crete, taking with it all the Venetian children of the city. After that, no more help came. By July 1571 life was so terrible within the town that the citizens petitioned the general to surrender. Bragadino replied by asking the Bishop of Limassol to say a public mass in the cathedral, with Bragadino himself as his server, and then appealing to the congregation to hold on for fifteen days more. Nearly all the food had gone by now. All the cats and donkeys had been eaten, and only three horses were left alive. The ammunition was almost spent.

For fifteen more days, nevertheless, they stuck it out as their general asked, ceaselessly bombed and repeatedly mined, quenching fires, repairing shattered revetments, fighting hand to hand battles now at one corner of the walls, now another, until the garrison was reduced to half-starved men, the Bishop of Limassol was dead like Paphos before him, and even the indomitable Bragadino was exhausted. Only seven barrels of powder were left in the magazines: on 1 August 1571 they raised the white flag on the ramparts.

The Turks are said to have lost 50,000 men in the siege of Famagusta, and in return they had practically razed the little town, leaving to this day that air of abandoned defeat we felt inside the walls. When at last Bragadino surrendered, Mustapha promised him that the garrison might sail for Crete with full honours of war. For what happened in the event, history has generally relied upon the word of the Venetian chroniclers: Turks say that Bragadino broke the surrender terms by putting some of his prisoners to death, but it is the Venetians' account that has prevailed, and here is their version of the end at Famagusta in 1571.

Mustapha Pasha ordered a fleet of twelve ships to embark the surrendered garrison, and on 3 August the embarkation began. Two days later Bragadino set off for the Pasha's camp to take him the keys of the city, before boarding the galleys himself. He wore his purple robe of office, and above his head was held the red umbrella which was the prerogative of his office. He was escorted by some three hundred of his officers and men. They were conducted to the Pasha's camp, where they were courteously required to give up their arms, and Bragadino and his senior officers were taken into Mustapha's pavilion. At first the Pasha was polite, but after a few moments of conversation he flew into a rage. He accused Bragadino of breaking the surrender terms, and of squandering thousands of Turkish lives by a needless and hopeless resistance.

Suddenly the Venetians were seized and bound, and the soldiers outside the pavilion were fallen upon by the janissaries and cut into pieces. Only a handful escaped, not always by the most comfortable means – Hercules Martenigo, scion of a famous aristocratic clan, became a eunuch's slave. Bragadino was made to kneel for execution, three times, but each time the axe was stayed at the last moment: Mustapha himself then cut off the Venetian's right ear, while a soldier removed his left ear and his nose.

Twelve days later, horribly mutilated and pitifully weak, he was dragged back into the city, and his old threat to the Pasha was turned against him. He was made to carry heavy sacks of stone and earth up and down the ramparts, kissing the ground each time he passed Mustapha. Then they tied him in a chair and hoisted him to the yard-arm of a galley, for the army and the citizens to see: and then, taunted all the way, hit by anyone who cared to, jeered at constantly by the Pasha himself, he was taken to the square beside the cathedral, opposite the palace, and tied face front to one of the Venetian pillars.

Mustapha Pasha sat in the loggia of the palace, and offered Bragadino his life if he would become a Muslim. Bragadino, one supposes, was past apostasy by then, and so in agony he faced the pillar, while an executioner flayed him alive in the sunshine. His head was stuck on a pike (where it shone like the sun, so Christian legend was to say, and gave forth a lovely fragrance). His body was quartered, and the various parts were distributed among the breaches the Turks had made in Famagusta's walls. His skin, stuffed with straw, dressed in his purple robe and surmounted by his red umbrella, was carried around the streets of the city on a cow, before being slung to the yard of a warship and taken on a triumphal cruise around the eastern Mediterranean, now truly a sea of Turks.

Finally it was taken to Constantinople by Mustapha Pasha himself, and presented as a trophy of victory to the Sultan. It was placed in the Arsenal in the Golden Horn, directly opposite the place where, 350 years before, the Venetian forces had broached the walls of Constantinople and begun their imperial history. In 1650 a citizen of Verona, Jerome Polidoro, was persuaded by the Bragadino family to steal it. It was brought to Venice, and laid at last, all torments ended, in the church of San Zanipolo. As for Polidoro, the Turks caught him and tortured him appallingly, but he was ransomed by the Bragadinos, and given a pension of five ducats a month by the grateful Signory.

So there came to an end the brief and unhappy Venetian domination of Cyprus, 1489 to 1571. Two months after the fall of Famagusta the Holy League achieved a great victory over the Turks in the battle of Lepanto, but it was too late to save the island. Hardly a Venetian was left in Cyprus then: only a few noble families, it is said, their lives spared by the Turks, melted into the peasantry and remained for another 300 years, from their village of Athenion in the central plain, the chief muleteers of the island. The Turks remained sole rulers of Cyprus until the nineteenth century, but they did not bring it contentment. Stagnant and divided the island festered on, until the memory of the Venetians was almost lost and nothing was left of them there but the ruined and fateful walls of fortresses, a church or two, a winged lion here and there. They had earned no gratitude, and gained little love, from their anxious generations in the bitter-sweet island.

But what, you may ask, became in the end of Caterina Cornaro, whose sad marriage all those years before had brought Cyprus into the Signory's grasp? She was lucky to have abdicated, as it turned out, for the second half of her life proved much happier than the first. She never married again, and a portrait of her in middle age, by Gentile Bellini, shows her massively shouldered and busted, with her hair cut short, her mouth resolute and her rather porcine eyes displaying a slight but distinctive outward squint. Instead she devoted herself to cultural and social pleasures, and became in later years a famous patron of the arts.

She remained a queen – of Cyprus, she signed herself to the end, of Jerusalem, and of Armenia. The Republic fixed her up with a pseudo-kingdom, a fief of the delectable little hill-town of Asolo, forty miles north of Venice. There she lived happily ever after with her devoted court, with twelve maids of honour and eighty serving-men, with a Negress to look after her favourite parrots and a little menagerie to enliven the gardens of her castle. For twenty years she was Lady of Asolo, visited constantly by friends and relatives, attended often by eminent scholars and writers, entertained by pageants and torchlight processions. She died in 1510, fifty-six years old, and they built a bridge of boats across the Grand Canal from the Cornaro Palace, from whose steps she had sailed upon the adventure of her life in 1472, to take her body to the church of Santi Apostoli near the Rialto bridge. On a wet and stormy night they buried her there: her corpse was dressed in the brown habit of the Franciscan order, but upon her coffin was laid the crown of Cyprus.

Shores of Greece

The Eye – sui generis – *tramps and argosies –*
Monemvasia – view of a battle – last fling –
lasting accomplishment

CYPRUS WAS THE eastern outpost of the Venetian Empire. Here
we turn. The surrendered soldiers of Famagusta never did set sail
westward for Iraklion, for they were enslaved by the Turks after
all, but in happier times the Venetian convoys from Egypt and the
Levant, when they left Cyprus behind them, were in their own
waters. From Cyprus to Crete – past the clumped blue shapes of
the Cyclades – west of Kithira and Matapan – until meeting,
perhaps, as they rounded the Peloponnese, with other vessels
homeward bound from Aegean waters, they reached the hinge of
the whole imperial construction, Modon. Modon, modern
Methoni, stood at the extreme south-western point of the Peloponnese, and acted as junction, supply point, information office,
command post, repair yard and recreation centre for all the
Venetian shipping on the eastern routes. It was the most spectacular of all the sea-castles of the empire. It was said to stand 'halfway
to every land and sea', and the Venetians called it 'The Eye of the
Republic'.

We will sail into it now, since our choice of transport is
absolute, with a convoy of the early fifteenth century, say, when
Methoni was in its heyday and the Venetian Empire itself still in
the ascendant. As we stand on the foredeck of our galley, homeward bound from Beirut perhaps, with its oarsmen heaving at the
oars below us and its captain languid on his high poop behind – as
we stand there in the sunshine of a medieval Grecian morning, the
lion of St Mark billowing above us, it is as though all the wealth of
east and empire is pouring home with us to Venice.

There are spices and silks from Syria on the galley over there; cotton from Cyprus, peppers from Egypt on the ship behind; monkeys for the menageries of the rich, incense from Arabia, hides, furs, enamelware from Constantinople; Mongolian slaves from the Sea of Azov, wines from Naxos or Mykonos; Cornaro men on leave from the Cyprus plantations, soldiers thankfully re-posted from Tinos or Frangocastello, delegations from Syros, Jewish bankers from Euboea, Greek icon-artists, merchants retiring after a lifetime in Alexandria, or going home to invest the fortunes they have made in Aleppo's bountiful profit margins.

Past the islet of Enetika we sail, itself a proclamation of sovereignty on the charts, and through the narrow channel past Sapienza Island, until we enter the great calm bay of Sapienza. Around us a mass of other shipping is assembled. There are war-galleys with prows like beaks, stocky square-rigged coasters, lateen skiffs from the islands, and as our convoy finds its berths, ship by ship, the bay is a bustle of small boats, and shouts, and rattling anchor chains, and whistles. We feel we have reached some great haven, some first chamber of Venice herself, where all will be safe and sure: and this is not surprising, for low-lying there across the water, ivory-coloured now that the evening is drawing in, the fortress-port of Methoni crouches fierce but reassuring, rather like a lion itself.

It is one of the great sights of Mediterranean travel. It stands on the tip of its own peninsula, above a half-moon sandy beach, and is a kind of screen or barricade of towers, one after the other along the water's edge. Flags fly from its turrets, sentries patrol its cat-walks, windmills whir, and its two big sea-gates, thrown open to the harbour, are alive with traffic in and out. The smoke of hundreds of houses rises above its walls, for the whole community of the port lives within the fortifications – its merchants and its agents, its priests and its soldiers, its ship-builders and chandlers and bankers, its thriving colony of Jewish silk-workers, its famous hostel of the Teutonic Knights where the pilgrims stay, its Commander of the Galleys and its all-powerful Bailie. Only a shambled colony of gypsies lives outside the walls, in those tents and shanties over the moat to the north, trading in pigs with the Greeks of the countryside (and supplying nearly all the bacon of

Venice). To the east a track runs away over the bony hills to Coron, Koroni, the Second Eye, on the other side of the Messini peninsula; to the north a road goes up the coast to the Venetian fortress of Navarino; but Methoni itself looks altogether self-sufficient, sustained by the sea and cap-à-pie.

When a convoy like ours puts in, the place is in ferment. Thousands of oarsmen and passengers go ashore. The shops and taverns within the walls are packed to bursting ('the very thought of the Muscat of Modon delights me,' wrote the fifteenth-century traveller Father Felix Fabri). Officialdom hums. Bemused strangers wander the streets of the city, or look out in wonder across the bare landscape. Spiced and woody smells arise, there is a babel of languages, pilgrims kneel in thanksgiving before the head of St Athanasius, 'Athanasius against the world', in the cathedral of St John. Officers present their requirements to the shipyard men, grandees their introductions to the Bailie, merchants their bills of credit to the banks. It is the *Stato da Mar* encapsulated: sharp, cosmopolitan, grand of style but purely practical of function.

Darkness falls, only the sentries patrol the walls and the night watch murmurs on the decks of the galleys, and when we wake in the morning the centuries have passed and we look out at a different Modon. Twentieth-century Methoni is not at all what it was. The great sea-fort is only a shell now, rotted and sombre above its beaches. The wide bay is empty. A raggle-taggle village has grown up outside the walls, where the gypsies used to be, with a plate-glass tourist hotel at the water's edge, beside the Bembo bastion. A bulldozer scrapes at the sand on the foreshore. A woman screams across the water to her husband on the jetty. In a *taverna* beside the sea the restaurateur, tooth-pick between his lips, serves you your fried fish distractedly, his eyes on the television above the bar. The hundreds of houses within the walls, the offices of empire, the warehouses, the pubs, the hostels and the barracks – all have vanished, leaving only grassy mounds here and there, a precarious wall or two, warrens of dark chambers in the earth, scuttled about by beetles, and chipped remains of the Venetian pillar of authority, *sans* lion, *sans* everything. The great sea-gates are crudely blocked with stones. Noble crests and sculpted animals look down dimly from the shadows, eroded by sea-winds.

Modon, now Methoni

But perhaps during the day, as sometimes happens, one of the great storms of the Cretan Sea will fall upon Methoni out of the south. The old walls shake with the thunder of it, the towers stand silhouetted magnificently against the scudding clouds, and it sounds as though all the winged lions that ever were, wherever the Venetians ruled, are mourning their lost dominion.

Methoni was the most important of the prizes the Venetians acquired, at the dissolution of the Byzantine Empire, upon the mainland of Greece. Behind it the feudal states carved out for themselves by the Crusaders soon degenerated into a protracted scramble for power and territory, and Greece was a welter of violence and intrigue. Normans, Burgundians, Italians, Germans and Spaniards marched and counter-marched across the classic lands, Frankish forts sprang up among the citadels of Argos and Corinth, Thebes and Sparta. In the fourteenth century the Greek Byzantines, temporarily restored to power on the Golden Horn, recaptured much of Greece: in the fifteenth century the Turks,

117

having taken Constantinople, inexorably advanced down the peninsula until all was theirs.

The Venetians could not be aloof to all this, but they remained detached. Here as everywhere, they were *sui generis*. Though from time to time they were drawn into the incessant conflicts of Greece, and Venetian armies went into action far inland, for the most part they pursued their specialized concerns single-mindedly, and kept themselves, as sailors should, at the water's edge. They were never interested in empire for empire's sake, and they chose their Greek possessions, like all the others, with an eye only to the trade and security of the Serenissima.

From Nauplia in the north-east to Patras in the north-west, at one time or another the Venetians held almost all the principal ports and harbours of southern Greece. Besides being staging-posts on the convoy routes, and bases for their naval squadrons in the eastern Mediterranean, these put most of Greece's seaborne commerce into Venetian hands – all the Latin rulers of the interior depended upon Venetian ships for their trade and transport. The possessions of the Grecian shore became part of the Venetian heritage. They called the Peloponnese the Morea, because it was thought to look like the leaf of the mulberry tree (*morus*), and this name was to recur constantly in the chronicles of the Signory until the seventeenth century. They called Methoni, the pivot of it all, 'the receptacle and special nest of all our galleys, ships and vessels', and when in 1500 it was lost to the Turks, the Council of Ten at home in Venice, ermine-dressed and velvet-capped though its members were, burst unanimously into tears.

Though all these colonies were fortified, against attack from the land as well as the sea, they were essentially trading stations, and their life depended upon the cycles of commerce between Venice and the east. Methoni was the point of convergence of the two main eastern shipping routes. One went northwards through the Aegean into the Black Sea, and further still, to the Venetian trading station at Tarfa on the Sea of Azov. The second went by way of Crete and Cyprus to Syria and Alexandria, where the Venetians had maintained warehouses since the twelfth century.

In the fifteenth century, at our own moment of entry into

Sapienza Bay, traffic along these routes was scrupulously organized by the State. Venice then was approaching the climax of her maritime power: in 1414, according to the Doge Tommaso Mocenigo, she possessed 3,000 small merchant ships, 300 large ones and 45 war galleys, with some 36,000 seamen. Two convoys each year left the lagoon on each of the organized routes, generally travelling together as far as Methoni. The Venetians preferred to make their long voyages in fast oared galleys, rowed by free men, rather than in the big sailing ships used by other powers, and the State convoys generally consisted of fifteen or twenty of these impressive vessels, escorted by lighter fighting ships. A convoy was a mixture of capitalism and state enterprise. The Republic organized it, stipulated the design of ships, provided the naval escort. Private enterprise put up the money and made most of the profit. Every man on board a merchant galley was to some extent an investor in the enterprise, since each was entitled to do his own trading on the side, and when a galley put into one of the eastern ports it was turned almost at once into a sort of floating bazaar, with bumboats milling all about, and local traders clambering over the gunwales to start bargaining.

The convoys were elaborately ordered. They were commanded by an admiral, and led by a fleet navigator, appointed by the Republic. The ship's secretary on each trading galley was an official appointee too, charged with keeping an eye on the books, and every aspect of the voyage was meticulously regulated, from oarsmen's rations to permitted loading levels or turn-around times. Every ship carried its complement of archers, making the entire convoy a fighting unit, and distributed through the fleet were chaplains, doctors and the young gentlemen-bowmen who, by an old Venetian tradition, sailed with the galleys as part of their education.

Shipboard life was earthy. The captain might live well enough, in his cabin aft, and so did any important passengers: but the rest of the ship stank terribly from the bilges below, and from the excrement of the sheep, goats, calves, oxen and pigs huddled together on deck around the open kitchen. The crews included every kind of vagabond and runaway, and for the inexperienced traveller a voyage was full of incidental hazards. When one young fifteenth-century Venetian went to sea for the first time he was warned by his elder brother against playing games with anyone on board (except possibly draughts with the chaplain), against being left behind when the sailing-drum sounded in port, against eating too much when they went ashore, and against consorting with the whores of Crete and Cyprus, all of whom were diseased.

Several times a year, then, one of these spectacular armadas appeared off the coast of Greece, as we ourselves appeared that morning. Every boy on the waterfront knew the names of the ships; every Rector, Bailie or Governor knew their captains; every prostitute had experienced their crews. Nothing could be more lovely than the sight of the great galleys, the liners of the Venetian trade, moving down the Grecian coast, ensigns aflutter, escort all around; and with their long sleek lines, their bright colours and the measured beat of their oars, seen from some high headland of Hellas, looking across to Kea, say, from the Lavrion peninsula, they must have looked hauntingly like the long-ships of the ancients, carrying their Homeric heroes through these same wine-dark seas.

In times of distress, and especially during the long advance of the Turks into Greece, the Venetian colonies around the coast played the part of havens. By 1460 the whole of the Peloponnese was Turkish except the Venetian colonies, and then refugees poured out of the mountain passes to take shelter within their walls. Deposed chieftains took ship there, or left their wives and children in Venetian care. Young Greeks joined the locally recruited companies of light horse, the *stradioti*, which provided the most spirited element of the Venetian land defences – Graitzas Palaeologus indeed, a Greek of famous name who heroically resisted the Turkish advance during the 1450s, was made commander of all the Republic's light horse. The presence of Venice, the stance of the winged lion over the city gate, seemed in those violent times to be a pledge of stability: Normans and Catalans might come and go, Turks might storm across the land, but there on the edge of the blue the towers of Venice seemed to stand inviolate. Sometimes it was truly so, and in some Venetian cities of Greece people could hardly conceive of life without the protection of St Mark. In others the Venetian tenure was brief, but so potent that in a short time an ancient comity might be altogether Venetianized, its past half forgotten and its future apparently secured.

One such place was Monemvasia, on the east coast of the Peloponnese. The Venetians ruled it for less than a century, from 1463 to 1540, and it was a famous place long before their time, but it might have been designed by nature for them, so perfectly suited was it to their manner. It was a steep almost treeless rock, connected to the mainland by a causeway perhaps a hundred yards long, and it had been inhabited always. The ancients had built a citadel on its windswept summit. The Byzantines had built a church there, naming it after Santa Sophia in Constantinople, and made it the seat of a bishopric. Corsairs of Monemvasia were notorious throughout the Middle Ages; wine of Monemvasia was famous, as malmsey, all over Europe. But the Venetians made it their own, and developed it into one of the most interesting of all their colonial stations.

Monemvasia means 'the only entrance', and you must still approach the place over the causeway from the mainland. It was heavily fortified in Venetian times, but today it hardly feels like a bridge at all, so narrow is the channel there. There is no doubt, nevertheless, about the insularity of Monemvasia. Its massive but shapely rock rises from the sea in a posture wonderfully apart. In its prime it bristled with armaments, from causeway to high summit, and even now as you pass through the double gateway in its walls, near the water's edge, you feel you are passing into some distinctly unwelcoming, if not actually hostile encampment.

The lower town of Monemvasia, enclosed within its own walls near the bottom of the rock, is predominantly Byzantine, and feels it. A little colony of Bohemians and expatriates lives there, and there is a café, and a modest pension (defined in one of the franker recent guidebooks as 'spooky'). Much of it, though, is in ruins. Crisscross and confusing run its alleys through the wreckage, like the runs of weasels or city foxes, and its houses are jumbled cheek-by-jowl on the escarpment above the sea, sometimes almost on top of each other, so that the lanes have to burrow and probe beneath them, here and there opening out into a little plaza with a church, or a neglected esplanade along the sea-wall. A goat nibbles distractedly among the toppled walls; the voices of

Stuttgart batik designers echo thickly down the alleys; from their shadowy terrace an elderly French couple with their spaniel contemplate, glasses in hand, the passing of the centuries in this place.

But higher, far higher up the rock the Venetians made their stronghold. A steep zigzag track leads there, and halfway up a huge iron-studded door, bullet-pocked, marks the entrance to the Kastro. Up this track, through this door, everything had to pass into the Venetian fortress: there is no other way. Through the dark gatehouse you must go, past the guard-post, and there as you emerge into the sunshine and follow the track to the crest of the rock, a scene of magnificent dereliction unfolds. Wherever you look on that high plateau, sun-bleached and scoured, scattered chunks of buildings stand. At the very summit of the rock are the ruins of the utmost guard-post, and from there the remains of the city, tight-packed across the bumpy plateau, have rather a Celtic look, old and eerie: as you lie among the cyclamen watching the fishing boats or following the fluttering antics of skylarks in the blue, you may fancy you hear a distant murmur of voices, and perhaps the sound of water too, drip-drop, drip-drop, in some ancient cistern far below.

It is probably no more than fancy, though, for of all the buildings on the summit of that rock, only the cathedral is still alive. The Byzantines built it on the very edge of the rock, where every approaching ship could salute it, perhaps the most superbly sited of all their churches: actually on the lip of a precipice, like a pledge to providence, looking up the lovely coastline towards Athens, Salonika and distant Constantinople itself. The Venetians recognized the glory of this structure, and embellished it with a handsome narthex, and when all else in the city was destroyed, the last shipload of malmsey had long sailed from the little harbour below, and Islam was supreme all over Greece, the church of Santa Sophia remained a noble echo of its great progenitor on the Golden Horn, and its cousin beside the Piazza San Marco.

It remains the single spark of animation among those structural skeletons. People come to its services from the lower town and from the mainland, laboriously climbing that track through the scarred old Kastro gate. Candles burn always beneath its dome, dimly illuminating the mosaics all around: on one wall there hangs a modern picture of the original Santa Sophia, restored to all its Christian glory by the artist's wishful fancy, overflown by the Virgin Mary, and surrounded by all those columns, statues, obelisks and memorials of The City to whose destruction Dandolo and his Venetians so long ago contributed.

On the other side of Greece, the western side, just inside the Gulf of Corinth stands the little port of Navpaktos. Though fortified from top to toe, it looks rather demurely southward across the gulf to the Peloponnesian mountains, and is a delightful little specimen of Colonial Venetian, at an opposite extreme from the stark fascination of Monemvasia. High on the hill behind stands its guardian citadel, and in intermittent bastions down the wooded slopes, resolving themselves near the bottom into trellised cottages, pergolas and pretty lanes, the fortifications run down to the harbour mouth, enclosing the town within their protective walls, and embracing indeed the little harbour itself, which has a lighthouse on its mole, and stern gun-platforms above its bobbing yachts. It is a very satisfying ensemble. In summer tourist coaches line up along its waterfront, wanderers from the north pile their rucksacks beneath the jacarandas of its square, and children clamber all over the harbour walls, looking at the guns.

In the days when the Venetians held this place, they commanded the Gulf of Corinth, the inner sea through which all ships must pass to the narrow isthmus joining the Peloponnese to the rest of Greece. Today many ships sailing to Athens from the west come this way, making for the Corinth canal, and there is seldom a moment when there is not a vessel in sight. A few miles to the west, where the ferry now crosses from Patras, are the Navpaktos narrows which are the entrance to the gulf, 'the little Dardanelles', and the small castles of Rion and Anterion which command them, one on each side. For the Venetians, this was one of the most important of the Greek coastal stations, but paradoxically it became a household name to them only when they had lost it to the Turks. For this was Lepanto, and from its roadsteads sailed the Turkish fleet whose defeat in the open sea outside the narrows provided the proudest of Venetian battle-honours.

The Turks took it from the Republic in 1499, thanks to the incompetence of Antonio Grimani, one of those admirals whose fortunes we followed in Chapter Three. He was exiled for his failure, only to become Doge later in life; the commander of the garrison was hanged in public outside the Doge's Palace. The Turks immediately turned Lepanto into their main base in western Greece; and so it came about that when, in 1571, the war between Islam and Christianity reached a climax in one of the most famous of all naval battles, it was from this archetypically Venetian port that the ships of the Turkish Grand Admiral sailed out to fight.

It was the time of the war in Cyprus, when Turkish mastery at sea and apparent invincibility on land seemed still to threaten the existence of Christianity itself. The Venetians had been driven from most of their Aegean possessions and all their strongholds on the Greek mainland. Even their territories on the Dalmatian coast, within the Adriatic, were hardly more than enclaves in enemy territory. Nicosia had fallen, Famagusta was invested. In this extremity the Venetians, the rearguard of western Europe, had appealed more desperately than ever for help from the Christian powers; in October 1571 the great confrontation occurred, between the battle-fleets of the Holy League and the Empire of the Ottomans.

From the highest point of Navpaktos fortress, among the aromatic pines and cypresses, you can see it all. From the calm waters of the gulf below you, where the ships go by for Italy or Piraeus, the Turkish fleet of some 280 galleys sailed, on the evening of 6 October, between the twin forts on the headlands to the open sea. They flew the long pennants of the Sultan of Turkey, the Bey of Alexandria and the great corsair Uluj Ali, Dey of Algiers, who was said to be a renegade monk from Calabria. They were rowed by Christian prisoners and their admiral was another of those semi-anonymous Turkish commanders – Ali Pasha is what the world calls him, and history knows no more. He took with him a sacred talisman, a tooth of the Prophet Mohammed mounted in a crystal ball, and above him there flew the grand standard of the Ottoman Empire, never yet captured in battle, inscribed with the name of God 26,000 times. He sailed against the advice of many of his captains, who wanted to stay safe under the guns of Lepanto, but he hoped that by destroying the Christian fleet he could not only seal the fate of Cyprus, but also lay Crete and all the rest of the Venetian empire at the Sultan's mercy.

Away to the west outside the narrows, far beyond the ferries plodding from Rion to Anterion and back again, where the bay of Patras broadens towards the open sea, your mind's eye may see the sails and flashing oars of the Christian fleet, assembling for the battle – ships from Spain, Sicily, Genoa, Naples, Malta and Venice. Their commander was Don John of Austria, twenty-four years old, natural son of the Emperor Charles V and half-brother to Philip II of Spain, a precipitate, conceited but undeniably dashing scion of the European chivalry. His command was a difficult one, for the allies frequently quarrelled among themselves, the Venetians and the Genoese were hereditary enemies, and just before the battle the disheartening news arrived by dispatch vessel from Cyprus that Famagusta had fallen.

Nevertheless the fleet we may dimly see, milling into their battle positions beyond the narrows, was the greatest ever assembled in the name of Christendom, with more than two hundred ships and 50,000 men. More than a hundred of the ships were Venetian, under the command of Sebastiano Venier, Captain-General of the Sea, and Agostino Barbarigo. Sixty had come from Venice herself, sixteen of them manned by convicts chained to the oars, the rest by free men. Five more were contributed by Venetian noblemen of the *terra firma*. Thirty came from Crete, seven from the Ionian Islands, eight from the Venetian possessions in Dalmatia.

The most striking Venetian contribution, though, was a flotilla of six great galleasses. These specialities of the Arsenal were a cross between the traditional galley, the backbone of Mediterranean fighting fleets for centuries, and the big sailing galleons used by the navies of northern Europe. They had four masts, three carrying lateen sails, one with a square sprit-sail protruding over the bows. The galleasses were very broad in the beam and this enabled them to carry, besides a heavy broadside, a circular structure in the bows, rather like a modern gun-turret, in which were mounted at least half a dozen heavy guns. They were hard to manoeuvre, and so we may fancy their great shapes, away out there to the west, being towed into their fighting stations by galleys.

By the morning of 7 October the two fleets were in position and 100,000 men were preparing for action. It was a Sunday, the feast of St Justina, and for the Christians this was a crusade. On every galley crucifixes were raised and men confessed their sins to the chaplains. Don John, in full armour, attended mass on board his flagship, the Spanish galley *El Real*, and later himself hoisted to its masthead a banner, bearing the image of Christ crucified, which had been blessed by the Pope. The Turks were assembled in a crescent, with two supporting wings and a flotilla in reserve behind; the Christians were grouped in three fighting lines, with thirty-five galleys in reserve and the six Venetian galleasses like champions in the van.

Hundreds of fanciful pictures illustrate the battle of Lepanto, and usually show its tactics neat and logical. Naval historians, too, make it all sound rational enough: how the two fleets clashed head-on, while the Turkish wings tried to outflank the Venetians on the Christian left, the Genoese on the right; how the great galleasses broke the Turkish impetus; how Don John, sailing from here to there along the line, pulled his fleet together and reinforced its worst-hit squadrons; how the issue was decided in the centre, when Spanish soldiers boarded the Turkish flagship and forced its surrender. I doubt, though, if we would see it very orderly from our vantage-point above Navpaktos. It was doubtless a terrible muddle, like most sea-battles from Actium to Midway, and the classic formations in which the fleets opened operations soon collapsed into savage hand-to-hand fighting across the splintered decks of broken and listing galleys.

Everybody, admiral or galley slave, was in equal danger, and little quarter was given. When the Venetians on the left captured the Bey of Alexandria after rescuing him from drowning, they beheaded him there and then, on the deck. When Ali Pasha himself surrendered his flagship, they hacked off his head at once and presented it to Don John, before mounting it on a pike and displaying it to the Turkish fleet. Barbarigo was killed by an arrow; so was Prior Giustinian of the Order of St John, commander of the Maltese contingent. (On the other hand one hand-to-hand skirmish, it is said, degenerated into a hilarious pelting of oranges and lemons between Christians and Muslims, both sides in fits of laughter.)

It was a fearful battle, all in all. Some 8,000 Christians lost their lives, and at least 20,000 Muslims. Thousands more Turks were taken prisoner, thousands of Christian captives were freed from their oars, and Ottoman sea-power was held for ever within the eastern Mediterranean. Christendom felt itself to have been saved, and in many parts of Europe even now you may see tokens of its immense relief – paintings of the battle in galleries everywhere, captured flags and trophies, a pulpit shaped like a galley-prow at Irsee in Bavaria, a stained-glass window at Wettingen in Switzerland. Even the flowering of the baroque style itself, so some historians suggest, owes its exuberance to the new hope of Lepanto.

The Venetians were the most delighted of all, for the news of the victory, raced to Venice in ten days flat, reached the lagoons the very day after the hideous story of Famagusta. It was hailed as one of the classic Venetian triumphs, proof that the old blood still ran high and the lion of St Mark had not lost his roar. It was, after all, the great Venetian gunships which had stood in the front of the Christian line and taken the brunt of the Turkish assault. All Venice went into celebration when the galley *Angelo Gabriele* sailed into the Basin with a huge Turkish flag and a long line of turbans trailing from its stern, its crew wildly firing off their guns and shouting 'Victory! Victory!' Tremendous services were held in the Basilica, mighty banquets were organized, an oratorio was composed, dozens of popular songs swept the streets, heady pageants paraded around the Piazza, Turkish prisoners were displayed in chains, supervised by a stucco lion and a lady in red velvet symbolizing Victory.

It was like Mafeking night in London 300 years later. All the barriers were lowered, all the classes mixed, and even the pick-pockets, we are told, took a night off. The euphoria lasted for months. Tintoretto painted a huge picture of the battle. Andrea Vicentino painted another, featuring himself as a floundering but impeccable officer up to his neck in water. Veronese painted a vast allegorical Victory which was placed directly above the Doge's throne. An altar was erected in the church of San Giuseppe, the entrance to the Arsenal was reconstructed, a whole new charitable brotherhood, the Scoula del Rosario, was established specifically to celebrate 7 October 1571.

All over the territories of the *Stato da Mar*, too, you may discover memorials of the battle and boasts of the part Venetian ships and sailors played in it. But in the event, if Lepanto possibly saved Europe, it did little to preserve the Venetian empire. Cyprus was lost anyway – as the Grand Vizier observed sagely in Constantinople, the Turk might have had his beard singed, but Venice had lost an arm. The Ottoman fleet was soon rebuilt, and if it never ventured to challenge all Christendom again, was strong enough to fall upon Venetian Crete eighty years later.

As for little Lepanto, Navpaktos, it was always to remain for the Venetians a metaphysical possession, so to speak, a colony in the mind.

Rather more than a century later, all the same, the Venetians did go back there. By then the Republic was in obvious decline, its wealth denuded, its fleets diminished, its hardy working people softened, its once dutiful nobility ever more selfish and irresponsible. The empire was almost lost – Iraklion had fallen in 1669, and all that was left were the Ionian Islands, Tinos, the ports of the Adriatic coast and three island-fortresses off Crete. The splendours of Methoni were long gone: Venice depended now largely on foreign-built ships and foreign mercenaries.

Yet when war with the Turks broke out again in 1684, the Venetians fought with unexpected aggression. German, Maltese and Italian troops were hired to reinforce the Republic's army of Venetians and Dalmatians, and it was decided to forestall Turkish offensives by a massive invasion of Greece. This was a startling decision, but there was a commander to hand of sufficient boldness to undertake the campaign: Francesco Morosini, the heroic defender of Iraklion fifteen years before. His conduct then had saved him not only from bisection or disembowelment by the Turks, but also from the dungeons or horrid islands usually reserved for Venetian generals who had surrendered their commands, and he was the national hero of the day. A fleet was prepared; an army of German, Venetian, Maltese, Slav and Italian troops was mustered; in August 1684, an invasion force landed at Koroni.

This was a triumph. Morosini proved himself once more an inspired leader, and there is a description of him personally turning the tide of battle, when things were going badly at Methoni, by the sheer grandeur of his carriage – that scarred old pillar within the fortress ruins is named for him to this day. Within a few months he had taken the whole of the Peloponnese, more than Venice had ever ruled before, had brought the winged lion back to Navpaktos, had crossed the Isthmus of Corinth to capture Athens, was planning an invasion of Euboea and was even thinking of going on to Crete. The Signory was overjoyed, and erected a bust of the general in the Doge's Palace, dubbing him Morosini the Peloponnesian. The Greek inhabitants of the Peloponnese were not, on the whole, so delighted: their religion had generally been tolerated by the Turks and they had unhappy memories of old Venetian arrogance. Nevertheless Morosini set up the usual elaborate administration all over the peninsula and for a while it seemed that the name of the Morea, so evocative to Venetian ears, would once again enter the registers of the Serenissima.

It lasted in the event only thirty years, but it left behind it the greatest single monument of the empire's declining years – the fortress of Palamidhi above the city of Nauplia, at the head of the Gulf of Argos. The Venetians had held Nauplia throughout the fifteenth century, and it had always been an important place – after the Greek War of Independence against the Turks, in 1831, it was to become the first capital of independent Greece. In 1685, when the Venetians returned there after 145 years, it was already dominated by the fortress of Akronauplia, and by the sea-castle which they themselves had built on the off-shore reef of Bourtzi (used by the Turks as a safe residence for their retired executioners). The Turks had strengthened the town still further and had crowned it everywhere with minarets (even Bourtzi had two) making it the toughest and spikiest looking place imaginable. Morosini decided, though, to build a far more formidable fortress on the high hill behind the town, to be the Venetian military headquarters for the whole of conquered Greece, and this was to prove the last masterpiece of the Venetian imperial adventure.

Nauplia is still the most Italianate of all the towns of mainland Greece. It played little part in the Greek War of Independence, in which so much medieval architecture was lost, and is full of blithe charm. The minarets have gone. You may take rooms in the executioners' island castle. The engaging waterfront is lined with tourist cafés, the Venetian barracks in the main square have been turned into a museum, two hotels have been built within the ramparts of Akronauplia. Picturesque hilly lanes run upwards from the sea and every other house is a *pension*. It is a lively little place, a prawn-and-retsina, souvenir-tile, excursion-round-the-bay sort of place.

But immediately behind it looms something much more sombre: Morosini's Palamidhi, touched up a little by archaeology but impervious to tourism. It was built long after the prime of Venice, and is rather a self-conscious stronghold, I think – a showy, virtuoso construction, expressing perhaps, despite its strength, some underlying sense of wasting power. But its style is undeniably terrific, and when the Venetians built it Palamidhi was easily the most powerful fortress in Greece – the only truly modern fortress, according to contemporary specialists.

Elaborately, in many layers, it crowns the bald hill. You can drive to its gates now round the back, but originally the main approach was by way of a covered track direct from the port, arched and loopholed for defence, which gave way in its upper reaches to a winding and precipitous stairway up the face of the rock. This is still there, is popularly supposed to have 999 steps (actually there are 857) and is still climbed every day by dogged, perspiring and all too often regretful visitors. No doubt this disagreeable clamber, imposed upon visiting plenipotentiaries, defeated generals or dilatory allies, tellingly emphasized the castle's consequence: certainly when at last you reach the final step, and pass through the intricate defensive gateway into the fortress itself, you are in no mood to scoff.

Inside all is cunning device. It must have seemed a futuristic fortress in the 1690s, set against the antique citadels of Greece. Eight self-sufficient lesser forts are contained within its immense outer wall, each with its own ammunition bunkers, cisterns, barracks and gun-stations, and in the heart of it all is a master-fort, with a huge reservoir, deep storage-rooms for food and munitions, and a field of fire covering all the outer-works. So, at least, the books say; but though I am sure there really was nothing accidental about the design of Palamidhi, every slit and cranny having a military purpose, nowadays it is hard to grasp its pattern properly, and sometimes its succession of gates and staircases, its beautifully dressed stone ramps, buttresses and archways, remind me rather of a Piranesi prison, whose staircases lead nowhere after all, and whose vaulted arches support nothing but themselves.

Palamidhi does not feel, like Methoni or Monemvasia, organic to its site, or to history. It doth protest too much. From the summit of its hill there is, to be sure, an almost stagey sense of command. The sea lies glistening at our feet, the mountains rise misty over the water, rain-shafts, perhaps, slant here and there, and across the plain you can see the tall rock-citadel of Argos, for so many centuries Nauplia's twin guardian of the gulf. But still it feels a place of contrived majesty, just as the whole last fling of Venice in Greece seems, in retrospect, unnatural – a gesture out of time. The Venetians were overreaching themselves, in their brave return to Hellas. The attack on Euboea failed, all plans for a Cretan campaign were abandoned and by 1715 the Turks were storming back again. Nauplia fell after the briefest of resistances. Monemvasia did not resist at all. The garrisons of Methoni and Koroni mutinied rather than fight. In three months it was all over; the empire of Venice in the Morea was ended. Palamidhi was its epitaph, and Morosini the Peloponnesian, who had gone home to become Doge, emblematically died in Nauplia during a return to the scene of his triumphs.

On a gate upon the lower fortress wall, three years before they left, the Venetians erected the most decadent of all the winged lions of their empire. You can see it there still, overgrown now with figs and wild magnolia, at the head of the steps from the town: a stunted beast, a runt of a lion, with a head too big for its body and a puny pair of wings.

★

We will not leave them there, though, for the Venetians created one more monument to themselves, more permanent even than the fortress walls of Nauplia, during their last years in Greece.

On 26 September 1687, a lieutenant from Lüneburg serving in Morosini's army found himself with his mortar unit on the summit of the hill called the Mouseion in Athens. The view from this high observation post was stupendous, and is easy to re-create now, if you care to walk up there through the scented woods. On the top of the hill, then as now, stands a first-century memorial to the Syrian philhellene Philopappos, and somewhere there the lieutenant posted his men. To the south, where you now see the shipping of Piraeus crowded like an invasion flotilla itself off the smoky port, he could see, through crystal air, the Venetian fleet at anchor off-shore – scores of the high-hulled, square-rigged vessels by now standard in the Venetian service, which had arrived there five days before with an army of 10,000 men. Where now the southern suburbs of the city straggle shapeless to the sea, he could still make out the lines of Themistocles' Long Walls, built 2,000 years before to link Athens with its port. To the north, where today the charmless capital extends mile after mile, street after street as far as the eye can see, for him there was only the little village that was Athens itself. Some three hundred houses was the whole of it, a hangdog little settlement, spiked by the minarets of its Turkish overlords, with the exquisite little churches of the Byzantines knobbly among the rooftops, and only the open countryside beyond, stretching away around the hill of Lycabettus towards the distant mountains.

Directly to the lieutenant's front, and directly before us too – the Acropolis! It is a ruin now. It was a fortress then, the Turks garrisoning it in force. The silhouette so familiar to us now was rather different in 1687, for the Parthenon itself, its dominant shape, was still complete: after consecration as a cathedral under the Greek emperors and the Frankish dukes, it had been turned into a mosque by the Turks and embellished with a tall minaret at its northern end. Then the sacred enclosure all around it was filled with a clutter of shacks, barracks and stores, into which the whole Turkish community of Athens, some 3,000 people in all, had withdrawn for safety. The exquisite temple of Nike, which we can see today rebuilt at the south-west corner of the Acropolis, had been dismantled by the Turks so that they could use its stones for defences. The glorious entrance of the Propylaea, now shattered, was partly a ruin even then, having been damaged by a chance explosion in a munition store, but was partly used as the harem of the Turkish governor, and had a square tower on top of it.

The Acropolis was an active fortress, commonly called 'the castle'. Turkish pickets held the steep slopes of the hill, there was artillery on the summit, and the Venetians, though they had easily occupied the rest of Athens, had so far been unable to dislodge the garrison from this remarkable redoubt. They had tried tunnelling into the rock and had succeeded only in losing their chief sapper, who fell down the cliff. They had tried bombardment, but their shells had mostly gone over the top of the hill, falling into the Greek houses on the other side and provoking angry demands for compensation. On 25 September, though, a Turkish deserter arrived at the Venetian lines with the intelligence that the Turks had now concentrated all their ammunition actually within the Parthenon; orders went out to aim specifically at that majestic target, and on the Mouseion hill the lieutenant from Lüneburg adjusted his sights.

It cannot have been a difficult target really. The range was no more than half a mile, and the brilliant Attic air made it seem closer still, and illuminated every detail. On the evening of the 26th the lieutenant got it right. The bang of the mortar; the whine of the projectile over the valley, a distant thump as it burst somewhere in the mass of the temple, and then, a mighty explosion, a cloud of flying debris, a shaking of the ground itself, and when the smoke and the rubble cleared, through a mass of flames the temple of Athene, the loveliest of all the temples the Greeks had ever built, was seen to be a roofless ruin. The whole ammunition store had gone up inside it, killing 300 Turks, including the commander of the garrison, bringing all resistance precipitously to an end, and scarring the Acropolis for ever.

The German mercenaries, it seems, were rather ashamed at what their fellow countryman had achieved, but the Venetians were apparently not so much distressed. Morosini, so one of his officers wrote, 'fell into an ecstasy' as he gazed upon the ruined Parthenon. He reported to his government that 'a fortunate shot' had given him command of the fortress, and he put a Venetian garrison up there at once, raising the banner of St Mark above the Propylaea. He had already earmarked for Venice the celebrated fountain-lion that had guarded the mouth of Piraeus harbour since classical times, but he thought the Serenissima should also have a trophy from the Acropolis itself, even to the world-weariest soldier some sort of ultimate objective. Unfortunately, when his engineers tried to remove the figure of Poseidon and the chariot of Victory from the pediment of the Parthenon, the sculptures fell to the ground in pieces. He sent home some other lions instead: one of them was headless, but as he airily remarked to the Signory in an accompanying dispatch, they could easily get another head from somewhere.

The Acropolis has never recovered from this tragedy. We scramble down the Mouseion now, down the zigzag path through the pine trees and up the steep slope of the Acropolis on the other side of the valley; as we climb the awesome steps to the sanctuary, pass between the pillars of the Propylaea and find ourselves upon the sacred rock itself, even now it is like walking into a battlefield, or entering a bombed city. The Parthenon stands there as the Venetians left it, roofless and gutted still, and the great empty space of the rock around is scattered with broken columns, bits of statuary, struggling trees and bric-à-brac, rather as though it has all been swept by blast. Even the perpetual chattering crowds fail to dispel the sadness of the scene, and the poisonous mist which swirls around the rock so often nowadays, driven up by the sea-wind from the chemical plants of Piraeus, suggests to me still the fumes of cordite.

The Lüneburg lieutenant's later career is lost to history, but alas, his accurate trajectory upon the holy hill was to prove the one Venetian accomplishment in Greece that the world would always remember.

Ionian White and Gold

*Tittle-tattle place – importance of Corfu – the
system – circumspection – signs of Venice –
gypsies – Jews – images and values*

MOST VENETIAN imperial chapters end with explosions –
shrieks too, drums, and recriminations. As we sail up the north-
west coast of Greece, though, out of Methoni's spectacular bay,
past the hill-top castle of Navarino, through the battle-waters of
Lepanto, along the harsh high shore of Epirus, we approach the
one great Venetian possession which was acquired painlessly,
beat off all foreign assaults, and remained a more or less loyal
subject of the Serenissima until the Republic itself faded away
from sheer decrepitude. The Greek island of Corfu is made for
pleasure or escape – 'a very small tittle-tattle place', Edward
Lear once called it – and by the restless standards of the *Stato da
Mar*, a pleasant enough refuge it was during the four centuries of
Venetian sovereignty. The climate was agreeable, the peasantry
was docile, the local gentry flexibly adapted to Venetian ways,
and by general consent Corfu was the most desirable station of the
Venetian colonial service.

In Corfu the Venetians, at least in the earlier years of their
dominion, were at their most statesmanlike. In the islands of the
Aegean, in Crete and Cyprus and the Grecian fortress-ports, they
seem always to be mere successors in the train of history: they
look back to Roman or Byzantine forebears, they blend often
enough vaguely into the mists of paganism, their admirals lost in
the company of the gods, their legends merged in yet more insubstantial myth. When they go, they are replaced by the blank and
unlettered presence of the Turks, like night descending. It is on the

island of Corfu that we first feel them to be forebears, trustees, one day to hand over responsibility to successors in their own kind.

I was rummaging one day in an antique shop in Corfu Town, the capital of the island, when I came across a curious local coin, grimy with a century's handling and slightly squashed around the rim. Polishing this unprepossessing object on the seat of my trousers, and helped by the spit and handkerchief of the shop-keeper, I discovered it to be inscribed with two majestic devices. On the one side it bore the emblem of St Mark. On the other there appeared the winged lion's direct successor in the iconography of imperialism, Britannia, holding a trident, a laurel leaf and a shield emblazoned with the Union Jack. The Turks, when they inherited a colony, obliterated everything Venetian; at least the British, recognizing the noble style of their predecessors, had the courtesy to acknowledge a line of descent.

The Venetians were allotted Corfu at the division of the Byzantine empire, but they failed to keep it for long and it fell into the successive hands of the Despots of Epirus, the King of Sicily and the Angevins of France until 1386. By then the local administration was so awful that the Corfiotes themselves appealed for Venetian protection, sending a delegation of local worthies to Venice to plead their case. The Venetians needed little persuasion; Corfu was the gate to the Adriatic, and with their long war against the Genoese just ended, they were on the point of taking the island anyway.

The Adriatic was almost a lake, in their eyes. It was the Gulf of Venice, and when each Ascension Day the Doge went out in his *bucintoro* to wed the sea, if it was in a morganatic way the universal ocean that he was marrying, in a more intimate and particular sense the Adriatic was his bride. The entrance to the Adriatic, the Otranto Strait, is only fifty miles across, and the sea within it really is distinct from the Mediterranean as a whole – physically and climatically different, lined on its eastern shores by the harsh escarpment of the karst, the limestone rim of the Balkans, and periodically churned into fury by that fearful wind of central Europe, the *bora*, which sends small ships scurrying for shelter, and has been known to blow railway wagons off their tracks.

For many generations it was the policy of the Signory that all traffic originating in this inner sea, 500 miles long and never more than 150 miles wide, should be channelled through the docks, banks and warehouses of Venice herself, *La Dominante*. Ships leaving Adriatic ports had to make deposits guaranteeing that they would take their goods to Venice, while in times of famine the Venetians held themselves entitled to seize food from any ship, wherever it had come from, encountered by their warships inside the Otranto Strait. The powers intermittently acknowledged this supremacy, and ship-masters of all nations, slipping past the watchful galleys of the Serenissima to enter the Adriatic, felt themselves to be in semi-private waters.

Corfu became the Gibraltar of Venice – the Pearl Harbor too, perhaps, for in later years the two squadrons of warships generally based there were the strike force of Venetian power. In their prime, their reach was long and swift. In 1517 the King of Tunis sent a rare and precious gift to the Sultan of Turkey – four eight-horse teams, each team of a different breed or colour, and each attended by eight slave-grooms of matched skin and costume. The consignment, valued at 200,000 ducats, was entrusted to a Venetian ship, but when it put in for provisions at Syracuse, in southern Italy, it was immediately surrounded by pirates. No matter. The Corfu command was alerted: at once three war-galleys left for Syracuse, and even before they had stormed into action the prudent buccaneers had dispersed, and the polychromatic stable proceeded on its way.

To Corfu, as to all other Venetian colonies, the greatest threat was the Ottoman Empire. The view from the waterfront of Corfu Town, on the eastern shore of the island, graphically illustrates the anxiety. The town stands cluttered above its quays, the bay is busy with ferries, freighters, motor-caiques and cruise ships, the island wanders bumpily away, clad in blues, greys and browns, littered with sweet mountain villages and distasteful hotels, and reaching a climax in the holy summit of Pantokrator, the Lord of All, dually crowned nowadays with a monastery and a radar station. Framing this happy prospect, though, is a line of mountains more remote – grimmer, grander mountains crowned with snow even in the spring and looking altogether alien and forbidding. They are the mountains of Albania, characterized by the fastidious Mr Lear as possessing 'a certain clumsiness and want of refinement'. In Venetian times they contained the implacable Turks, in ours they enclose the most xenophobic and suspicious of the states of Europe, friends to nobody, churls to all. Only the narrow strait of the Corfu Channel, three miles wide at its narrowest point, separates them from the island.

It is a queer feeling nowadays to look across the water to those impenetrable highlands, and doubtless it sometimes gave the Venetians uneasy sensations too. There stood the Great Enemy. Those mountains were an outcrop of the great land mass which ran away to Constantinople itself, the centre of Islamic power. Corfu bristled like a porcupine in the lee of that tremendous reminder, and the Turks repeatedly attacked it. One great raid, in 1537, reduced the population from 40,000 to 19,000, and in 1715, when the Venetians fell back upon the island after their withdrawal from the Peloponnese, 30,000 Turks besieged Corfu Town for forty-two days and came within an ace of capturing it. They never succeeded, though. The town was a very figure of martial resolution, and the Serenissima spent millions of ducats on its fortifications – in the sixteenth century it had 700 guns.

Its focus was the Old Fort, the twin-peaked citadel which appears in hundreds of old maps and prints, and which sheltered within its walls the palace of the Venetian governors, the naval command and the Latin cathedral. It never did fall to an enemy (though Nelson suggested it might be taken by running a frigate ashore and storming the ramparts from the riggings, rather as Dandolo engineered the assault on Constantinople). Like so many imperial fortresses, it occupied the whole of a small peninsula, separated from the mainland by a ditch, and backed by a wide open space kept clear as a field of fire. Time has softened its grim outlines now, brooding there on its peaks, and in the summer evenings, when the fireflies waver about the shrubberies, and a band plays perhaps upon the promenade at its feet, it seems hardly more than a romantic fantasy: but it was no conceit in its day, and suggestively at the flank of it, beside the moat, you may still see the mooring-places of the galleys, the fists of the Republic.

After the fearful Turkish raid of 1537, and just before Lepanto, the Venetians built another fortress, the New Fort, on the other side of the town. Dominated by these two great strongholds and by hill-top forts commanding the landward approaches, in Venetian days this was a true garrison town, and the great man of Venetian Corfu was not the Governor, nor the Latin Archbishop, but a functionary called the Proveditor-General of the Levant, a military commander whose writ ran throughout the Venetian colonies of the east. When this grandee arrived at the start of his term of duty, protocol afforded him an almost mystical welcome. A special volume of etiquette was printed to govern the arrangements. The heads of both the Latin and the Greek churches were to be on hand to greet His Excellency. A Corfiote noble was to compose a panegyric upon his virtues. The Jews were to lay carpets along the streets through which he would pass from the harbour. The remains of St Spiridon, patron saint of the island, would be available for him to kneel before. More Jews, with bouquets of flowers, were to bow low as he entered his palace in the citadel to take up the immense responsibilities of his office.

Such was the importance of Corfu in the Venetian pattern of self-esteem and the Venetian strategy of survival. In the Golden Bull by which, in 1387, they declared their possession of the island they undertook never to leave it and to defend it against all enemies; and this commitment they honoured to the end.

Venetian noblemen ruled Corfu, of course – a Bailie and two councillors stood at the top of the administration, as in Crete – but here more than in their other colonies they allowed the indigenes some real share in government. A council of island noblemen disposed of almost all the local jobs, even the captaincy of the Corfu war-galleys: it was a Corfiote captain who captured the Turkish admiral's flagship at Lepanto (and another, taken prisoner himself in the same battle, enjoyed the privilege of being flayed alive for Venice).

Though most of these island swells were Greek Orthodox by religion, many of them claimed Venetian descent, and many more were happy to use Venetian titles. They had their own Golden List of nobility, modelled upon the Venetian Golden Book, and they successfully beat off successive attempts by the bourgeoisie to get a share of the power; in 1537, when many noblemen lost their lives in the Turkish raid, by direct instruction from the Signory the order was repleted from the ranks of the middle-class, but in no time at all these new aristocrats became just as haughty as their predecessors. In an attenuated form the Golden List was to stay in existence long after the end of the Republic. In 1797, when Venice fell, 277 families were represented in the register: by 1925, when its last issue appeared, twenty-four remained. Of them three traced their origins to Venice itself: the others had sprung from every part of the old empire – from Crete, the Peloponnese, Cyprus, Dalmatia, even Constantinople – all drawn here, long before, to this Hellenic island in the lee of Islam, by the presence of the Serenissima.

By and large the Corfiote nobles formed a useful client class for their Venetian overlords, and they were assiduously humoured in return. Even the peasants seldom complained in Corfu, and performed with becoming grace exhibitions of loyalty at public functions. This showed restraint, for here as everywhere, the administration was not noticeably sympathetic to the common man. The last thing the Venetians wanted in their empire, especially in its later years, was an enlightened working class, and in the 1756 budget for Corfu and its sister islands, for example, out of a total expenditure of 421,542 ducats only 822 ducats went on genuine social improvements. Schools scarcely existed in the island, and since the official language was Italian, in the Venetian dialect, ordinary people were quite out of touch with affairs of state and policy.

Corruption crept in too, here as everywhere. The class of impoverished Venetian noblemen called the Barnabotti provided most of the expatriate officials, and they were notoriously venal. Judges were often bribable. Tax collectors were often crooked. The Bailie lived in great style, escorted at all times by liveried servants, serenaded at his dinner table by his private band, but the garrison was often reduced to thieving and beggary, so sporadically was it paid, while the navy kept its accounts in balance by undertaking commercial transport on the side. During the 1537 fighting, when the Old Fort was closely invested by the Turks, the Venetians had no compunction in driving old people, women and children out of the gates into no man's land, where they wandered forlornly between the opposing armies, the women vainly crying for help, the men displaying to the soldiers on the walls, so eye-witnesses reported, the wounds they had suffered fighting for Venice in previous conflicts.

Yet faith in Venice herself, that distant majesty of the lagoon, remained undeterred. Deputations frequently made the journey north, to argue Corfiote cases before the Grand Council in the Doge's Palace, and generally they seem to have found redress. The Venetians remembered always the grim example of Crete, with its interminable record of rebellion, and were inclined to be conciliatory to the Corfiotes. Venetian Bailies were repeatedly enjoined to treat the local people fairly and sometimes agents were sent out to report secretly upon the state of the island.

The Signory did not forget, either, that in Crete the Venetians themselves developed political ideas beyond their station. The commanders of the two town fortresses, so a seventeenth-century English traveller reported, had to swear not to communicate with each other during their terms of office, to make sure they could enter into no treasonable compact, and once the Republic felt obliged to decree that no more monuments were to be erected to Venetian governors of the island. The rulers of Corfu were to be, however prominent in their functions, non-persons in themselves: the Signory wanted no vivid demagogues up there in the fortresses, who might be tempted to go the Cretan way, and proclaim an island republic of St Spiridon.

'With regard to the Greeks,' wrote a French observer in Corfu, 'the Venetians are infinitely more jealous than disdainful. The vivacity and natural perspicacity of the Greeks, the superiority of their native talents, and their marked aptitude for the arts and sciences, appeared dangerous to a jealous Government . . .'

This was probably true. They treated this volatile population, especially in their more experienced years, with distinct caution. Here as in Venice itself, citizens were encouraged to spy upon one another, and to make use of the lion's head post-boxes, the denunciation boxes, which were affixed to walls at convenient corners of town. In particular the Venetians trod carefully when it came to the susceptibilities of the Greek church, and they were more successful than usual in their dealings with the Orthodox community. They knew by now that the Greek clergy was invariably a political body too, the seedbed always of patriotic sentiment, and they well understood the power of the village priests – almost nothing terrified a Corfiote peasant more than the possibility of excommunication, freely dispensed by local parsons (and profitably rescinded).

They accordingly brought the Greek church actually into the Establishment of the colony. It is true that they deprived it of its titular archbishopric, transferring that to their own Latin prelate, but they allowed the Greeks their own sort of metropolitan, the Chief Priest, elected to office by a body of local clerics happily entitled The Sacred Band. They also astutely cherished the island's own saint, St Spiridon, who wielded so immense an influence upon the Corfiotes that half the local boys seemed to be named for him. Spiridon was a fourth-century Cypriot bishop whose miracle-working corpse had been brought to Corfu in the fifteenth century; a church and a cult arose around him: he was credited with all sorts of wonders, from the ending of plagues to the discomfiture of pashas, and he became the central figure of the Orthodox faith on the island, its pride and its protector.

The Venetians fulsomely cultivated him. In 1489 they proposed to remove his corpse to Venice and were dissuaded only by the unanimous appeals of the people, but they never made that sort of error again. When in 1715 he saved the island from the Turkish invasion, the Senate itself sent a silver lamp to be hung in gratitude above his altar (where it remains). And when, four times a year, the embalmed corpse of the saint was processed in its ebony casket around the town, the Venetian Bailie, his councillors and the Proveditor-General carried the canopy that shaded it. A salute of twenty-nine guns was fired from the Old Fort. The warships in the harbour saluted and when the procession moved along the sea-ramparts, galleys were rowed in parallel alongside. While the saint was carried high on the shoulders of the priests, while choir and acolytes intoned their litanies, while the sick were rushed by their hopeful relatives into the path of the procession, trusting that the mere passage of Spiridon over their prostrate forms would be enough to cure them – while all these symptoms of Greekness swayed and proliferated, solemnly bearing their canopy walked the Venetians, looking, we may reasonably assume, eminent but a bit embarrassed.

The Venetians may have been wary of the Corfiotes, but they loved Corfu. So delectably set there, so benign of climate and beguiling of silhouette, not too far from home, not too close for discomfort, it provided a perfect setting for the colonial enterprise, for a merchant setting himself up as a country gentleman, or a servant of state ready to retire from his labours. It was almost like another island in their own lagoon: and indeed when in 1753 the Sardinas family of Corfu were elevated to the nobility for their services in battle, they were simultaneously elected to the pages of another Golden List, that of their native island of Mazzorbo, an almost indistinguishable settlement some five miles north of Venice.

Corfu Town remains recognizably Venetian. Because the Republic held it continuously for 400 years it has an air of civilized constancy and well-being unique among Greek towns. It is hemmed in still between the two fortresses, and its much-loved Esplanade, arcaded by the French in later years, provided with bandstands and gravel cricket pitches by the British, is nothing more than the open field of fire decreed by the engineers of the Old Fort. Tall, jumbled and hung with washing are the houses of Corfu, aggrandized sometimes by the shadowy outline of a *palazzo*, long since declined to flats or tenements, and crowned here and there with authentically Venetian campaniles, from whose belfries on Sunday mornings properly cracked and fruity bells ring out across the water.

Here are the shady flagged streets of Venice, the arcaded shops, the alleys of ample vegetables and sweet-smelling breads, the skulking market rats, the ingratiating grocers, the nodding black-shawled women, the strolling bravos, the glimpses of sacred pictures through the glazed inner doors of crooked churches. The Venetians brought to Corfu, besides their forts and war-galleys, their coffee-houses, their concerts, their operas and their taste for cultivated dalliance: by the eighteenth century it was the duty of

the Venetian naval commander not only to supervise the upkeep
and disposition of his ships, but also to arrange for the annual visit
of the Commedia dell' Arte players.

'All the bad habits of the Corfiotes,' a British administrator was
to write, 'come from the Venetians.' He was thinking, no doubt,
partly of their somewhat languid temperaments, and certainly
there is something very Italianate about the leisurely evening
stroll of the Corfiotes up and down the Liston, the paved promenade beside the Esplanade, fast-talking ladies arm in arm, lines of
students linked across the pavement, solemn men in Homburg
hats, paper under their arm, gravely discussing events in Athens
up and down, up and down beneath the trees. The custom was
introduced to Corfu by the Venetians, who made it the privilege
of the Corfiote nobility and actually named the promenade the
Liston after the Lista d'Oro. (And if, by the way, you want to
consult that catalogue, where better than the library of the
Reading Club, which is housed in a delectable small Venetian
palazzo overlooking the bay, and is rich enough in leather, prints,
smells of wood and furniture polish, hospitable librarians and
savants sunk in ancient narratives, to make the most dedicated
scholar of Venetiana, fresh from the libraries of San Marco itself,
feel comfortably at home?)

In the country too, for all those Turkish incursions, there are
signs of Venice still. Not only did the Venetians build, at the very
end of their stay, the island's first proper roads, but by offering
subsidies they clothed all Corfu with the olive tree, whose dark
green foliage and now wrinkled trunks set the very tone of the
countryside today and seem as immemorial as the rocks themselves. Some of these trees are said to be survivors of the original
plantings 600 years ago, and if you want to get a true idea of
Venice's aesthetic impact upon the island, try walking up one
of the wooded hills that overlook Corfu Town from the south: for
there, looking down over the blue waters that the galleys once
patrolled, one can see the red roofs and white walls of the
Venetian presence, the bell-towers and the castles, framed between the leaves of the most ineradicable legacy of them all, the
olive, which once and for all plucked this island from its Balkan
hinterland and made it part of the Mediterranean idea.

Corfu is another Venetian possession where you may see Venetian country houses – not medievally castellated like the Naxos tower-houses, but serene and modestly bucolic, couched in almond trees and gladioli, with wistaria winding its way up the garden cypresses, and anemones sprouting in the shade. At Kothokini, for example, in the rolling country south of Corfu Town, there is a house of the Sardinas family, those counts of Corfu and Mazzorbo. It is not a very big house and has rather a ship-like air to it, even to a flagpole; but it is unmistakably squirely in manner, having a private chapel in its cobbled yard, a big barn, and a little hamlet clustered respectfully around its walls – the Sardinas had the right to give sanctuary to fugitives from the law, and prospered for over several centuries from the fees they charged, not to mention their monopoly of the Corfu salt-pans.

It is a lovely place. Sardinas still own it, and it has kept its style intact. Its low-ceilinged rooms are shabby but gentlemanly, stuffed with quaint curios, and there are family crests about the place, and old portraits, and pedigrees on parchments. It is like Longhi's Venice transplanted. On a hot afternoon it seems to dream there: as the loud Greek music thumps away from the village radios over the wall, and you sit in the rambly garden with your host beneath the pergola, so there drifts over you the sense of privileged seclusion that must have seduced the Sardinas in the first place.

They were, so to speak, exotics in this simple setting. The holiest Venetian shrine of Corfu is the little church of the Blessed Virgin at Kassiopi, on the north coast. Its site has always been sacred to seafarers. The Romans built a temple there, and for many centuries sailors made a point of stopping there on their voyages to and from the east – Nero offered oblations at Kassiopi on his way to compete as a lute-player in the Isthmian Games at Corinth. A very early Christian church succeeded the temple, and when it was destroyed by the Turks in 1537 the Venetians replaced it with one of their own.

This became exceedingly holy too. Later in the century a young man was unjustly condemned for theft and blinded by order of the Venetian judges. Fraught with pain and despair he wandered sightless around the island until he reached Kassiopi, and there spent the night within the church. He was awakened by gentle

145

hands pressed upon his eyes, and when he opened them he saw the Virgin Mary standing kindly over him. The vision faded, his sight remained, and the news was taken at once to the Bailie, who recognized the event as a miracle and hastened to Kassiopi to make amends. A Mass is celebrated still, every 8 May, to commemorate the day.

But beside the door of the church the Venetians erected a marble plaque rather truer to their memory, I think, than the tale of the blinded boy. It was placed there when the church was rebuilt in 1538, and recorded that, the building having been destroyed by 'cruel Turkish pirates', it was reconstructed by three pious Venetians: Niccolò Suriano, Proveditor of the Fleet, Filippo Pasqualigo, Commander of the Adriatic Sea, and Pietro Francisco Malipiero, Commander of the Triremes.

Sometimes in the interior of Corfu, in some shaded clearing among the olives, you may notice a tented encampment pitched higgledy-piggledy beneath the trees; and when you stop the car to take a closer look, like jackals out of the wood the gypsies will fall upon you, carrying their babies in their arms – whining, crying, pushing their skinny fingers through the windows, beating on the windscreen, swarming wildly all around, and eventually pursuing you out of sight, as you proceed shakily on your way, with hideous but fortunately unintelligible curses.

Blame the Venetians. The gypsies were encouraged to come to Corfu because of their skill in horse-breeding, and probably nowhere else in Europe did they acquire such standing. Gypsies thrived elsewhere in the Venetian Empire – at Nauplia they were given particular rights of tenure, at Methoni, as we saw for ourselves, they prospered in pigs. Nowhere else, though, were they so institutionalized as they were in Corfu, where every grade of society was somehow fitted into the imperial structure.

There they constituted a feudal fief of their own, under a baron appointed by the Venetians – 'an office of not a little gain', so a Corfiote historian assures us, 'and of very great honour'. Very great power too, for the gypsy baron had almost complete authority over his feudatories. They were his private army. They were his corps of servants. He could punish them how he liked, short of killing them. In 1502 we hear of a Corfiote sea captain receiving the fief as a reward for running the blockade of Methoni, which had just fallen to the Turks; later it went to one of the island's most eminent scholars, for his services during the Turkish invasion of 1537. Every May Day the gypsies came to town to do honour to their lord. Drums beating, fifes squealing, they marched through the streets carrying his feudal banner above them, and setting up a maypole outside his house, sang a peculiar ditty in his praise, and handed over their feudal dues.

In return for all this the gypsies had valuable rights of their own. They could not be conscripted for the galleys, or made to do forced labour for the Republic. They formed their own military unit, under a gypsy commander, and throughout the four centuries of Venetian rule, thanks to these ancient privileges, their horse-copers' skills and no doubt their evasive woodland ways, they flourished exceedingly. No wonder they have reverted to the predatory now.

A different destiny awaited the Jews of Corfu, whose ghetto still stands in the shadow of the New Fort, in the tangle of narrow streets behind the bus station. It is difficult to identify because since the Nazi occupation of Corfu in World War II it has shrunk from a large and cultured community to a few shops and houses and a solitary synagogue. Almost all its inhabitants were shipped away to slave camps or gas chambers. In the Venetian heyday, though, the Corfu ghetto was the richest and most influential in the empire, and held a peculiar fascination for the Venetians because Judas Iscariot was popularly supposed to have been a Corfiote – a lineal descendant was commonly pointed out to the more gullible travellers, as one of the island's sights.

The Venetians could never escape Jewry. In all their chief possessions and trading posts they found clusters of Jews, clannish and disputatious, at once disconcerting and indispensable. Jews were the intermediaries and interpreters of their commerce – the Jews of Turkey in the sixteenth century nearly all spoke four or five languages, and sometimes ten or twelve. The Republic was always ambivalent towards them. Perhaps the Venetians felt a little too close to Jewry for their own comfort, for there has always been, in my own view, something Hebrew in the bearing, the enterprise, the style, the separateness and even the look of the Venetians. Much Jewish blood, I do not doubt, went into Venetian veins in the course of their centuries of intercourse with the Levant, and the oriental strain that everyone noted in things Venetian was often less Muslim or Byzantine than Jewish.

At home in Venice the Jews were powerful, but rigidly circumscribed. Shylock could finance his argosies to the east, but the chances were that he was obliged to return at dark to the Jewish quarter of the city, the first of all the ghettos – originally on the island of Giudecca, which took its name from the Jews, then in the north-western corner of the city, on the site of a disused iron-foundry (a *getto* is a metal-casting). It was the Venetians who invented the idea of a special costume to mark out the Jews – first it was a yellow hat, then a red – and the Jews were harshly taxed, deprived of all civic rights, and once, in 1572, expelled from the Republic altogether.

Not for long, though, because Venice could not do without them. They controlled much of the city's trade, in spices, woollens, sugar and silks, and they were irreplaceable on Rialto, the central money market. They were respected, too, as people of learning and finesse, and consulted for their scholarship as for their way with money. The rules that governed them were often waived or winked at, and in the daytime they were to be seen on the streets of the city looking anything but persecuted – their ladies, it was said in the sixteenth century, 'gorgeous in their apparel, jewels, chains of gold and rings . . . having marvellous long trains like princesses that are borne up by waiting women'.

As at home, so in the colonies: the Jews were generally safe under Venetian rule, if they were seldom easy. The Venetians, being independent sorts of Christians, did not often regard the Jews with the savage fanaticism common in Europe then, but at the same time Jews played a prominent part in the demonology of their empire. Jewish women were blamed for the immorality (and hence disloyalty) of the Cretan cities – in the sixteenth century a Gentile caught there in sexual intercourse with a Jewess could get ten years in the galleys, while the Jewess could be burned. It was a Jewish axeman who had murdered Erizzo, after the fall of Euboea in 1470, and a Jewish executioner who had flayed Bragadino in 1571. It was the Jew, Joseph Nasi, who was generally supposed to have instigated the Turkish attack on Cyprus: certainly he was for many years a formidable commercial rival to the Venetians, with his network of associates all over the east, his agents from the Levant to western Europe and his access to the Sultan's ear. Another Jew, actually born a Venetian subject, signed on behalf of the Sultan the treaty that gave Cyprus to the Turks; indeed it was partly the association of Jews with the humiliating loss of Cyprus, and with the slow whittling away of Venetian power in the east, that led to the expulsion order of 1572.

But the Jews were never expelled from Corfu. Like the gypsies, they were special there. They had been on the island since the end of the twelfth century, when a Greek-speaking Hebrew colony was established and a synagogue was built – the first example of Greek demotic prose is said to have been a translation of the book of Jonah made by its rabbis. When in 1386 the Corfiote deputation went to Venice to ask for the protection of the Republic, two of the six delegates were Jews; under the Venetians the community grew and flourished and became vital to the workings of the colony. A second synagogue was built. The ghetto, though walled and gated, became the richest quarter of town. The Jews adopted the language of their rulers and were principal bankers and traders of the island. Without them its financial system would have collapsed; it was not Venetian benevolence, but plain self-interest, that exempted the Jews of Corfu from the banishment.

Even here their status was anomalous. Rich and influential though they were, they were forbidden to own land, they were obliged to wear the star of David on their clothing and they were liable always to be enlisted for the more degrading tasks of state, like manning the galleys, or performing that familiar chore of medieval Jewry, executing people. The Greeks were not discouraged from their ancient prejudices against them, and every Easter Saturday, as a substitute for actually stoning them, made a point of dropping old crockery noisily out of their windows, preferably upon passing members of the community.

Still they multiplied and were useful. They fought bravely in the Turkish siege of 1715: the Venetian mercenary commander, the German Count Johann von der Schulenburg, was so impressed that he suggested to the Signory the settling of more Jews in the island, if only for their military aptitude. By the end of Venetian rule in Corfu the Jews were said to have constituted more than a quarter of the whole population, making the island the nearest thing to Zion that existed. Nobody mourned the fall of Venice more than the Jews of Corfu, and with reason, for never again, under any successor government, did they achieve such power and prosperity, and in the end the worst of all the empires, arriving similarly out of the north, took them away and killed them. To the end their vernacular remained the Venetian dialect of Italian.

A few have come back since, and one of the synagogues is alive again. Next door to it the president of the community has a television shop, and a few other Jews keep shops and run businesses in the neighbourhood. They do not seem very happy. They still hear the clatter of the crockery on Easter Saturday. They show you their Auschwitz tattoos and conduct you round the synagogue with a trace of sad resentment.

Six other islands – Paxos, Cephalonia, Levkas, Homer's Ithaca, Zakinthos and distant Kithira, around the point of Greece – constituted with Corfu the Venetian possession of the Ionians. Zakinthos, Zante, which after 1500 took the place of Methoni as principal port of call on the eastern route, prospered by the export of currants to England, and on it the Venetians built what is said to have been the loveliest of all their colonial towns, a perfect set-piece around a bay: hardly a stone remains of it, for it was utterly destroyed in the great earthquake of 1953. Cephalonia had a great castle and in later years a dear little opera house, visited frequently by companies from Venice. Ithaca, left entirely empty after a Turkish raid in 1479, was repopulated by the Venetians and, although only ten miles round, boasted a Captain of the Island and one full-blown noble family. As for Kithira, the Eye of Crete, far away to the south, it had a garrison, three castles and, in 1545, 1,850 inhabitants; most of its budget, its Rector once reported, went on the courier service by which it kept Iraklion informed of possible Turkish attacks.

All these islands remained Venetian until the fall of the Republic in 1797, and the Venetian style was deeply imprinted on them. In the 1920s it was said that the general social pattern of Corfiote life, from land tenure to snobbery, was still fundamentally Venetian: Venetian titles were still commonly used, Italian was widely spoken. Venice kept these islands *western* islands, during the long Turkish domination of Greece, and to this day the Greek patois of the mainland is full of Turkish idioms, but the patois of the Ionians is thick with Italianisms. When the curtain goes up in the Cephalonia theatre this evening, when the lights go on in the exquisite waterfront houses of Corfu, when the coffee is brought into the Kothokini drawing-room, and the diligent old scholars of the Reading Club, adjusting their bifocals, search in the shelves for another volume of Saint-Sauveur's *Voyages Historiques, Littéraires et Pittoresques* – at all these moments the more benevolent shades of imperial Venice stir and smile complacently.

Throughout the Ionians Venetian rule was to be remembered, all in all, affectionately. It had kept them from the Turks, it had respected the Orthodox faith, it had brought periods of prosperity, it had given the islands the most beautiful towns in Greece. But most important of all, more by diffidence than by design it had preserved in trust the Hellenism of the islands, and so for once carved itself an honourable place in the rolls of empire. The Venetians may not much have admired the Greek manner of life and they did their best to temper it with their architecture, their protocol, their alien social forms, their operas and their pageantries. They were not much interested in Greek classicism, except for those tangible artefacts, like headless lions or convenient column-heads, which they could ship away to ornament their palaces at home. But under their aegis Corfu, like Crete before it, became a haven and a refuge for everything that was alive and creative in Greekness.

Especially after the fall of Crete, artists, scholars and thinkers from every part of the Greek world came to the Ionians, sometimes only on their way to Venice itself, sometimes for good. So did the *stradioti* who, deprived of their billets on the mainland of Greece, settled in their hundreds on Zakinthos, bringing their horses with them. During the years between the fall of Iraklion and the Greek *Risorgimento* in the nineteenth century, these islands were the bastions of Hellenism, the place where the Greek dimension was kept in being. It was no accident that, if Venetian Nauplia was the seat of the first independent Greek government, Venetian Corfu was the home of the first Greek president.

The Venetians left the Ionians peacefully if in obloquy, pushed out by Napoleon, and their place was presently taken by the British, whose manners were not dissimilar and whose intentions towards the islands were much the same. When, in their turn, the British voluntarily left in 1864, the islands became the most cultivated and progressive parts of the new Greece, and for this the Venetians could properly claim credit. They had ruled the Ionians for four centuries, and their chief achievement was to leave them, as they found them, unmistakably Greek.

Just this once, then, the Venetian empire formed a link in history's chain, handing on a tradition from one era to another. One of the best-known Venetian monuments in Corfu is the Kardaki fountain, on the outskirts of Corfu Town. It is an antique waterspout on the flank of a hill above the sea, used for the watering of ships and richly Venetian in flavour. Crumbled in its fronded grotto a winged lion lurks, guarding the spout with raised paw and belligerent glare, and when the light is right it is easy to see the galley crews of the Corfu Squadron rolling their barrels up the twisty path to its fountain, horse-playing around the conduit perhaps, or dousing their sweaty heads in its cool water.

But agreeable though such fancies are, another and more ethereal presence really dominates the place. For 2,000 years before the Venetians built their fountain, the waters of Kardaki had bubbled through the precincts of a temple to Apollo on the hill above. For countless generations before the oarsmen of Venice toiled their way up that path, Greek sailors sprang ashore here, sweating and swearing too, to water their own galleys. It needs imagination to see the Venetians at Kardaki, but it requires no inner vision to conjure the images of Greece. They live there still, grand and ageless, in the green-blue of the sea, in the dapple of the trees, in the softness of the island air and the shrill passionate chatter of the children, playing immemorial Grecian games on the pebbles down below.

152

Adriatica

*Dukes of Dalmatia – Korčula – pragmatic
imperialism – the lion-house – navy towns –
on pirates – a piece of grit – a puzzle – a fable
by the way – aesthetics – a shimmer in the
distance*

NOW, LEAVING THE twin peaks of Corfu Town behind us,
moving cautiously northwards through the Corfu channel,
where the binoculars of the Albanians, we may be sure, like the
cannon of the Turks before them, are trained upon our passage,
murmuring a prayer as we pass the sailors' church at Kassiopi, we
sail through the Otranto Strait and enter home waters. Everything in the Adriatic points towards Venice at its head, and we are
swept northwards, in the twentieth as in the fifteenth century,
irresistibly by the magnetism of the lagoon.

The Venetians seldom kept footholds for long on the western
shore of the sea, the flat Italian shore, but never throughout the
whole course of their imperial history, from the thirteenth century to the eighteenth, were they without ports and bases on the
eastern shore, what is now Yugoslavia. This magnificent coast,
which they called generically Dalmatia, was predominantly
Catholic by religion, and they regarded it almost as an extension
of their own island estates, just as they regarded the Adriatic as a
sort of magnification of their lagoon. Duke of Dalmatia was the
very earliest of the Doge's external honorifics, and it was to regain
Venetian control of Zadar, halfway down the coast, that the
Fourth Crusade first veered off its course to the Holy Land.

It is a vastly complicated coast. The shoreline of Yugoslavia,
from Istria in the north to the Albanian frontier in the south, is
rather more than 400 miles long as the gull flies; but it is 2,000
miles long if you follow all its island shores and inlets –

'a co-efficient of indentedness', says my Yugoslav handbook, 'of 9.7'. There are said to be 725 islands, sixty-six of them inhabited, and 508 reefs and crags. Ethnically it was complex too – in Venetian times the hinterland people were all Slavs, but the Roman Empire had left a deposit of Latins in the coastal towns – and politically it was precarious: sometimes the Hungarians pushed down to the shore in one of their periodic spasms of expansion, and later the inevitable Turks pressed upon it from over the mountains.

For several centuries, though, the Venetians were effectively its suzerains, giving a territory here, gaining one there, ruling sometimes by direct force, sometimes by delegacy or persuasion, baffled sometimes by opponents too tough to crack, but never giving up, from start to finish. If they lost the mastery of this coast they lost the Adriatic too, and they were willing to fight any enemy, Byzantines, Magyars, Turks or common pirates to retain their authority over it – just as, in later years, the British were willing to risk any ignominy to keep control of the routes to their Indian Empire.

As India became to the British, so the Slav shore of the Adriatic Sea became to the Venetians – almost a part of themselves, linked by so many bonds and images, by such ancient associations, that the one seemed indivisible from the other, like a villa and its garden. Critics of the Venetians liked to call them 'Slavs and fishermen', and this is why: for the traffic was reciprocal, and if Venice profoundly affected the look and feel of Dalmatia, Dalmatia irrevocably influenced the character of Venice.

There is scarcely a mile of that tortuous shore, scarcely one even of its 659 *un*inhabited isles, which does not possess some token of Venice, a campanile, a name, or just the ghostly score of prows and keels on a sandy beach, where the galleys once careened. Let us, as we sail up the coast ourselves, put in first at one of the most Venetian of all its seaports, to stand for all the others: the island town of Korčula, Curzola to the Venetians, or Korkyra Negra, which lies some 300 miles north of Corfu, and was once its dependency.

I first arrived in Korčula late on a winter evening, and the little town looked very dark, almost deserted, piled on its hillock above the sea, and guarded still by its circuit of walls. There was dim light and muffled movement outside the walls, where the supermarkets are, and the cafés around the bus station; but up the steep steps to the Land Gate, through the little piazzetta inside, into the crooked lanes beyond, I met not a soul. Only when I reached the tall shape of the cathedral, in its cramped square in the centre of the town, did I hear the sound of organ music: so I pushed open its creaking door and went inside.

If we had been on the planet Mars I would have known that the Venetians had got there first. The cathedral of St Mark at Korčula is not exactly a clone of its greater namesake, for physically there is not much resemblance, but it has inherited every essential characteristic of the Basilica. A handful of nuns were singing a hymn when I entered, in very screechy voices, led by a solitary priest at the altar and accompanied at the harmonium by a sister of substantial physique and deliberate *tempi*. It was very dim in there, but all was familiar to me. The mosaic floor heaved beneath my feet, like the ancient chipped images on the floor of the Basilica; the stone seemed to be glowing in the half-light, like the substances of San Marco; all around me I sensed, rather than saw, those tall columned monuments, gilded and grandiloquent, by which the Venetians loved to remember their servants of state.

All Korčula is like that – full of allusions and reminders, rather Proustian in fact to those who have ever tasted the Venetian madeleine. The town is built to an ingenious crooked grid, like the skeleton of a fish – skew-whiff to prevent the winter sea-winds sweeping through the transverse streets from one side of town to the other. Time, though, has fretted the edges of the plan, with balconies and protrusions, with substitutions and decay, and today wandering around the little place, which is only a few hundred yards across, is a very Venetian experience. Ships show sometimes at the end of shadowy streets. The cathedral bell rings the centuries away, clang-clong-clang through the day and night. Ever and again a Korčulan cat, descended without a doubt from ship-borne forebears of Giudecca or Cannaregio, moves from gutter to dustbin with the true Venetian slink.

★

From such places, from Budva and Kotor in the south, from Split and Zadar, from Fiume and Pula in the far north, the Venetians maintained their adamant control of the coast. They seldom ventured far from the towns: their frontier was the grey-white wall of the karst, running parallel with the sea a few miles inland, and even the coastal plains between the ports they generally left alone. Their system was pragmatic, sometimes fumbling. In earlier times they generally allowed the local authorities, land-owners, churchmen, to keep their dignities, simply requiring the promise of support in wartime, and some symbolic annual tribute – oil for the Basilica from Pula, for example, marten skins from Vis, raw silk from the isle of Rab.

Gradually, however, they took over. They did not at first abolish the local offices of authority: instead they arranged that Venetian nominees should occupy them – local worthies first, later, more often than not, noblemen sent from Venice. One by one the semi-independent townships of Dalmatia, often enjoying civic dignities they had inherited from Roman times, were trans-formed into Venetian colonies. Venetians assumed all the import-ant offices, loyal locals were mutated into honorary Venetians, or even admitted into the Golden Book of the metropolitan aristocracy.

To achieve this hegemony the Venetians had to beat off, or eventually buy off, the Hungarians, but once it was done they never let go, and used Dalmatia with energy to the end. They stripped the forests in their insatiable demand for ship-timber. They shipped mountains of Istrian stone to build their houses. They despoiled whole landscapes to make clear fields of fire for their garrisons. They shamelessly exploited the maritime skills of the Dalmatians, paying their locally recruited sailors far less than other nations did. They obliged the local ruling classes to speak Italian, further separating the towns from their countrysides: in Trogir (Trau in those days) specially-imported language teachers instructed the nobles, and the names of local families were compulsorily Venetianized – Cubranović, for instance, into Cipriani. The Venetians even filched the sacred relics of the coast: an arm of St Ivan (some say for the sake of the ring upon its hand), a foot of St Trifone and for a time the remains of a singularly obscure martyr called St Euphemia, of whom nothing whatever is known except that she *was* a martyr.

They put down rebellions with their usual enthusiasm. Dandolo himself set the standard when he threw the whole weight of the Fourth Crusade against Zadar, sacking the town, setting it on fire and destroying all its fortifications. Thereafter the Venetians were always tough with their Dalmatian dissidents. 'Proceed against the culprits,' Vincenzo Capello was instructed, when sent to put down a rising in Hvar in 1514, 'with whatever severe censure is in keeping with justice and the dignity of our state, bearing in mind the security of our interests': which, being interpreted by the commanders of punitive expeditions, meant wholesale hangings and exiles. Here, as in Corfu, the secret denunciation was a tool of policy and the local Venetian governors, variously entitled Counts, Captains or Podestas, were autocrats within their walls.

Yugoslavs like to say that the Venetians gave Dalmatia nothing but the habit of blasphemy, and certainly they always remained aliens along this shore, inhabiting small castellated beachheads on the edge of the Slavic world. But if there was frequently disaffection with their rule, there was much loyalty too. Over 500 years and more the Dalmatians grew accustomed to their dependency. Venice was their overlord, but also their customer: produce from leather to vegetables flowed ceaselessly northward to the lagoon – the sailors of the island of Brac used to load their ships with wine and operate them as floating saloons on the canals of Venice. Besides, the existence of the empire gave their men of talent boundless opportunities to rise above that narrow strip of shore below the karst. Dalmatian architects became European figures. Dalmatian artists fulfilled themselves in Venice. We read of a Dalmatian archbishop of Famagusta, and the traitor who tried to betray Khalkis to the Turks in Chapter Three was a gunner from Korčula.

Certainly when the time came for Venice to go, there were regrets here and there along the coast. In Istria in the north the loyalty never faded, and flickers on even today in a longing for Italy. At Perast in the south, when the Venetians left at last, the people buried the banner of St Mark with a solemn requiem

beneath their church altar. It was another century and a half before
the Dalmatians, their memories soured by later wars and occupations, began to chip the winged lion from its plaques and
entablatures.

The winged lion! The lion of St Mark first went into action on
the Venetian flag, it is thought, during an early expedition to
Dalmatia, and along this coastline is the supreme collection of his
images, stamped upon its structures in a thousand different styles,
moods and postures.

Architecturally he was a blessing – so elegant but so muscular,
he gave class to any rampart and admirably finished off the most
meticulous arch. He was the symbol sometimes of peace, sometimes of war; he was religious by origin, distinctly secular by
intent; sometimes he carried a flag, sometimes a sword, sometimes the Doge's hat and nearly always, awkward though it
sometimes was for the composition, the gospel of St Mark open
or closed between his paws. If it was closed, it was an ominous
sign of Venetian displeasure, a record of punishment, a threat of
retribution, or perhaps just a reminder of Venetian military
power. If it was open, with its serene slogan, PAX TIBI MARCE,
EVANGELISTA MEUS – 'Peace to you Mark, my evangelist' – it
was a pledge of protection and order, even sometimes of justice,
that everyone understood. (The book in the paws of the huge lion
outside the Arsenal in Venice was open – but blank.)

Winged lions of innumerable sub-species were erected in Dalmatia, and many are still there. Occasionally only a gap remains
where the lion once stood, or his entablature has been filled
instead by the red star of Communist Yugoslavia. His face may
have been gouged off, or his rump removed. Generally, though,
even now he remains anatomically complete and provides a sort
of leitmotif for any journey up the Dalmatian shore. Sometimes
he is elongated, sometimes he is squashed into rectangularity, as
in a distorting mirror. Sometimes he offers a somewhat sickly
smile, like those in rare photographs of Queen Victoria or
Lord Kitchener. Sometimes he faces one way, sometimes the
other, and sometimes his wings are curved sinuously behind his
tail, or under his belly. Sometimes he is symbolically amphibious,

backfeet in the sea, forefeet on land; sometimes he is only just a lion at all, but is more like a mangled sort of griffin, or a frog.

There was a lion at Trogir whose book said: 'Let God arise and let His enemies be scattered.' There was a lion at Rovinj whose book said: '*Vittoria* Tibi Marce, Evangelista Meus.' There was a lion at Budva who seemed to have *two* books. There was a lion at Piran with the inscription: 'Behold the winged lion! I pluck down earth, sea and stars . . .' The mightiest of all the lions of the *Stato da Mar*, I think, is the one above Sanmichele's Land Gate at Zadar, for many years the Venetian headquarters on this coast; on the other hand among the least successful is a late example on the loggia down the street, which was erected in 1792 and is depicted front-face – he grins toothlessly, points at his book with what appears to be a hoof, is surrounded by plumped-out feathers, like a turkey, and bears on his head a lightning conductor in the form of a palm tree.

The Trogir lion, it is claimed, miraculously closed his book when the Republic fell, and long afterwards, among the simpler Slavs, the beast retained magic powers, and was affixed to peasant houses, in ever cruder copies, to keep the worst at bay.

This is a sailor's coast. It grows sailors as other lands grow farmers or miners, and its waters run with ships. Everywhere the ferryboats labour to and fro, the holiday hydrofoils streak away, the fishing boats hurry home with the evening catch. Sometimes, round a point, you come across a bay jammed tight with ships under refit – big Russian liners on stilts out of the water, tankers assaulted by swarms of welders. On remote island shores or in unexpected creeks you discover little country shipyards, like garages, with a solitary tall-funnelled steamer in dry dock, perhaps, or a crane protruding above the pines. Small grey warships cluster at jetties. Steady old steamers convey their villagers, animals, trucks, motorbikes and crates of garden produce patiently between the islands.

As it is now, so it was in Venetian times. Dalmatia was the true source of the Republic's naval power; half the crews of Venetian ships came from Dalmatia, seamen whose sea-going experience was unrivalled in the Mediterranean and who were later to man most of the Austrian navy too. The towns of this coast were navy towns. Hvar, Lesina then, was the headquarters of the Venetian Adriatic Fleet, and had an arsenal to arm its ships, and a theatre to keep its sailors happy. Poreč, Parenzo in Istria, was the head-quarters of the Guild of Venetian Pilots: proud to be so perhaps, for the guild-men were very, very grand, especially those super-pilots, the *pedotti grandi*, who were alone permitted to guide the great galleasses in and out of the lagoon.

Many of the proudest civic memories concerned triumphs at sea in the Venetian cause. Lepanto in particular was the Trafalgar of this shore, to be remembered by old men in chimney-corners and commemorated municipally. Hardly a cathedral of Dalmatia lacks its memorial to the local heroes of the battle, and the mementos are inescapable. Here is a galley lantern perhaps; here an angel made of captured cannons; here an escutcheon won by courage of arms that day. The ceremonial Land Gate at Korčula, through which I passed a page or two back, was erected to commemorate Lepanto. So was the column of St Justina at Koper, old Capodistria, at the other end of the coast. On the Sea Gate at Zadar a plaque recalls the glorious reception given to the city's galleys when they returned cock-a-hoop from the battle, and in a shadowy gateway at Trogir an old cock's head on a wooden hand, once a Turkish figurehead, has been displayed ever since 1571 as civic booty of the victory.

At the southern end of the Yugoslav coast, near the Albanian frontier, the line of the shore is dramatically disrupted by a vast sea-fiord, the Gulf of Kotor – Cattaro to the Venetians – which breaks into the land mass there in a volcanic sort of way. What seems at first to be just another bay turns out, when you sail into it, to be a theatrically gloomy pair of salt-water lakes, connected one with the other only by a narrow channel, the Verige Strait, and towered over by the Lovćen mountains of Montenegro. This sombre haven was for many generations a familiar base of the Venetian navy: they closed the Strait with chains to give the inner lake absolute security, and at Lepantani, on the spit between the lakes, they maintained what would now be called a rest and recreation centre – the name is supposed to be a corruption of *le puttane*, 'the harlots'.

On the east shore of the gulf there is a place called Perast which played a particularly important part in Venetian naval history. It is hardly more than a hamlet, strung out along the waterfront, with the statutory Venetian campanile, a café or two beside the road, a palm tree here and there, scattered solitary cypresses on the bare hill above. Perast though was always a favourite retreat of sea-captains in the Venetian service, and they gave the place a certain stature, building their pleasant villas on terraces above the water, where they are mostly crumbling away now in flower-scent, bird-song and cock-crow, and are reached by crooked stone stairways clamped with iron. Some were consequential enough to have coats-of-arms above their doorways; one or two were proper little palaces, balconied and trellised, and in their heyday I would think, looking as they do boldly across the water, prominently telescoped too.

At this highly nautical place a school for sailors was established in a big house on the waterfront, watched over by the retired salts all around. For many years it produced officers in the Republic's service, so successfully that Perast-trained seamen included many of the best-known Venetian professionals. In 1626 Peter the Great of Russia, laying the first foundations of the Russian Navy, noted this old record of accomplishment, and sent his first naval cadets to be trained at Perast: he went to England to learn how warships should be built, but he looked to this Venetian sea-hamlet of the Adriatic to acquire for his empire, in its turn, the arts of seamanship.

Pirates of many sorts infested the shore – Genoese, Catalan, Arab, Turk, even English and Dutch sometimes. In the period between 1592 and 1609 alone seventy ships bound for Venice were taken by pirates within the Adriatic: sometimes their seamen resisted strongly, sometimes they preferred to rely upon their insurance and abandoned ship at once. As early as the tenth century Slav pirates had raided Venice itself, carrying off all the brides from a mass wedding taking place in the church of San Pietro di Castello, and in successive centuries the pest was never quite stamped out – driven out of one den, the pirates simply set up their base somewhere else. In 1571, Lepanto year, the Sultan Selim II actually installed a pack of Arab pirates at Ulcinj, south of the Gulf of Kotor, to harass Venetian shipping; they brought their Negro slaves with them, and the black people you sometimes see in Ulcinj now are their descendants.

The most melodramatic of all these varied miscreants were the people called the Uskoks, whose fearful memory lingers around their old lair of Segna, in the north, renamed Senj now but still crouching rather frowardly over its half-moon bay. The Uskoks were indisputably ghastly. The name probably comes from the Serbo-Croat *uskočiti*, to jump, and the Uskoks were originally Christian refugees from the eastern side of the mountains, who had escaped from the Turks by guile and violence, and set themselves up to prosper by similar means on the Dalmatian shore. They were epic villains. Their greatest fighting leader, Ivo, was supposed to have routed 30,000 Turks with a handful of comrades and to have come home from another battle holding his own severed left hand in his right. The Venetians said they were supernaturally guided, too, by wise women in caves.

The Uskoks took to sea the same skills and prejudices that had preserved them on land. Fanatically anti-Turk and anti-Muslim, they were never averse to Christian booty either, and with their long hair and trailing moustaches, and the iron rings they sported in their ears, they became the terror of all mariners. Uskoks liked to nail the turbans of Turkish prisoners to their heads and sometimes cut out the hearts of their still living captives (we read of a Venetian commander whose heart, in fact, was the pièce-de-résistance of a celebratory banquet). Captains would often run their ships aground rather than risk such a fate: 'as if Whale should flie from a Dolphin', scornfully commented an English traveller, who had perhaps not himself come face to face with a long-haired, iron-earringed Uskok on the high seas. Senj became a haven for rascals and runaways from many countries and its whole community was brutalized. The priests of Senj piously blessed the pirates' enterprises. The citizenry at large contributed financially to the cost of them and shared cheerfully in the profits, one-tenth of the loot going to the Franciscan and Dominican monasteries.

During the Uskoks' heyday, in the sixteenth century, they enjoyed the protection of the Hapsburg dukedom in Austria, and sold their captured goods in the great international market of

Trieste, from where they were distributed throughout the Hapsburg possessions. This was particularly infuriating to the Venetians, who fought the rascals with ever-increasing anger both at sea and on land – after one victory over them, they displayed the heads of luckless Uskoks on stakes all around the Piazza San Marco. But the shallow galleys of the pirates, rowed in relays by ten oarsmen each side, were exceedingly hard to catch, and it was only in the early years of the seventeenth century that they were eliminated at last: in their very last adventure of all, when only a handful of desperadoes was left to man the galleys of Senj, they seized a final Venetian ship, for old times' sake, and made off with its cargo, worth 4,000 sequins.

So crippling was piracy to Venetian trade, during its worst periods, that the Signory cast around for alternative routes to the east, avoiding the most dangerous parts of the Adriatic. In the past Venetian merchants had often shipped their goods to Durrës, then Durazzo, on the Albanian coast, and taken them in caravans over the former Roman road, the Via Egnatia, which ran across Thessalonia and Thrace to Turkey. In the winter, too, the Venetian postal routes ran from Kotor over the Montenegrin mountains to Constantinople. In the sixteenth century the Venetians created a parallel route from Split, much further to the north, enabling them to by-pass most of the Adriatic altogether.

This was a truly imperial conception, undertaken on an imperial scale, and it was proper that it should be based upon the imperial city of the Roman Emperor Diocletian, himself a Dalmatian born and bred. Virtually the whole of Split, which the Venetians called Spalato, consisted of the emperor's vast waterside palace, long since taken over by the citizenry and converted into a marvellous warren of houses, shops, halls and piazzas, with Diocletian's mausoleum as a cathedral in the middle. It was a Venetian Jew, Daniele Rodrigo, who first suggested that this extraordinary place, then hardly more than a picturesque backwater, should be the base of the new route: in 1591 the Signory authorized him to make it so.

He set about it with style. An entire new town was built outside the Diocletian walls, with hostels and warehouses for merchants, customs houses, hospitals and a quarantine station. The fortifications of the port were rebuilt. The roads into the interior were developed. A new kind of galley was designed for the short sea-run between Venice and Split, shallow-drafted, manned by a relatively small crew of 120 sailors and forty soldiers. Every other month one of these ships, the container ships of their day, made the double voyage: as soon as it reached Venice to unload, its crew was shifted to another vessel and sailed immediately back to Split.

The scheme worked brilliantly. Caravans with hundreds of horses plodded down the mountains to the seashore from places as far away as Armenia, Persia and even India. For the first time silks, spices, hides, woollens, carpets and waxes reached Venice from the east overland, a smack in the eye not only for the Adriatic pirates, but also for rival merchants of the west, laboriously sailing their caravels around the Cape of Good Hope. Split never looked back, became the principal port of the Dalmatian coast for the rest of the Venetian period, and is now the liveliest and most cosmopolitan coastal town of Yugoslavia.

Credit it to the Uskoks! There were no pirates like those sea-devils: trying to stop their predatory passages through the Adriatic, a Venetian senator once cried, was 'like trying to stop the birds flying through the air with one's bare hands'. There are said to have been, even in their prime, no more than a thousand fighting Uskoks, but nobody would ever forget them.

One great piece of grit impeded the Venetian mechanism of authority on the Dalmatian coast: the sea-city of Dubrovnik – Ragusa then – whose merchants were so enterprising, whose fleets ranged so far, that the very word 'argosy' comes from the name of their port. During the twelfth and thirteenth centuries Dubrovnik was nominally under Venetian suzerainty, and a Venetian governor was installed there; but it was never reconciled to the Signory's rule, presently rejected it, and alone among the city-ports of the littoral, remained a bitter rival until the end of the Venetian Republic.

If you would like a suggestion, a sort of mirage perhaps, of the medieval meaning of Dubrovnik, disembark at the peninsula village of Cavtat, which lies some ten miles south of the city across the bay of Lokrum. From there you can see the place in context. To the right the limestone mountains rise sheer and treeless, to the left is the green island of Lokrum, and half-hidden from the open sea upon its own inlet, the walled city of Dubrovnik shows like a white blur at the water's edge. It has a very steely look from there, a private and plotting look, secreted as it is between the highlands and the sea, within its screen of islands.

A hard city it remains too, to my mind, when you cross the bay and land upon its quay, beneath its high fortifications. It is very beautiful, but hard. It lacks the yield or leniency of Venice. Built of a glittering and impermeable marble, enclosed with superb city walls, tilted slightly with the lie of the land and corrugated everywhere with battlements – tightly packed there within itself it has acquired none of the give-and-take of great age, but seems in a way a perfectly modern place, dogmatically planned and didactically displayed to visitors, like a model town in a trade fair.

Much of it was destroyed in a sixteenth-century earthquake, but it was all rebuilt, and the Dubrovnik we see today is still in all essentials the Ragusa which was so long a thorn in the side of Venice. Superficially it seems Venetian itself, and most visitors probably believe it to *be* Venetian. Its city fathers were inevitably influenced by the Serenissima, the force which made all this coastline look north for its examples. Though the people of Dubrovnik were Slav almost to a man, they assiduously Italianized their city. They imported artists and craftsmen from Italy, they adopted the latest Italian styles in dress, in literature, in modes of living. They even devised Italian genealogies for themselves. They based their constitution upon the Venetian pattern, though being even more vulnerable to the ambitions of potential despots, they decreed that their Doge, called the Rector, should hold office only for a month at a time and that he should leave his palace only if accompanied by a band and by twenty-four attendants in red liveries.

But it was only a veneer really, and Dubrovnik does not feel Venetian for long. Its people never gave up their Serbo-Croat language, so that all the influences of the Italian Renaissance were subtly mutated here, and the city remained pure Slav at heart. Its famous central street, the Placa, is austere and metallic, like a parade ground. Its Rector's Palace lacks the voluptuous festivity of the Venetian touch. Its pervading style, for all its fineness of detail, is somehow defensive, as though it is conscious of being all alone in the world, and its citizens, who have always loved it with a peculiar intensity, talk about it even now almost as though it is an independent republic, beleaguered by change.

Indeed it was a prodigy of European history, and in his day St Blaize, its patron saint (who had the particular ability to cure the common cold), was almost as powerful a protector as St Mark of Venice. Today there is another Dubrovnik outside its walls: the holiday villas spill along the coastline north and south and clamber up the hills above the great Dalmatian Highway. During the great days of its power, though, Dubrovnik consisted simply of the little walled city itself, perhaps half a mile across or two miles in circumference; yet such were the skills of its statesmen, its economists and its seamen that this remote and minute state became a world power, one of the great maritime forces of its day.

At the end of the sixteenth century Dubrovnik tonnage was probably as great as Venice's, and Dubrovnik ships, men and merchants cropped up all over the world. Here is a Ragusan converted to Islam, defending the Indian fort of Diu against the Portuguese at the start of the sixteenth century. Here is one sailing from Lisbon in command of a Spanish Armada ship, and another making his fortune in the Potosi silver mines of Peru. Merchants from Dubrovnik were active all over the Balkans, with hundreds of trading colonies in Bulgaria, Serbia, the Danube provinces, Constantinople, and they were well-known in England too. So many Dubrovnik gentlemen went abroad to be educated that the two orders of the hierarchy were dubbed the Salamanchesi, after Salamanca University, and the Sorbonnesi, after the Sorbonne, and Dubrovnik diplomats tacked so adeptly between the world's chanceries that cynics nicknamed their state the *settebandiere*, the Republic of the Seven Flags.

It was true that every year a train of noblemen set off over the mountains to pay the city's tribute to the Sultan in Constantinople, but in fact this was a particularly independent little republic. It was governed by its aristocracy, generally speaking, with remarkable enlightenment. Slave trading was outlawed very early. Torture was forbidden. A civic home for old people was founded in 1347 and there was a high standard of education. Patriotic feeling was intense; there are no records of revolution, and the Ragusan republic outlived that of Venice itself.

Dubrovnik never exactly went to war with Venice, but there were skirmishes now and then, and relations were always cold between the two powers, Ragusan captains habitually disregarding Venetian pretensions to command of the sea. The Venetians built a series of watchful fortresses around the perimeter of the little state: the Ragusans for their part were so anxious to distance themselves from Venetian territory that in 1699 they actually ceded to the Turks two strips of their own land, north and south of the city, to form a *cordon sanitaire* between Saints Blaize and Mark. The Ragusans were not in the least expansionist – theirs was the purest sort of merchant state, living entirely by its wits and its trade. Nor were they xenophobic – they generally employed foreigners as state secretaries (and among unsuccessful applicants for the job was Machiavelli). But they were jealous of their separateness and maintained it successfully, through the powerful climax of Venice, all through the long decline, until a French sergeant, reading out a Napoleonic declaration in 1806, declared the extinction of Ragusa as a state.

They gained much over the centuries by this brave detachment, but perhaps they lost something too. They gained no doubt in self-esteem and social well-being, and did more to assimilate western progress into their native culture than did any of their subjugated neighbours of the coast. But they lost, I suppose, that sense of wider unity, comity and purpose that can be the saving grace of imperialism. Dubrovnik was to remain always a lonely kind of place, with the prickliness that isolated communities often have, and a certain wistfulness too. Few citizens of Dubrovnik would admit it now, just as few Ragusans would have allowed it then: but one misses the winged lion on the walls of this determined little city, and with it that warmth of the Venetian genius which, with all its faults, brought its own light, pride and fantasy wherever it settled.

Grit on the foreshore: high in the mountains above, an enigma which the Venetians never quite solved. Above the Gulf of Kotor, almost within sight of Dubrovnik, stood the Black Mountain, Crna Gora in the Serbo-Croat, Monte Negro in the Venetian dialect. Going home weary after the making of the world, God took with him a sack of unused stones, but the sack burst on his way across the skies, and so Montenegro was made. Bears lived up there in the mighty pile of rocks, lynxes, wolves, tree frogs, vultures, great wild boars, Illyrian vipers and monstrous trout in mountain lakes. And up there too lived the most baffling of Venice's neighbours in Dalmatia, the Montenegrins, who were sometimes enemies, occasionally allies, but always to be kept at arm's length.

For most of the Venetian period the Montenegrins possessed no coastline of their own, and they looked down resentfully upon the Venetian settlements around the Gulf of Kotor from the high eyrie of their homeland, the mountain massif of Lovćen, in whose inaccessible and unlovely recesses they built their village-capital, Cetinje. The way there from the gulf was daunting, but thrilling too. The Venetian town of Kotor huddled beneath the very flank of the mountain, in shadow half the day, rushed past by a mountain stream like an Alpine village: immediately behind it a dizzy zig-zag path clambered up the sheer face of Lovćen in a series of seventy-three narrow and precipitous loops. To strangers this rough mule-track looked impossible, but it was the only way to Cetinje from the sea, and up and down it travelled all the limited commerce of Montenegro, on the backs of mules and donkeys, on the shoulders of men, so that at any time of day, if you looked up the mountain face from the quayside at Kotor, you might see small black figures crawling along the rock-face far above.

The track was called the Ladder of Cattaro, and though nowadays it starts in a different place and is a road with only twenty-five rather less disconcerting loops, it is still startling enough. To imagine what the journey must have been like for the Venetian merchants, diplomats and spies who reluctantly climbed their way to Cetinje over the years, it is best to make it at the beginning of winter, when the snows have fallen on the high ground but have not yet blocked the highway. The world shifts then as you climb. At the bottom it is the Mediterranean world –

towers and villas the Venetians built, oleanders beside the sea. At the top it is the Balkans, white, stony and uncertain. As you round the last bend in that twisty road, you find all about you a blasted sort of landscape, corrugated here and there with what look like the runnels of ancient avalanches, waterless, apparently soil-less, and stubbled only in sporadic patches with arid and thorny shrubs. This is the Black Mountain. You pass one windswept settlement, crouched in a declivity in the snow plain, and there is nothing more, not a hut, not a barn, until suddenly in the middle of the wasteland you see before you, in its own cold scoop among the hills, the village of Cetinje.

From here the Montenegrins projected their unyielding defiance against all comers, and particularly against the Turks. For generations they were the first line of Christian defence against Islam and alone in the Balkans they never gave in, decorating their streets with the skulls of Turks and inculcating their children with patriotic ferocity. They were ruled in their heyday by prince-bishops, Vladikas, fighting prelates who combined all authority, spiritual and secular, in one mighty office, and unlike the Venetians they believed strongly in the power of individual personality. Bards sang the praises of Montenegrin chieftains, not at all the Venetian practice, and the greatest of their heroes, the Prince-Bishop Petar Njegoš, would not long have survived the cautious safeguards of the Venetian constitution: a learned theologian, a gifted linguist, a scholarly jurist, a crack shot, the first poet of Montenegrin literature, six feet six tall, he was the idol of his people and was buried flamboyantly at his own wish on the very top of Mount Lovćen itself, where his mausoleum remains. Swaggering, boastful and terribly superstitious, the Montenegrins were armed to the teeth always, and their bearing was described by an English writer, as late as 1911, as being 'soldier-like and manly, though somewhat theatrical'. The Venetians viewed them with predictable ambiguity. They were Christians, after all. They were doughty enemies of the Turks. Also Kotor was their only outlet to the world and they brought business to its bankers, merchants and agents. It was Venetian money that enabled the Montenegrins to raise the ransom for their Prince-Bishop Danilo, when he was condemned to crucifixion by the Turks. It was a Venetian press which, in the year 1493, in the Montenegrin monastery of Obod, printed the first book in the Serbo-Croat language, less than half a century after the invention of printing. Rich Montenegrins, tiring of their perpetual siege-life in the mountains, sometimes retired to Venice, and several Montenegrin chiefs were ennobled by the Republic.

On the other hand they were exceedingly difficult neighbours. Their yearning for a sea-outlet was a running threat to the Venetian position on the coast, and the houses of Kotor and Perast had to be fortified against the more lawless of their guerilla bands. At the same time the Venetians, pursuing their generally ambivalent policy towards the Turks, were chary of allying themselves too closely with such uncompromising enemies of Islam, and they repeatedly rebuffed the Montenegrins, deceived them or left them in the lurch – refusing to help when their armies were on the point of annihilation, letting them down in diplomatic negotiations, and once actually colluding with the Turks in a plot to assassinate their Vladika.

Yet it could be said that only the furious determination of the Montenegrins, during the fifteenth, sixteenth and seventeenth centuries, saved the Adriatic coast, and so possibly Venice itself, from the Turks. To the very end of the Venetian empire the Montenegrins were fighting up there, and you can feel this heroic heritage still in the windy streets of Cetinje. There is a raw challenge in the air. Peter Njegoš' barracks-like palace, called the Biljarda after the billiard-table laboriously conveyed to it, by order of the Tsar of Russia, up the Ladder of Cattaro, still crouches comfortless beneath the slope of the hill: on the white summit of Lovćen, deep in snow, you can still make out his lonely tomb.

Unfortunately long after the Venetians had left the Gulf of Kotor a later prince of Montenegro, Nicolas, gave the little capital a very different significance, for he aspired to join the egregious company of monarchs who then lorded it all over Europe, and in 1910 proclaimed himself a king. The powers took him seriously. The King of Italy married one of his daughters, the King of Serbia another, two more became the pair of Grand Duchesses who introduced Rasputin to the Russian court. Grandiose legations were erected in the village streets of Cetinje and Nicolas built himself a palace stuffed to every corner with the signed portraits, the chivalric orders, the mementos of Tsars, Empresses and Queen Victorias essential to every royal home. So the capital of the Montenegrins, which had so tantalized the Venetians down the mountain, became in the end the capital of Ruritania: until World War I, that mighty scourer of pretension, swept all away to oblivion, leaving only museums behind.

This (by the way) is the manner in which, in the year 1484, the son of the Prince Ivo the Black of Montenegro married the daughter of the Doge Pietro Mocenigo of the Venetian Republic:

The Prince wrote to the Doge thus: 'Harken to me Doge! As they say that thou hast in thy house the most beautiful of roses, your daughter, so in my house there is the handsomest of pinks, my son. Let us unite the two.' And the Doge replied, 'Yea, let us,' and Ivo the Black went to the palace of the Doge in Venice with handsome gifts of gold, and the wedding was arranged for the following autumn. 'Friend Doge,' said Ivo, 'then thou shalt see me with six hundred choice companions, and if there is among them a single one who is more handsome than my son Stanicha, then give me neither bride nor dowry.' The Doge was much pleased and Ivo sailed away to Montenegro.

But as autumn approached, Stanicha was stricken with a terrible smallpox, and his face was pitted hideously, and all his beauty destroyed. Ivo the Black told the Doge nothing of this, but when there came a message from Venice saying that all was ready for the nuptials, he assembled his 600 men to go to Venice: and they were the handsomest of all men, with lofty brow and commanding look, from Dulcigno and from Antivari, the eagles of Podgoritza and all the finest young men as far as the green Lim.

'What say you, brothers,' asked Ivo of them, 'shall we put one of you in place of Stanicha for the nuptials, and allow him on our return half the rich presents which will be given to him as the supposed bridegroom of the Doge's daughter?' The young men approved, and Obrezovo Djuro was declared the handsomest of them all, and elected to play the part. So they embarked for Venice crowned with flowers.

171

They arrived in Venice and the Doge Mocenigo was struck with amazement at the beauty of Obrezovo Djuro, whom he took to be the prince's son. 'Surely he is the handsomest of them all,' said he, and so the wedding was celebrated, and there was feasting and festivity for a whole week. 'Friend Doge,' said Ivo at the end of the week, 'we must return to our mountains,' and the Doge gave to Djuro, whom he took to be Stanicha, a golden apple as a token of wedlock, and two damasced fusils, two tunics of finest linen wrought with gold, and much besides, and so they sailed away with the Doge's beautiful daughter back to the Black Mountain.

When they reached the Black Mountain, the bride was shown her real husband Stanicha, ugly from the smallpox. 'Here is your real husband, my son Stanicha,' said Ivo the Black: but she was very angry at the deception, for half the costly presents that the Doge had given must stay with Djuro, and she had embroidered with her own hands the tunics of gold. 'If I must be Stanicha's wife,' said she, 'then Stanicha must fight Djuro to recover the last tunic of gold. If not, I will pluck a thorn, I will scratch my face with it, and with the blood I will write a letter which my falcon will carry swiftly to great Venice.'

So Stanicha killed Djuro with a javelin through the head. War followed in the Black Mountain and Ivo could see the whole plain covered afar with horses and riders cut in pieces. The young men rose so furiously on behalf of the murdered Djuro that Stanicha was forced to leave the mountains for a foreign country far away; and his bride went home to Venice a virgin.

A particular aesthetic governs the Dalmatian coast, corroded though it is in many parts by the stain of tourism. It lies partly of course in the splendour of the landscape, that incomparable combination of sea, island and limestone barrier. It is partly the climate too, generally so benign, shifting suddenly to seething seas and scudding clouds when the *bora* falls upon the Adriatic like the breath of fate. Perhaps it is partly the nature of the inhabitants, almost all Slavs now even in the towns, tough and stocky people, made a little more drab by the exigencies of Communism and given to particular violence in war, who slump themselves opposite you at the dining-table grim and unresponsive, but can be coaxed with patience into true bonhomie.

But what chiefly gives the coast its tang, and makes it like no other shore, is the particular blend of the Latin and the Slav which is the gift of Venice to Dalmatia. History has expunged some of it: hardly a trace of the Italian cuisine is noticeable now and the Italian language has been systematically eradicated even in those places like Zadar, Rijeka and the ports of Istria which became Italian again between the two world wars. But in the long string of towns which graces this shore one can detect a particular sinewy allure which could arise, I think, only from this particular association of temperaments. I accept absolutely the theory that Vittore Carpaccio was from Koper in Istria, for the cool spareness of his vision, so different from the exclamatory style of a Titian or a Tintoretto, or the gentle mysteries of a Giorgione, perfectly reflects the Dalmatian mix of ornate and naive, sea and karst.

There is a similarity but not a sameness to all the towns. Each has its piazza, recognizable still as the centre of Venetian power. Each is likely to have one of those elegant little loggias, pillared, tile-roofed and possibly en-lioned, which were sometimes used as lesser courts of justice and sometimes as lodging-places for travellers. There is probably a handful of patrician houses still standing, distant cousins to the *palazzi* of the Grand Canal, escutcheoned as often as not though long since divided into flats or handed over to People's Consultative Syndicates. There is also certain to be, proudly in the middle of town and still an active centre of Christian devotion, a cathedral.

One cannot really call the cathedrals of Dalmatia Venetian buildings. Most of them were built, or rebuilt, under the aegis of Venice, and Venetian architects frequently worked upon them, sometimes modelling them upon Venetian originals. But their particular magic comes, nearly always, from the touch of the Slav upon the Italianate. They are very sensual buildings, almost always, made of glowing marble or soft sandstone, intimate with little side-chapels and dark chancels, curiously embellished with images sacred and profane, instructive or merely frivolous. If spiritually they sometimes seem, like the one at Korčula, minia-tures of the Basilica San Marco, physically they are often boldly individualistic or even eccentric, marked by the preferences of some local artist, or conceived by local circumstance.

The cathedral of San Lorenzo at Trogir, for instance, seems at first just a singularly beautiful example of medieval Venetian architecture, from the period when Romanesque dovetailed into Gothic. Set in a neat ensemble of piazza, loggia and patrician house, like a close, it is not too hard to imagine it transferred to some *campo* of Venice itself. But within its heavily arched narthex, shaded deeply against the sun, an altogether alien marvel reveals itself: an elaborately, almost violently carved great porch, of a style so roughly vigorous that no Venetian artist could ever have made it. It was the work of the thirteenth-century Croatian sculptor Radovan, and it is guarded by two of the burliest and most truculent lions of the Venetian Empire – Slav lions through and through, on guard like mercenaries.

The cathedral of Šibenik, Sebenico to the Venetians, is another declaration of independence. The principal architect of this famous building was a Dalmatian who had studied at Venice and is known by his Italian name of Giorgio Orsini; he married a Venetian and possessed houses in several Venetian territories. But his cathedral turns out to be, despite a certain initial impact of *déjà vu*, very un-Venetian after all. Its interior, especially, is like nothing in Venice. It rises in a series of steps from narthex to altar, but not in the graceful manner of Santa Maria dei Miracoli in Venice: the dark nave does not glide upwards to the high altar, but rather stumps there, step by step through the twilight. Outside, too, the posture of the church, when you look at it longer, is strangely bold and muscular, a little piratical perhaps, and around the back seventy sculpted heads, said to be those of citizens too stingy to contribute to the cost of the building, gaze out at the passers-by astonishingly like the decapitated heads of captured enemies, some moustachio'd and unrepentant, some innocent and aghast.

But the most startling expression of this hybrid aesthetic is to be found in the island-town of Rab, Arbe to the Venetians, some fifty miles north of Zadar and reached by ferry from the old Uskok nest of Senj. Rab is a tiny place on a promontory, perhaps half a mile long and three narrow streets wide, but its silhouette was familiar to every Venetian mariner along this coast, and is unmistakable now. Four tall campaniles are its emblems, all in a row along its western shore, and they give the place an oddly eerie effect, even when the tourists crowd its beaches.

Wherever you walk down the spine of the town, pine-scented from the woods that edge it, those four tall towers seem to beckon you on, like markers – down the flagged and wheel-less lanes, under the old stone arches wreathed in creeper, past the dark little loggia in the middle of town, past quaint crested palaces and high-walled gardens, until at the end of your walk, near the tip of the promontory, you discover before you the ribbed Italianate façade of the little cathedral, on its own piazzetta beside the sea.

There is a little belvedere beside it, pleasantly shaded, where you may lean over the water and watch the boats go by; but your eye is not likely to wander for long, because above the main door of the church is the true focus of the whole island, the object to which, you realize now, those four grave towers have been guiding you all along. It is the starkest and saddest, perhaps the truest of Pietàs, in which a grief-stricken Virgin cherishes a Christ still writhing from the pain of the cross. Nothing could be further from the ample and confident faith of Venetian Christian art. It is a chunk of the karst that is mounted there, carved with a bitter vision.

Northward through the off-shore islands, as the coast with its indentations unfolds itself to starboard: the treacherous gulf called Boiling Bay, where indeed when the wind gusts from the north the waves do seem to bubble, hiss and steam, as though there is fire beneath them; Rijeka, which used to be Fiume, where the Venetians built themselves, in the church of San Guido, a remarkably inaccurate copy of their beloved Salute; Pula, a naval base all its life, Roman, Hungarian, Austrian, Italian and now Yugoslav; until there stands to the north the bumpy peninsula of Istria. This was the nearest to home of all the possessions of the *Stato da Mar*, separated from Venice itself only by Trieste and the lagoon-shore of Venezia Giulia.

This is where Dalmatia ends, and now the little seaside towns are more exactly Venetian. They gave to the Doge one of the earliest of his ancillary titles, DUX TOTIUS ISTRIAE, and they remained Italian until the end of World War II. They were confirmed irrevocably as Yugoslav only in 1975, when their future was settled with that of Trieste, and they have powerful sizable Italian populations still. Even today it is hard to remember that Capodistria is Koper now, Parenzo Poreč, Rovigno Rovinj. A powerful sense of nostalgia informs them, dingy as they are with Communism's patina, and every weekend their inhabitants pour in their thousands over the frontier to Italy, to stock up not just with jeans, confectionery and spare parts, but also no doubt with the sense of style and colour to which so many centuries of Venetian rule accustomed them.

This rather melancholy peninsula – for centuries it was repeatedly ravaged by plague – was always familiar to Venice. It was only a day and night's sailing to the lagoon, even in the Middle Ages, and more than any other imperial settlements, the Istrian seaports feel like illusions of Venice herself. Sometimes their appearance now in this still alien setting, with a splash of authentic Venetian red, perhaps, and a pattern of real Venetian machicolation on the skyline, and a perfect little replica of St Mark's Campanile rising above the rooftops, backed by such sober hills and pine forests, and often hemmed in by modern office blocks, tourist hotels and Corbusian apartments, can be sadly unsettling.

There is an easy cure, though. You must do as the Venetians did. Climb the high ground behind Koper, say, on a fine spring day, when the sea is flecked only with little curls of foam, and the long line of coast is clear as pen-and-ink. Settle up there among the conifers with a picnic and a pair of binoculars and presently, when the sun is just beginning to set, you may make out through the glasses an indistinct grey blur upon the horizon to the west, faintly picked out perhaps, in fancy if not in fact, with a shimmer of gold. There is a stack of buildings on a waterfront, surely. There is a suspicion of a tower. Isn't that a gilded angel there, that faint spot on the lens, that golden dust-flake?

It is no nostalgic copy this time, no extension of style, faith or strategy. It is the real thing out there. We have reached the end of our sea voyage, and we are looking at Venice.

Post-Imperial

Back the imperial way – effects of empire –
falling into place – ethnics – out of the sun
at last

So we sail across the bay of Trieste to that glistening destination over the water, guided now if not by the actual flash of the
sun on the summit of the great Campanile, as seafarers used to be,
at least by the shining knowledge of its presence there. Many
ships still sail up the Gulf of Venice to *La Dominante*: tankers
taking oil to the refineries of the lagoon, freighters for the busy
docks of the city itself, cruise-liners booming disco music, hydrofoils from Trieste, and now and then warships of the Italian navy,
whose vessels are still the most beautiful of all, streaking lean and
elegant, like the galleys before them, to anchor tonight off the
Riva degli Schiavoni, the Quay of the Slavs, only a stone's throw
from the Arsenal.

We will return the imperial way too, through the sea-gate of the
Lido, as the Crusaders did, and the bravos of the Cyclades, and
Petrarch's courier-ship from Crete trailing its captured banner,
and poor Caterina Cornaro, and Morosini home from defeat and
from victory, and all the countless argosies, galleasses, pilgrim
galleys and troopships that returned, at one time or another
during the long story of the Venetian Empire, triumphant or
humiliated to the lagoon.

An abandoned but still glowering fortress greets us as we pass
through the sea-gate, emblazoned of course with a gigantic lion of
St Mark – the fortress of San Andrea, which was designed by that
same Sanmicheli who built the walls of Zadar and Iraklion, and
whose guns, by injudiciously firing on a French frigate in 1797,

177

gave Napoleon the *casus belli* he wanted to end the Venetian Republic. Round the point we sail, into the calm waters of the lagoon, sheltered against the open sea by the long line of the Lido islands, and there before us resplendent in the morning, the sun glinting from its golden domes and baubles, from its forest of campaniles, from the periwigged presence of the Salute and the grand mass of the Doge's Palace – there before us is the Serenissima once more. More than ever, now that we have travelled her lost dominions, does she seem an imperial city, stashed and gilded with the spoils, memorials and attitudes of the long adventure. She rules nothing in fact, being only one of twenty Italian regional centres, but she retains the charisma of command, and has hung on to the booty.

We disembark where Dandolo set sail, nearly eight hundred years ago, and the sense of permanent occasion is as exciting now as it was when we started. The Piazzetta remains a quay fit for princes or Crusaders. The chimerical winged lion, St Theodore with his despondent amphibian, welcome us back from their column-heads above the sea. Dandolo never came home from Constantinople, except perhaps as a bag of bones, but if he were to be resurrected now he would easily recognize the scene about him, and doubtless rejoice at the evident success of the imperial enterprise he launched. He was a terrible old man, but he loved his city and the city still loves him: there is a monument to him, in Latin, on his modest house near the Rialto bridge, No. 4172 San Marco, and from his day to our own there have always been Dandolos in Venice eager to claim him as an ancestor.

We are back where our journey began, but now we recognize the effects of empire all around us. Venice has not, like London, shrugged off the memory of its mighty mission. In an aesthetic sense at least, this city still holds the east in fee, as the place where orient and occident seem most naturally to meet: where the tower of Gothic meets the dome of Byzantine, the pointed arch confronts the rounded, where hints and traces of Islam ornament Christian structures, where basilisks and camels stalk the statuary, and all the scented suggestion of the east is mated with the colder diligence of the north. Augsburg met Alexandria in these streets long ago, and nobody fits the Venetian *mis-en-scène* better than the burnoused sheikhs so often to be seen these days feeding the pigeons in the Piazza, leading their veiled wives stately through the Merceria, or training their Japanese cameras upon St Theodore like that contorted sightseer in the old picture.

Everywhere around us are the brags of empire – Venice, George Eliot remarked once, was 'a creature born with an imperial attitude'. The Doge's Palace is full of them, in huge allegorical studies of Venice Crowned By Fame, Sitting on the World with Lion, Surrounded by Virtues Receiving the Sceptre of Dominion, or in depictions more specific, like vivid reconstructions of the sack of Zadar, or Vettore Pisani taking Kotor in 1378. Outside, just beside the Porta della Carta, are the four little knightly figures, embracing each other in porphyry, which we saw the Venetians loot in Constantinople on page 40. Nearby are the ornamental columns from the same page and all around are the marble slabs like veined silk, the porphyry panels and the miscellaneous pieces of antique carving brought home from the Crusade as ballast.

The Piazza, when we look at it now, is pure empire. The very shape and scale of it bespeaks a consequence grander than any city-state's: Napoleon's finest drawing-room in Europe was really a lobby for the eastern Mediterranean. Tremendously out of scale above us stands the Campanile, no longer the one that Dandolo knew, for that fell down in 1902, but still recognizably a beacon tower as well as a belfry, upon whose summit the angel stands sublime beneath his halo, to salute the captains as they pass. On the loggetta at its foot Jupiter, playing the part of Crete, Venus personifying Cyprus, lie in attendance upon a Venice disguised as Justice: nearby are the three bronze flagpoles from which on State occasions flew, according to the current state of empire, the flags of Cyprus, Crete, Euboea or the Peloponnese. The great square all around is as crowded, as variegated, as endlessly entertaining and as wickedly expensive as ever it was in the days of dominion, when it was habitually frequented, we are told, by 'Turks, Libyans, Parthians and other monsters of the sea'.

Presiding over it all, as ever, is the Basilica, no longer the Doge's private chapel, nor even alas a state church, but still the seat of the Venetian Patriarchate, still the shrine of everything

Venetian, and still an eclectic and magical jumble of many rites, anomalies and nuances of the Christian faith. Its façade seems almost to sag with the weight of the gold ornament, statuary, fragments of ancient art, grace-notes of marble and afterthoughts of architecture added to it since Dandolo's day, so that its still graceful and airy outline looks as though it is straining to move, but is held down by the sheer weight of its magnificence. The shallow Byzantine domes of the thirteenth century have been covered with more bulbous cupolas now, giving it a much more eastern look, and upon each of these there is a device of golden frivolity, giving the whole a last exuberant touch of sparkle.

Into this inimitable building, over the eight centuries since we began our voyage, the Venetians have packed shiploads of loot. The treasury is a jackdaw's nest of stolen reliquaries, chalices and sacred ornaments, bones, fingers, hair-locks and blood-phials of countless saints, exquisite altar-pieces from the lost churches of Byzantium, marvellous vestments and episcopal rings from Greece, the Aegean and the further east. The Zen Chapel, once the State entrance to the building, is supposed to be walled with the marble and verd-antique tombstones of Byzantine emperors. The Pala d'Oro, the great gold screen behind the high altar, with its 1,300 pearls, 300 sapphires, 300 emeralds and 15 rubies, is studded with the lovely enamels the Crusaders took from Constantinople, and in its centre the figure of the Emperor John II Comnenus, its original patron, has been metamorphosed into the Doge Ordelafo Falier.

In her own chapel to the north of the high altar is the Nikopoeia, that most holy prize of empire. If she served the Byzantine emperors well and long, she served the Venetian Republic better and longer. The Venetians adopted her, like the Byzantines, as their Madonna of Victory; before her image supplicatory Masses were held at the beginnings of wars, Masses of thanksgiving after victories. She was adorned by the Venetians beyond her original simplicity, and set in a sumptuous frame, but still from its recesses her lustrous eyes looked out, smoky but reassuring, to bless the admirals before they sailed, or congratulate the loyal *condottieri*.

In 1979 some of the jewels from the Madonna's frame were stolen by a pair of young toughs from the mainland, who had concealed themselves inside the Basilica when it closed for the night, and rushed out with their trophies when the caretaker opened it in the morning, giving him as they passed, like janissaries at Nicosia, a valedictory clout on the head. The jewels were soon recovered, but I happened to be in Venice on the day of the theft, and went along to the Basilica to attend the Mass of repentance and supplication that the Patriarch immediately held. Never was history so poignantly played out. A profound sense of sadness filled the fane, nuns sighed and priests blew their noses heavily, as they mourned the desecration of that particularly cherished piece of stolen property.

Much in this city falls more easily into place, once you have travelled the imperial routes. What are those crumbled relief-maps affixed to the façade of Santa Maria Zobenigo, and why are they there? They are the fortresses of Split, Corfu, Iraklion and Zadar and they are there because members of the Barbaro family, patrons of the church, fought actions in all those places. What recumbent hero is this, high on the wall of San Zanipolo, attended by Roman soldiers? It is the fighting Doge Pietro Mocenigo, formerly Captain-General of the Sea, whom we met with his galleys at Cyprus on page 96, and whose epitaph is frank and simple: *From The Booty Of Enemies*. Does the funeral church of San Michele, on the cemetery island, look curiously familiar? It does: it is thought to have been based on Orsini's masterpiece, the cathedral at Šibenik.

The remains of Morosini the Peloponnesian, brought home from Nauplia, lie as you might expect beneath the biggest funeral slab in Venice, in the church of San Stefano, around the corner from the Campo Morosini. The remains of Pisani, victor of Chioggia, and Venier, victor of Lepanto, lie near each other in San Zanipolo, the first beneath a fourteenth-century stone statue, the second beneath a twentieth-century bronze. The remains of Jacopo Pesaro the Bishop-Admiral lie in his own family chapel in the Frari – he did everything in style, and close beside him is the marvellous altarpiece, showing the Pesaro family prostrate before the Virgin and Child, which he himself commissioned from Titian when his fighting days were over. Look hard at the tomb of

Bragadino in the south aisle of San Zanipolo. It is surrounded by symbols of fortitude and virtue, lions winged and wingless, cherubs, coats of arms, and on its bas-relief is portrayed the general's terrible end, his degradation before Ali Pasha at the gate of Famagusta, his flaying alive beside the cathedral in the city square. In the heart of the composition, though, is a small stone urn: within it there lies, peaceful at last, the hero's poor scarred skin, brought home from Constantinople at such risk and sacrifice.

The greatest of all the winged lions, the one who must have roared the loudest through the storm at Methoni, stands guard above the gate of the Arsenal, the power-house of the entire imperial undertaking. He is attended by four wingless lions, all trophies of empire. On the far right is the now re-capitated lion which Morosini mentioned in his dispatch from Athens on page 134. On the extreme left is the lion who used to spout water from his mouth on the harbour-front at Piraeus, and who gave his name indeed to the Port of the Lion there: he is inscribed on his flank with a runic inscription, cut it is thought during some Grecian engagement by members of the Varangian Guard who protected the Byzantine emperors so formidably in Chapter Two.

The Arsenal behind them is a shipyard to this day. It has been greatly extended in the centuries since its foundation, but if you stand on the wooden bridge outside its twin protective towers, you may look inside to see exactly the dockyard from which, in the years of empire, the warships of Venice emerged with such phenomenal profusion. They sailed to the open sea beneath your feet, only pausing at the quayside commissariat, we are told, to be provisioned, victualled and armed for all the contingencies of the trade routes. Ships are still prepared for sea in there, and in an iron shed there very likely lies, being touched up for the next civic ceremony, the latest descendant of the Doge's *bucintoro*, flash and grandiose as ever.

Here is the church of the Greeks, with its precarious leaning tower over the Rio dei Greci, and its attendant Hellenic Institute. It was to this nucleus of Greekness, founded by Cretans and Corfiotes, that the exiled writers, philosophers and theologians came, and it possesses a famous collection of pictures from the Veneto-Cretan school. Around the corner is the Scuola of the

Schiavoni, the charitable guild of the Slavs. They were powerful in Venice, providing many of the workers of the Arsenal besides many sailors, and they commissioned one of their compatriots to decorate the building for them: Carpaccio the Istrian, whose exquisite fantasies of saints, cities, dragons and little dogs make the building one of the loveliest things in Venice.

You cannot evade empire in the streets and shrines of Venice. There are captured Turkish flags in museums, and great wooden models of colonial fortresses, and imperial pictures everywhere, and scattered across the city, it is said, are the bodies of fifty saints, and segments of many more, most of them brought home as imperial spoils, some snatched in the nick of time from the Turks – like the head of Athanasius the creed-maker, which we last came across at Methoni on page 116, and is now at rest in the imperial city. The best-remembered of the Doges are still those, like Dandolo, Morosini or Venier of Lepanto, who sailed with their fleets on their imperial ventures. The greatest of the Venetian artists were not above portraying imperial events. And we are not in the least surprised to learn that Bajamonte Tiepolo, whose attempted coup d'état in 1310 was thwarted by a stone mortar dropped on his standard-bearer's head by an old lady in the Merceria – we are not at all surprised to discover that this villain had previously been in trouble among the colonials of Methoni.

The name of the Querini-Stampalia Palace, on the Grand Canal, is a reminder that many aristocratic Venetian families had colonial stakes: the Querinis were feudarchs of Stampalia in the Aegean. The name of the Palazzo Vendramin-Calergi, now the municipal casino, is a reminder that many a colonial clan made its fortunes in the metropolis – the Calergis were originally Greeks from Crete. The Natural History Museum, between the Rialto bridge and the railway station, was once the Fondaco dei Turchi, the Turkish merchant headquarters established here in 1621, in the lull between the loss of Cyprus and the Ottoman attack on Crete.

Few women figure in the annals of the Venetian empire (or for that matter of Venice itself) but the one tragic heroine of the tale, Caterina Cornaro, is certainly not forgotten in the city. Her last Venetian palace, now the Monte di Pietà, the municipal pawnshop, is still called the Palazzo Cornaro della Regina (if only to differentiate it from the fifteen other palaces that perpetuate her family name). A day trip to Asolo, Caterina's pastoral fief in the hills, is a favourite optional extra of the package tour. Caterina herself is assiduously pointed out by guides in Gentile Bellini's famous painting, in the Accademia gallery, of a Miracle of the True Cross at the bridge of San Lorenzo: there she kneels, plump, pious and tightly stayed, on the edge of a canal with her row of waiting ladies. Caterina's reception as Queen of Cyprus is portrayed in bas-relief in the church of San Zanipolo, where the keys of Famagusta are handed over to her on the tomb of her protector Mocenigo. Her corpse has been moved a few hundred yards down the street from the church of the Apostoli to the church of San Salvatore; but there, in her luxuriant funerary chapel, the sacristan still rolls the carpet back with a reverential flourish, to show you where the poor Queen lies, wrapped in her rough habit.

If you can read the imperial text in the substance of Venice, you can read it in the people too. Venice is never more herself than in the high days of the summer season, when the city is jammed to the last attic bedroom with its profitable visitors. This is how it was when *La Dominante* was still dominant. Today's sightseeing hordes are yesterday's pilgrims, itinerant traders, sailors, supplicants. The Hotel Danieli, the Pensione Accademia, the Youth Hostel on Giudecca are only successors to the hostelries which, in Enrico Dandolo's day, occupied the whole southern side of the Piazza. Florian's and Quadri's, the cafés whose string orchestras compete so vigorously across the square, stand in the line of the shops which, in 1580, introduced coffee to its first European customers. The Biennale Festival of modern art, the Film Festival on the Lido, are natural descendants of the Great Whitsun trade fair of Venice, where the merchants of east and west met to exchange orders, display samples and indulge in industrial espionage.

There are Jews still in the ghetto of Venice, more prosperous now than they have been for generations, and their synagogues have been handsomely restored. There are still Greeks to worship at their church of San Giorgio. The Armenians, many of whom followed the Venetian flag step by step before the advance of the Turk, have their own island monastery, church and school – the chief Armenian Catholic school in existence, to which students come from Istanbul, Damascus and Teheran. Above all the Slavs, who did so much of the work of the Venetian Empire, are recognizable everywhere to this day.

In 1797, when the Republic was at its last gasp, a stout message reached the Doge from Dalmatia: 'Put on your crown,' it said, 'and come to Zara!' Later still it was Slav reinforcements from Dalmatia, sailing into Venice at the last minute, who offered the final chance of resistance to Napoleon: the Doge Ludovico Manin was much too frightened to use them, and indeed was terribly scared by the *feu de joie* which those loyal colonials fired in salute outside his window. By then Venice was half-Slav, and it remains hardly an Italianate city in the popular kind. Those thoughtful blue eyes, those hefty shoulders of bargees and market-men, come from the coasts of Dalmatia, so long the recruiting-grounds of the Republic; and the gondolier himself, the very herald of Venice, often has in his veins the sea-salt blood of Perast or Hvar.

There is another strain too, that one senses rather than notices: something subtle and evasive, a twist of courtesy, a wry shrug of the shoulders, to remind one that through it all, boldly though they flew the banner of the evangelist, proudly though they represented Christian civilization against the Turk, the Venetian imperialists were never out of touch, nor altogether out of sympathy, with Islam.

> . . . her daughters had her dowers [so Byron wrote]
> From spoils of nations, and the exhaustless East
> Poured in her lap all gems in sparkling showers . . .

We will end with the most marvellous booty of it all, and the most moving (for the Nikopoeia, after all, failed to preserve the Venetian Empire as she failed to save the Byzantine, besides letting me down disastrously when I appealed for her support in the 1979 Welsh devolution referendum), more majestic than the lion of Piraeus (which looks, as a matter of fact, rather lugubrious and lick-spittle, like a blood hound), more dazzling even than the sheen of the Pala d'Oro, more touching than the little emperors, hand in hand in the Piazzetta. The four Golden Horses of Constantinople, the Stallions of St Mark, were the very epitome of loot, the very standard of national self-esteem.

In all recorded history there were no such imperial trophies as these. They were scarred by the fortunes of time and war. They had lost much of their ancient gilding. They were mounted wrongly on their gallery on the façade of the Basilica, in two couples instead of a single quadriga. But they were to remain for 800 years the supreme symbol of Venice, powerful but always magnanimous. If the winged lion stood for Venetian authority, the Golden Horse represented the generosity and constancy of Venice – La Serenissima, the Most Serene. When in 1379 the Genoese admiral Pietro Doria lay with his fleet at the very gate of the lagoon, he boasted that he would never leave until he had 'bridled the horses of St Mark': within the year the siege was lifted, Doria was dead and all his ships and men had ignominiously surrendered.

Whoever made the Golden Horses, the Venetians took them as their own, and they entered the sensibility of the city like no other images. Tintoretto included one as the charger of a Roman centurion, in his monumental Crucifixion. Carpaccio mounted St Martin on another. Canaletto took them off their gallery, in a famous caprice, and re-erected them on pedestals in the piazzetta. Poets from Petrarch to Goethe celebrated them: 'blazing in their breadth of golden strength', was John Ruskin's vision of their presence up there, and Max Beerbohm said they made him feel *common*.

Through the long Venetian decline the horses remained unchallenged, for Venice was never invaded and never suffered a successful revolution. Only with the fall of the Republic in 1797 were they removed, for the first time in six centuries, and shipped away to Paris: there, after some years between the Tuileries and the Louvre, they were taken in procession, escorted by camels and wild beasts in wheeled cages, to be mounted on the Arc de Carrousel as the most marvellous of all Napoleon's battle trophies (though he uncharacteristically rejected a suggestion that he might himself be added in effigy to the quadriga, driving a chariot).

They were returned to Venice after Waterloo, but their pride was never the same again, because Venice herself had lost her independence for ever. They had been bridled at last. Only for a few months in 1848, when the half-Jewish Venetian patriot

Daniele Manin led a heroic but abortive rebellion against Vienna, did they recover their symbolic meaning: when Venice finally became part of the Italian kingdom, after the *Risorgimento*, they remained up there on their gallery as beloved friends, but never again as defiances. They were removed for safety's sake in each of the world wars, and then in 1977 it was decided by the administrators of St Mark's that they ought to be indoors, away from the fumes and the salt. To the sorrow of millions of lovers of the Golden Horses, it was decreed that they must be taken from their pedestals, restored, and kept for ever as museum pieces in the rooms behind the gallery.

There they are now, out of the sun at last. Through the door of their last resting-place you may see their forms, proud as ever, silhouetted against the half-light from the windows. Their hoofs are raised, as always, in a noble gesture of greeting, companionship or compassion. Their heads are turned still, fraternally towards each other. But the life has gone out of them at last, as the power and purpose have left Venice. The Venetians used to say that whenever the Golden Horses were moved, an empire fell – the Byzantine Empire in 1204, the Venetian Empire in 1797, the Napoleonic Empire in 1815, the Kaiser's Empire in 1918, Hitler's Empire in 1945. This their last move, though, is no more than an obituary gesture, a long farewell, a recognition that the glory of Venice has gone, and only the forms remain.

Four replicas are their successors, made of bronze in Milan. They are skilful copies, perfect in proportion, exact in scale, aged by a patina artificially applied. But they are lifeless things. They lack the bumps, the scratches, the suggestions, the mighty experience of the Golden Horses of St Mark. They never saw old Dandolo storm ashore at the Golden Horn, nor welcomed the great galleys, aflame with flags and profit, home from the seas of empire.

Gazetteer

Arbe, Yugoslavia: *Rab*
Astipalaia, Cyclades Islands: *Stampalia*
Bocche di Cattaro, Yugoslavia: *Boka Kotorska; Gulf of Kotor*
Boka Kotorska, Yugoslavia: *Bocche di Cattaro; Gulf of Kotor*
Byzantium: *Constantinople; Istanbul*
Candia: *Crete*
Candia, Crete: *Iraklion*
Canea, Crete: *Khania*
Capodistria, Yugoslavia: *Koper*
Cattaro, Yugoslavia: *Kotor*
Cephalonia, Ionian Islands: *Kefallinia*
Cerigo, Ionian Islands: *Kithira*
Cetinje, Yugoslavia: *Cettigne*
Cettigne, Yugoslavia: *Cetinje*
Chalcis, Greece: *Khalkis; Negroponte*
Constantinople, Turkey: *Byzantium; Istanbul*
Corfu, Ionian Islands: *Kerkyra*
Coron, Greece: *Koroni*
Crete: *Candia*
Curzola, Yugoslavia: *Korčula*
Dubrovnik, Yugoslavia: *Ragusa*
Dulcigno, Yugoslavia: *Ulcinj*
Durazzo, Albania: *Durrës*
Durrës, Albania: *Durazzo*
Euboea, Greece: *Evvoia; Negroponte*
Evvoia, Greece: *Euboea; Negroponte*
Fiume, Yugoslavia: *Rijeka*
Gulf of Kotor, Yugoslavia: *Boka Kotorska; Bocche di Cattaro*
Hvar, Yugoslavia: *Lesina*
Iraklion, Crete: *Candia*
Istanbul, Turkey: *Byzantium; Constantinople*
Ithaca, Ionian Islands: *Ithaki*
Ithaki, Ionian Islands: *Ithaca*

Kea, Cyclades Islands: *Keos*
Kefallinia, Ionian Islands: *Cephalonia*
Keos, Cyclades Islands: *Kea*
Kerkyra, Ionian Islands: *Corfu*
Khalkis, Greece: *Chalcis; Negroponte*
Khania, Crete: *Canea*
Kithira, Ionian Islands: *Cerigo*
Koper, Yugoslavia: *Capodistria*
Korčula, Yugoslavia: *Curzola*
Koroni, Greece: *Coron*
Kotor, Yugoslavia: *Cattaro*
Laurium, Greece: *Lavrion*
Lepanto, Greece: *Navpaktos*
Lesina, Yugoslavia: *Hvar*
Levkas, Ionian Islands: *Santa Maura*
Lissa, Yugoslavia: *Vis*
Methoni, Greece: *Modon*
Modon, Greece: *Methoni*
Morea, Greece: *Peloponnese; Peloponnisos*
Napoli di Romania, Greece: *Nauplia; Navplion*
Nauplia, Greece: *Napoli di Romania; Navplion*
Navpaktos, Greece: *Lepanto*
Navplion: *Napoli di Romania; Nauplia*
Negroponte, Greece: *Euboea; Evvoia*
Parenzo, Yugoslavia: *Poreč*
Patrai, Greece: *Patras*
Patras, Greece: *Patrai*
Perast, Yugoslavia: *Perasto*
Perasto, Yugoslavia: *Perast*
Piran, Yugoslavia: *Pirano*
Pirano, Yugoslavia: *Piran*
Pola, Yugoslavia: *Pula*
Poreč, Yugoslavia: *Parenzo*
Pula, Yugoslavia: *Pola*
Rab, Yugoslavia: *Arbe*

Ragusa, Yugoslavia: *Dubrovnik*
Rethimnon, Crete: *Retimo*
Retimo, Crete: *Rethimnon*
Rijeka, Yugoslavia: *Fiume*
Rovigno, Yugoslavia: *Rovinj*
Rovinj, Yugoslavia: *Rovigno*
Santa Maura, Ionian Islands: *Levkas*
Santorin, Cyclades Islands: *Thira*
Scutari, Turkey: *Usküdar*
Sebenico, Yugoslavia: *Šibenik*
Segna, Yugoslavia: *Senj*
Senj, Yugoslavia: *Segna*
Šibenik, Yugoslavia: *Sebenico*
Spalato, Yugoslavia: *Split*

Split, Yugoslavia: *Spalato*
Stampalia, Cyclades Islands: *Astipalaia*
Tenos, Cyclades Islands: *Tinos*
Thira, Cyclades Islands: *Santorin*
Tinos, Cyclades Islands: *Tenos*
Trau, Yugoslavia: *Trogir*
Trogir, Yugoslavia: *Trau*
Ulcinj, Yugoslavia: *Dulcigno*
Usküdar, Turkey: *Scutari*
Vis, Yugoslavia: *Lissa*
Zadar, Yugoslavia: *Zara*
Zakinthos, Ionian Islands: *Zante*
Zante, Ionian Islands: *Zakinthos*
Zara, Yugoslavia: *Zadar*

Chronology

DOMESTIC AND MAINLAND	DATE
Fourth Crusade sails from Venice	1202

By the end of the thirteenth century the Venetian Republic had established its independence, evolved its system of aristocratic government, and made a start in building the city of Venice as we know it now.

Church of San Zanipolo begun	1234
Establishment of patrician autocracy	1297

Throughout the fourteenth century Venice was involved in a vicious struggle with its chief commercial rival, Genoa, against a background of political instability at home. It ended triumphantly with the defeat of the Genoese at Chioggia, on the threshold of Venice, and the consolidation of patrician oligarchy in the capital.

Tiepolo conspiracy against the Republic	1310
Frari church begun	1330
Present Doge's Palace begun	1340
Doge Marin Faliero beheaded for treason	1355
Genoese surrender at Chioggia	1380
Venice acquires Bassano, Belluno, Padua, Verona	1403–5

With Genoa defeated the Venetians seized for themselves territories on the adjacent mainland and by the middle of the fifteenth century had established a mainland empire reaching almost to Milan. The end of the century was the climax of their success, exciting the envy as well as the admiration of all Europe.

Birth of Gentile Bellini	c.1429
Birth of Giovanni Bellini	c.1430
Venice acquires Treviso, Friuli, Bergamo, Ravenna	1454
Birth of Carpaccio	c.1460

DATE	IMPERIAL AND OVERSEAS	
1202	Fourth Crusade subdues Zadar	
1204	Constantinople captured	
1204–10	Venice acquires Crete, Euboea, Koroni, Methon: Venetian citizens acquire Cyclades	At the time of the Fourth Crusade, though the Venetians were already commercially powerful in the eastern Mediterranean, their overseas territories were limited to scattered seaports on the coast of Dalmatia. The Crusade gave them a string of fortresses, islands and seaports in and around the Aegean and made them an imperial Power.
1386	Venice acquires Corfu	
1388	Venice acquires Nauplia	The defeat of their rivals, the Genoese, in home waters gave the Venetians extra freedom of movement, and through the
1420	Venetian control of Dalmatia confirmed	fourteenth century, and well into the fifteenth, their imperial expansion continued.
1453	Turks take Constantinople	
1464	Venice acquires Monemvasia	
1470	Turks take Euboea	

DOMESTIC AND MAINLAND	DATE
Birth of Giorgione	c.1471
European League of Cambrai against Venice	1508
Birth of Tintoretto	1518
Birth of Veronese	c.1528
Church of the Salute begun	1630
Birth of Tiepolo	1696
Birth of Canaletto	1697

During the last three centuries of her history, despite periods of astonishing artistic fertility, Venice consistently declined in power and virility at the centre. Though her constitution remained inviolate, her strength was whittled away by shifts in world power and the burdens of her commitments. In the eighteenth century she subsided into carnival and excess until Napoleon Bonaparte, declaring himself an Attila to the State of Venice, contemptuously abolished the Republic.

FALL OF THE VENETIAN REPUBLIC   1797

DATE	IMPERIAL AND OVERSEAS
1482	Venice acquires Zakinthos
1489	Venice acquires Cyprus
1500	Turks take Koroni and Methoni
	Venice acquires Cephalonia

The rise of Turkish power, though, was already threatening them and the fall of Constantinople to the Muslims was soon followed by the first loss of Venetian territory, in Euboea. Although this was really the turning-point of their imperial history, they continued to acquire new possessions, pragmatically, until the end of the fifteenth century.

1540	Turks take Monemvasia and Nauplia
1566	Turks take Naxos and Cyclades
1571	Turks take Cyprus
1571	Battle of Lepanto
1650	Turks besiege Iraklion
1669	Turks take Crete
1684–7	Venice takes Peloponnese from Turks

The last three centuries of the Venetian Empire were centuries of retreat. Despite the part the Venetians played in the Christian victory over the Turks at Lepanto, and despite a brief resurgence of imperial energies in Greece, and later in action against the Muslim corsairs of North Africa, Venice was outclassed by the superpowers of east and west. With the loss of her eastern colonies one by one to the Turks, by the time of the fall of the Republic she was hardly more than an Adriatic seaport once again.

1715	Turks take Tinos
1716	Venice surrenders Peloponnese to Turks
1785	Venetians bombard Tunis
1797	**END OF THE VENETIAN EMPIRE**

Bibliography

My original research for this book consisted in the main of a protracted and indolent potter through the Venetian seas. Readers familiar with the subject will recognize all too easily my debt to less escapist scholars, but for newcomers here is a list of the books I have found most useful:

BRADFORD, ERNLE, *The Companion Guide to the Greek Islands*, London and New York 1963.
The Great Betrayal: Constantinople, 1204, London 1967.

CHAMBERS, D. S., *The Imperial Age of Venice*, London 1970; New York 1971.

FOSS, A., *The Ionian Islands*, London 1969; Levittown, New York 1970.

FREELY, J., *Naxos*, Athens 1976.

FREEMAN, E. A., *Sketches from Subject and Neighbour Lands of Venice*, London 1881.

GUNNIS, R., *Historic Cyprus*, London 1938.

HAZLITT, W. C., *The Venetian Republic: its Rise, its Growth, its Fall*, London 1915.

HILL, G., *A History of Cyprus*, Cambridge and New York 1940–52.

HODGKINSON, H., *The Adriatic Sea*, London and New York 1955.

HOPKINS, A., *Crete: Its Past, Present and People*, London and Salem, New Hampshire 1977.

JACKSON, F. H., *The Shores of the Adriatic*, London and New York 1906.

JONGH, B. de, *The Companion Guide to Southern Greece*, London 1972.
The Companion Guide to the Greek Mainland, London 1979.

LANE, F. C., *Venice, A Maritime Republic*, Baltimore 1973.

LAURITZEN, P., *Venice*, London 1978.

LORENZETTI, G., *Venezia*, Rome 1956.

MACLAGEN, M., *The City of Constantinople*, London and New York 1968.

MILLER, W., *The Latins in the Levant*, London 1908.
Essays on the Latin Orient, Cambridge 1921.
Murray's Handbook to Greece, London 1884.

NORWICH, J. J., *Venice, the Rise to Empire*, London 1977.
Venice, the Greatness and the Fall, London 1981.

PARADISSIS, A., *Fortresses and Castles of Greece*, Athens 1972–6.

PEROCCO, G., and SALVADORE, A., *Civiltà di Venezia*, Venice 1973.

ROITER, FULVIO, *The Orient of Venice*, Padova 1982.

RUNCIMAN, STEVEN, *A History of the Crusades*, Cambridge and New York 1951–5.

SMITH, MICHAEL LLEWELLYN, *The Great Island*, London and New York 1965.

SPANAKIS, S. G., *Crete*, Iraklion 1965.

SUMNER-BOYD, H., and FREELY, J., *Strolling Through Istanbul*, Istanbul 1972.

VILLEHARDOUIN, G. de, *Chronicle of*

the Fourth Crusade, tr. F. Marzials, London and New York 1908.

WEST, R., *Black Lamb and Grey Falcon: The Record of a Journey through Yugoslavia in 1937*, London 1942; New York 1955.

YOUNG, M., *Corfu and Other Ionian Islands*, London and New York 1971.

YUGOSLAV LEXICOGRAPHICAL INSTITUTE, *The Yugoslav Coast*, Zagreb 1966.

The translation of an anonymous Cretan poem on page 83 is by Michael Llewellyn Smith, from his book *The Great Island*, (Longmans, 1965). The Euripides translation on page 92 is by T. F. Higham, and comes from *The Oxford Book of Greek Verse in Translation*, (Oxford University Press 1938). The maps on pp. 10, 33, 53, 66, 73 are reproduced courtesy of the Museo Storico Navale, Venice.

Index

196

Index

Index

Index